Double Exposure

A Life Visible in Two Genders

Meredith Lee / Derek Moo

This is a work of memoir, relying upon the author's imperfect recall around specific memories and events. Some names and identifying details have been changed for privacy reasons.

No AI was used in the creation of this book. This includes all of the text, editing, layout, cover design and cover image.

The use of any part of this work to train generative AI is strictly prohibited.

First published by Dream Workshop in 2025
Frankston, Victoria, Australia
https://dreamworkshop.space

Copyright © 2025 Meredith Lee / Derek Moo.
Cover image and photos by Meredith Lee / Derek Moo.
Source photo of mirror and camera by Doug Steley.
Artwork on Derek's T-shirt copyright © 2023 Art by Veya.

All rights reserved. No part of this publication may be reproduced without prior written permission from the publisher.

Lyric excerpt from "Neverland" copyright © 2004 Steve Hogarth.
Used with permission.

ISBN: 9781764267809 (paperback)

A note about language and spelling used in this book:

This book was written and published in Australia. As such, English words with regional and cultural variations (such as *realise* and *realize*) appear using their Australian spellings. However, US English spellings are used in some places where it makes contextual sense to do so, such as dialogue between American students. It feels much more egregious to incorrectly portray a person speaking with the wrong "accent" than it does to have a few spelling inconsistencies here and there.

The term *doll,* as applied to a transgender woman, has a history in African-American and Latina LGBTQIA+ culture. I was completely unaware of this fact until quite recently, and the cultural usage of the word (as in "Protect the Dolls") has not influenced the events of my life or the content of this book.

The word I use to describe myself – *dual-gender* – is an explicit choice: I don't like the term *bi-gender,* purely because there is still a twelve-year-old boy inside me somewhere; *bigender* is often written without the hyphen and I can't help but read that as *big ender.* Funny penis wordplay! Hur hur snigger snort.

On footnotes:

Some readers love them, some readers hate them. If you're one of the latter, feel free to ignore the footnotes in this book. They are not essential reading; they are intended to be bonus content for people who like to look in every cubbyhole and do all the side quests.

Sensitive Reader Advisory

My wish is for you to find hope within these pages. However, there are parts of my story that intersect with depression and suicide, and some readers may find them distressing. Below is a list of Australian resources that may be able to provide help in a crisis.

Lifeline
13 11 14
www.lifeline.org.au

Beyond Blue
1 300 22 4636
www.beyondblue.org.au

QLife
1 800 184 527
www.qlife.org.au

Suicide Call Back Service
1 300 659 467
www.suicidecallbackservice.org.au

Dedicated to all the transgender people,
in all their multitudes of colours and styles,
whose eggs have not yet cracked.

You are not alone.

CONTENTS

Part 1   3
    1. Gift   5
    2. Threshold   7
    3. Surprise   15
    4. Visible   18
    5. Undiscovery   23

Part 2   35
    6. Dolls Are For Girls   37
    7. Paper Dolls   41
    8. Jon   48

Part 3   55
    9. Jennifer   57
    10. Amy   64
    11. Lauren   79

Part 4   97
    12. Chrysalis   99
    13. Duality   108

Part 5   113
    14. Lisa   115
    15. Soapboxes   123
    16. Prescience   130
    17. Dating   135
    18. Together   139
    19. Party   144
    20. Prickly   148

Part 6 — 153

21. Click-Clack — 155

22. Belonging — 161

23. Melonworld — 168

24. Sydney — 173

25. Reckoning — 193

26. Escalating — 198

27. Tiptoeing — 205

28. Clandestine — 211

Part 7 — 217

29. Mover — 219

30. Navigating — 227

31. Daybreak — 232

32. Midnight — 236

33. Still Life — 241

Part 8 — 251

34. Bellie — 253

35. Flying — 262

Part 9 — 279

36. Impasse — 281

37. Neverland — 285

38. Oxygen — 288

39. Answers — 293

40. Daylight — 298

Part 10 — 305

41. Fragile — 307

42. My Other Self — 311

43. Plebiscite — 320

44. Nevermore	333
45. Disclosure	338
46. Official	343
Part 11	355
47. Body	357
48. Emergent	375
49. Conspicuous	379
50. Trans Enough	400
Part 12	413
51. Spotlight	415
52. Dance Like Everyone Is Watching	421
53. Present	431
Supplemental	435
Stones Unturned	437

Foreword

People are amused when I tell them that I used to be shy. I think I always knew that I wanted to be seen authentically, and perhaps when I was younger I instinctively understood that I didn't yet know myself well enough to present myself honestly and confidently. So I just stayed in the background, trying to avoid attention whenever I felt unsure about revealing too much.

Today I am known to be outspoken and easily excitable. I wear my convictions on my sleeve, unafraid to show my passion when I find something engaging. Sometimes I can be too forthright for comfort, but life is too short and unpredictable to waste any more time hiding. Understanding and continually re-evaluating this maxim has led me to create the book you are reading now.

The impact of writing this book was somewhat surprising to me. I began this project thinking I would simply be writing "my story", but unpacking my emotions and reflecting upon my choices and experiences has given me an appreciation for this existence that goes beyond mere thankfulness; the writing became part of the journey and developed its own sense of meaning and purpose.

I also discovered that a work of memoir has its own way of deciding what gets written, regardless of whatever ideas the author has in mind. The words come out indifferent to the consequences; the decision whether to

Foreword

include them in the final draft is a question for later, and that question can be a delicate one. I am not the only one affected by the existence of this book, and at times I have wondered whether I'd be able to publish it at all.

It's important to position the experiences I write about in the context of late twentieth and early twenty-first century American and Australian society. Any generalisations I make here are framed and influenced by the culture I grew up in and continue to live within. My struggles, my insights, my freedom or lack thereof – even my silly jokes would be different if I was writing from a different place and time. Nonetheless, I hope that I have managed to capture some meaningful truths in these pages. I certainly hope to convey *my* truth, and add my voice to the ongoing cultural conversations that make it to my corner of time and space.

I can't predict how this book will be received. People who already know me may be in for some surprises, and every reader, regardless of how familiar they are, will bring their own biases and experiences to their interpretations of my words. This book may challenge you to re-think your ideas and expectations not only around gender, but around identity and relationships and human nature itself. It may also provide hope, and comfort, and encouragement to live your life more authentically. It's a daunting prospect to reveal everything written in these pages. But it is worth telling my story because I know there are others like me who do not feel free to claim and express their truths. It's important to appreciate what is possible, no matter how difficult or unlikely it may be.

Part One

Chapter One

Gift

Late 1985

I am lying face down but it feels like I am floating. There is bright white light all around me, like in the movies when someone goes to Heaven. Everything is in a soft-focus haze, but the sensations and feelings I am experiencing are bold and immediate. Joy and contentment and bliss without any specific manifestation. Just… there, inside me, their presence unmistakable.

I think this is Love?

There is a girl underneath me. Lesley. One of my Year 10 classmates. I've never really considered her as a romantic possibility, so I don't know why my sleeping brain decided to choose her for this dream. Nevertheless, she is more beautiful than anything I have ever known.

This is Love.

My soul is overflowing.

There is a pureness around us and I breathe it in, absorbing it through my skin, swimming in it as it infuses throughout my being. It envelops and sustains us, Lesley and me, as we simply exist in this blissful moment of a lifetime.

This is Love.

It's so vivid, so powerful. I feel, beyond what words can describe.

I awaken.

Confusion.

Disbelief.

Reality.

Then, a monumental, overwhelming, unbearable sense of loss.

I remained listless and depressed for weeks following that dream. Fifteen years old and grief-stricken over a Love that never happened.

Or did it? Are my dreams to be discounted as unworthy of real emotions?

I never figured out why my brain decided on Lesley. She wasn't someone I ever interacted with much. The best guess I have is that it could have been anyone from my life – Lesley's image was simply a randomly convenient way to present the symbolically important girl in my dream.

The significance of the dream girl, however she is named, is another story. Well, with the benefit of many years of hindsight, I will decide that it's *this* story, really. Eventually.

Chapter Two
Threshold

There is a space between worlds where truths flicker and glow in a brief instant of understanding. Where secrets can be sown, nurtured, and harvested, and eventually, maybe, set free. To be celebrated.

I am drawn to this space.

What does it cost to be yourself?

I am a creature of habit. I like the stability of a comfortable routine, of familiar faces and greetings, of an environment where I feel like there is a place for me. I've spent years cultivating treasured little corners of time and space, regardless of whatever else my life demanded.

When I was younger, I'd always imagined I would find someone to share my routine with. The comfort of faithful companionship to go with the closeness of a loving partner. Something that so many stories and movies told me would happen.

Threshold

Maybe the price you pay to be yourself is not necessarily something you lose. Maybe it's something you never gain.

The reality of living one's truth can be stark and unforgiving. I know people who have lost their routine and much more. Who have had to start over from nothing. Rendered strangers by the rejection of others, or even through their own uncertainty and associated actions. Cast adrift as a consequence of showing themselves, or even simply trying to find themselves.

And then, what do we lose when we cannot share ourselves fully, even when it is safe? What if we want to open up, yet are too afraid? What if the other party doesn't want to know? Who pays the cost then?

I ask myself all of these questions and some of my answers are disappointing; still I know that I am one of the lucky ones.

I am a family man. A daggy dad, with a wife and two children whom I adore and care for. I can often be found tinkering with some random household fixture, or attending to various domestic duties, taking pains to ensure my family enjoys a life free of unnecessary hardship. Sometimes I build things, as an outlet for my occasionally restless creativity: a carved wooden fidget spinner, a homemade folding desk fan, a receptacle to hold my wife's crutches in the bathroom. I've even made a portable drumkit using materials I found at the hardware store.

I am a beautiful woman. A social butterfly, celebrating sisterhood, feminine energy and heartfelt connections. I treasure moments with close friends sharing our deepest secrets, being in each other's company with no expectations to act, or perform, or problem-solve. Simply sharing our existence, and appreciating who we are. I am uninhibited, and frivolous, and unapologetically sexy. I am fancy, drawn to frills and lace and fetching looks, captured posing for public exhibition: Look at me. This is me.

I am quiet, and thoughtful, and outspoken, and opinionated, and nerdy, and glamorous. I am all these things at once. The space between is my workshop, my studio, my wardrobe, my crafting table. A threshold where the threads of my lives meet, and intertwine to become something more.

* * *

Autumn 2021

The words emerge in sporadic bursts on my laptop screen as I attempt to capture this experience. It looks like a cliché – a solitary man sitting in a café, struggling to produce the next literary masterpiece – but I happen to like it, and I am self-consciously aware that I have chosen the circumstances of this setting. Sometimes we have to create the things we desire.

This establishment is a regular habit of mine. A local space where customers are known by name and coffee preferences are remembered without prompting. The kind of place where community can put down roots.

It feels lively today but the energy is unhurried; Fiona, the barista, has time to reorganise the pastry cabinet in between coffee orders. The morning light coming in from the street is softly grey and muted. At the window table, a woman and her young son are silhouetted against the passing world, looking adorable as they sip their drinks in their matching fedoras. Fiona absent-mindedly brushes a stray hair from her face, the lights above her glinting off the backs of her earrings as she moves. My long black has been cooling as I write; the remaining half is only just warm to my lips. It still comforts me as I sip what's left, wondering how long I should wait before ordering another.

This is my Sunday morning. It's the kind of thing I tried to share with my wife Lisa when we first started dating, but she never really took to it. Sleeping in was always much more attractive to her. So, like many of the things I am drawn to, it remains quite personal. I sit and observe the world, soaking in the energy of the day, the light, the people and their quiet conversations, the clinking and clanking of dishes and pans, against the ever-present aroma of coffee and a soundtrack usually filled with the groovy sounds of yesteryear.

Across the room I see a couple sitting quietly, a man and woman each reading their own book, sharing nothing more than the actual table and the silence between them. I wish that they could be myself and Lisa – more than twenty years together and we've never developed similar leisure habits. But I'm content to sit here alone, happy to inhabit my solitary space in the midst of this busy café. It's in moments like these I feel closest to my own existence, my heart connected to the wider world, people both familiar and strange, feeling their presence and walking reverently amongst the lines that weave our stories.

My story. I want to write the kind of story that makes people cry. Not through tragedy or sentimentality, but simply through connecting. Through *knowing*. When I read a memoir that hits home somehow, when the author's experience, even half a world and half a lifetime away, still speaks to me – when the tears come because I *get* it – I want to share this feeling with others.

Writing my story is the scariest thing I have ever done. I am terrified of revealing myself so openly. Yet without honesty, my story is not worth telling. If I omit the scary things, I may as well be sitting in an anonymous hotel room, drinking cheap instant coffee. Unsatisfying and not worth sharing.

Honesty is scary. For the writer, and sometimes even for the reader.

"Still going on that?" Fiona startles me as she stops at my table and peers at what's left of my coffee.

"Oh. Umm." I quickly take the final lukewarm mouthful and hand her the empty cup. "Could I please have another one?"

Fiona smiles. "Are you working on your memoir? I can't wait to read it."

"You're not the only one." I close my eyes and lean back. There is such a long way to go yet. I am learning to trust the process, and to trust this space where truths emerge in their own time.

I am privileged to live two lives in one: a dual-gender existence. If people are lucky enough, they get to meet both of me. Derek today, Meredith tomorrow.

It wasn't always this way. For years, the space between my lives was an unknown land, a void through which I hastened on my way from one existence to the other. It felt dangerous; men were not supposed to become women, nor the reverse. I dared not reveal too many details of my origin to those on either side, lest the knowledge be used in some way to complicate my passage: questioning my motives, shunning my presence, or forbidding my transit altogether. So I dashed across the unseen landscape under cover of darkness, trying to ignore the sneaking suspicion there might be something worth discovering if I only dared to take time and look.

I was too busy making sure there was no-one *else* looking.

I found deserted lots behind industrial estates where, on a quiet Saturday afternoon, I could park my car and nobody would see me change.

I learned which neighbourhoods had sleepy streets with high fences against the road where, late at night, I could stop on the way home and nobody would see me change.

I hung the washing up to dry and strategically obscured my female garments behind towels and large t-shirts.

When I had to discard things, I found random locations with public trash bins. I couldn't risk the chance of accidental discovery, however unlikely, if someone needed to retrieve an item from the household rubbish.

All of this secrecy took its toll. Over the years I found myself increasingly frustrated and resentful about this ever-present cost. To whom was I paying? It didn't seem worth it. So I began choosing instead to risk the consequences of visibility, coming out to friends one by one – and I found acceptance and relief. And I found joy.

Slowly, the space between my worlds emerged as a colourful landscape of possibility, no longer shrouded in darkness and no longer just a place to be skipped over without a second thought.

I think back a few years to the first time I came here as Meredith. The café staff had known about her, and had seen photos, but were delightedly surprised to see Merri in person.

"Good morning!" I stood in front of the counter with a nervous, expectant smile.

Fiona broke into a wide grin. "Merri! Oh my gosh, it's so good to see you! You look fantastic!"

"Thank you." Fiona's enthusiasm made me feel warm on the inside. I was dressed as if to attend a high tea: pink and black floral dress, petticoat, dainty bows on my heels, flower in my hair. "I thought it was about time you got to meet me."

"Well it certainly is. I've heard so much about you." She laughed, because it was true. Once I'd started risking my secret, I felt compelled to share Meredith's existence with kind and caring souls like Fiona. I found that there was something about opening up and being vulnerable that felt more than just liberating. Being free also brought me closer to others.

I took my usual spot and relaxed into the setting, nursing my coffee as I pondered the meaning of identity and the way we craft our presentation to the world. After a few moments lost in thought, I noticed that an attractive woman in a pretty dress had come to order a takeaway coffee.

I'd seen her here a few times before, and she always had a similar look: retro style dresses and cardigans, not unlike what I was wearing today myself. I'd wanted to compliment her in the past, but making unsolicited comments on a woman's appearance is something I am very careful about when I'm out in the world as Derek.

On this day, I had no such reservations. The rules are different when the social and cultural baggage is different, and it felt wonderful to be free of the unspoken assumptions I usually have to mind.

"Excuse me." I did feel a bit awkward getting her attention from where I was sitting, even though it was only a few metres away.

She turned to look at me.

"I just want to say that I love your dress." I smiled sheepishly. "It's beautiful."

She smiled back, looking pleased and slightly relieved, as if she'd been expecting me to say there was a run in her stockings or that there was food on the sleeve of her cardigan. "Oh! Thank you! I love your dress too! And your shoes!" Her eyes widened a bit as she took in the height of my heels.

"Thanks," I replied. My shoes felt comfortingly feminine, reassuringly cradling my feet in their delicate posture. Great for sitting pretty; not so practical for walking around with a takeaway coffee. I could appreciate this woman's pair of cute, sensible flats. "I've noticed you before and you're always dressed so nicely. Are you heading to church or something?"

"Oh no, not at all. I dress like this every day. No need for an occasion!" She stated this proudly, almost defiantly. I was clearly not the first person to comment on her style. "I don't go to church anyway."

How did that saying go? I found myself reciting it out loud. "Life is short; wear the pretty dress." I raised my coffee as a toast to our mutual appreciation for fashion. "Have a lovely day."

She nodded as Fiona handed her the takeaway cup. "You too, thanks!" And she swished out the door, petticoats bouncing as she walked.

How much of our presentation is for others – for the circumstances, for strangers we wish to attract (or repel), for our peers, for our friends and family – and how much is for ourselves?

How much does it affect how our lives intersect?

Threshold

I finish my second coffee and think about how I look to other customers. I sit in this same seat nearly every week. Sometimes I'm wearing nothing worth noting: today, it's a T-shirt, shorts and a hoodie, cheap running shoes and my hair tied back. A man dressed in unmemorable man clothes. Sometimes I'm wearing a casual skirt, or a glamorous party frock, or a sexy, sharply tailored office ensemble. A woman of many fashions. A person of multiple truths. Yet I am still the same on the inside. The café is still the same beautiful space. The coffee is always excellent, the service is always friendly, and the atmosphere is always inviting.

Here in this space, I have uncovered memories, learned unexpected truths, and questioned long-held beliefs. And I have discovered joy in the freedom to be myself. I am so very fortunate to have such freedom.

I am sitting here alone, but I want to share this with everyone.

Chapter Three
Surprise

I'm eight years old, surrounded by hundreds of other kids on the bleachers, sitting in the hot California sun as we wait for the summer day camp staff to organise us into our activity groups.

I don't know anyone here so I just kind of hang around the kids nearest to me and keep mostly quiet.

One of them looks at me curiously. "Are you a boy or a girl?"

I don't know if this is supposed to be an insult or if it is a genuine question. I also never considered that my appearance might be ambiguous. I'm just a kid, largely unconcerned with social customs, and whilst I think my face is dorky looking, I never give much thought to my clothes or my haircut.

The question doesn't mean anything to me, so I have no emotional response to it. I answer as if I am completing a survey or a school registration form.

"I'm a boy," I say.

Surprise

* * *

It's sometime in late 1996 and I'm out for lunch with a colleague. A fellow American, Denise is a career woman in her late thirties who's been in Melbourne for two years; I'm a young man of twenty-six just finding his feet in the city. I'm eager to learn from another expat's lived experience.

"How are you two ladies doing today?" The server approaches us from behind my chair. I smile with anticipation. It's my ponytail – I've been letting my hair grow out for the last eighteen months.

The server's face turns from friendly to mortified as she comes around beside our table and realises her faux pas. "Oh, I'm so sorry!!!" She looks a bit scared that I might protest angrily.

"It's fine, really." I hope that my smile is reassuring. I actually love it when this happens. It tickles the part of my brain that likes to be subversive and make people examine their assumptions about the world.

Denise looks amused but I don't know if she expects me to consider it insulting to be mistaken for a woman. I don't, of course. I've always wondered why so many people think such a reaction would be normal. Why? Do those people think there is something wrong with being a woman? If I'm insulted by this, then it's on behalf of all the women in the world.

I'm still a man, though. As far as I know.

* * *

I keep glancing over at Jackie as I unload my trolley onto the conveyor belt. She hasn't noticed yet. The couple in front of me have a large haul and Jackie is busy scanning everything through and chatting to them at the same time.

It's a beautiful Saturday morning in August. Late winter in Melbourne, 2019. Jackie has been ringing up my groceries nearly every weekend for quite a few years now. Sure, I could line up for one of the other cashiers working here, but Jackie is always friendly and she remembers her regular customers.

Her regulars don't usually change gender on random visits, though.

I approach the register as the previous customers depart. "Hello!"

Jackie looks at me without recognition for an instant, and then I watch the gears turning as she processes what she's seeing.

"Well, hello! This is a surprise!" She seems genuinely delighted. "You look fabulous!"

"Thanks," I say. "I'm being my other self today." I smile as I say my name, the one I've chosen because I love the way it sounds. "I'm Meredith."

Jackie nods approvingly. "Well, it's nice to meet you Meredith. To what do we owe the pleasure of seeing you today?"

I'm dressed in a pink and purple floral skirt, sheer white blouse and pink cardigan, and dusky pink heels. It's a bit much for doing the Saturday morning errands, really.

"I just felt like being pretty today." I shrug. I do have plans to meet a friend later but there's no particular reason to be Meredith instead of Derek. I can't really articulate my reasons for being female even when given time and space to reflect, let alone whilst making small talk at the supermarket checkout. I simply feel the need to be feminine, and it manifests itself in this socially-coded way.

I'm still a man, though.

Who also happens to be a woman.

Chapter Four
Visible

I grew up in the 1970s and 1980s, an era when *transgender* wasn't a widely known term. The distinction between sex and gender was rarely acknowledged, and the word *transsexual* was used to describe someone who changed genders. I don't remember the word *gender* itself being used much outside of clinical or technical contexts.

Inevitably, *transsexual* referred to someone who was "a man becoming a woman" (according to the language used at the time). Transmasculine people – "women becoming men" – didn't seem to exist at all (I never learned of any until my mid-twenties). Transsexuals were also portrayed as rare, lonely individuals – I had never heard of anything like a community in the way that we think of LGBTQIA+ folks today.

As a child, I lived a sheltered existence in middle-class American suburbia. Most of what I learned about trans women was from glimpses of tabloid newspapers and daytime television talk shows, where transsexuals were sensationalised for shock value. They were treated as aberrations, freaks to be gawked at, or at best, human interest stories to be remarked upon for their bravery. The subtext was very clear: deviance was bad.

My father followed professional tennis, and it wasn't uncommon to find the sports section of the newspaper left open on the kitchen table. One day, when I was six years old, I happened upon an article about Renée Richards, a tennis player who had transitioned from male to female. Even though I usually found newspapers boring, the subject made me curious, so I had a read.

Subconsciously, of course, there may have been a lot more going on than I was aware of. I don't remember having a particular interest in tennis, or in Renée Richards specifically as any kind of example or role model, but I definitely heard and read about her more than once. Something mentioned in those reports stuck with me, although I didn't know why at the time.

One of the articles touched briefly on the medical aspects of transitioning. The message I got was that if you were transsexual, you would have a shorter life. The details involved things like hormones and cancer and complicated risk factors, but my young mind simply equated "shorter life" with "unhappy". I wondered why someone would want to be transsexual if it meant you would die sooner.

Of course I didn't realise yet that being trans wasn't a choice. This lack of understanding meant that I was unable to identify the knot in my chest that arose when I accepted the media's message. I actually feel it again as I write this, in sympathy with my younger self, and I now recognise it as unexpressed anxiety. As a child, not consciously aware of my own transgender nature, I was somehow still afraid of what would come from following that dangerous path.

I didn't know enough to be sceptical of the media, so I took everything at face value. I see now that those articles were framed as cautionary tales against gender nonconformity – regardless of how Ms. Richards' life, or the lives of anyone else who transitioned, may have actually unfolded. The risk of dying sooner was a consequence of the choice transgender people made – but I never saw anything that addressed the risk of self-harm or suicide for trans people who were denied the chance to transition.

There was another feeling, too, that I also didn't recognise or identify at the time. Instinctively wanting to escape the anxiety, I must have chosen an alternative.

It was disappointment.

The belief that transitioning was dangerous made me completely dismiss the idea of ever thinking I might want to be female. It wasn't ever going to be an option, so without really understanding why, I was disappointed that I'd never get the chance.

There's a saying: "You can't be what you can't see." With no visible representations of trans women living "normal" lives to show me that such an existence was possible, I spent my childhood mostly unaware of my affinity for the feminine. Whenever any hints would surface I simply assumed they were personality quirks – I had no other context for them. I was emotional and I cried easily. I preferred to play with one friend at a time instead of hanging around with a potentially rowdy group of boys. I liked aesthetically pretty pictures and drawings, and loved the colours of butterflies and flowers. And I was secretly fascinated by beautiful female dolls.

These quirks of mine could have come from a child of any gender, but they suggest to me that I would have welcomed the idea of being transgender if I hadn't been frightened away from the possibility. In the late 1970s my peculiarities would certainly be more expected from a girl than from a boy, and somehow I managed to avoid expressing myself strongly enough for my femininity to be particularly noticed or remarked upon. With nobody else pointing it out, I remained oblivious for years.

* * *

At university in the mid-1990s, I found myself drawn to women's studies and feminist analysis while I completed my sociology degree alongside my mechanical engineering course.[1] It would be a few years before my own gradual awakening to the possibility that I might be transgender, and I did feel very much like the odd man out (literally) when sitting in a lecture hall full of women.

I relished being different, though, and I was proud that I possessed some kind of understanding of the feminine that I suspected my male peers did not. Luckily, my tendency back then to be shy and socially awkward probably helped me to avoid situations where I might have allowed this pride to come out as hubris. I don't remember ever trying to show off my insights, even though I would have had the opportunity amongst my engineering peers. If I'd tried, I'm sure the memory of it ending badly would be burnt into my mind!

Any sociological analysis has to make generalisations about large groups of people: the way they tend to think, and act, and respond to societal pressures. As my studies progressed, I began to wonder why I felt that the women's descriptions fit me so much better than the men's descriptions did.

None of my classes ever mentioned transgender people outside of the footnotes. If they had, I might have realised that there were other options for descriptions to compare myself to.

I distinctly remember stating one day – perhaps to a friend, or maybe just to myself – that if I woke up the next day in a female body I wouldn't mind, and I would feel like the same person as before. I was a person first and foremost, and I just happened to be housed in a male body.

I did not connect this statement with the idea that I might be transgender. Indeed, I was convinced that my gender didn't matter at all,

---

[1] I can't believe I've never realised this until now, but how much more of a stereotypical male-and-female combination could I be? I could have been the poster child for dual-gender before I even knew it was a thing.

when it came to my existence as a human being. I was well aware of how the *external* world treated gender, but because I hadn't yet started exploring it, I had no idea how much my gender could impact my *internal* experience of being a person.

You can't be what you can't see. I had been growing up, learning, gradually painting a picture of myself, and one of my primary colours was invisible.

Invisible, but still present.

Half a decade later, I was crossdressing in private, but I still didn't consider myself transgender. I simply knew that I liked wearing feminine outfits and feeling beautiful. I knew very little about the transgender world, and whilst I'd read about the existence of an underground community, it was as far away and fantastical as an alternative reality from a science fiction movie.

My concerns were much more immediate and tangible: I considered myself lucky to be in a relationship with a woman who didn't mind me wearing short skirts and high heels around the house. She wasn't comfortable with anything beyond this, however, so I didn't go any farther. The fear of upsetting her was enough to keep me from actively seeking out any information or advice about my feminine inclinations.

After a couple of years together, Lisa and I got engaged. I hoped that she would become more relaxed about my crossdressing with time. However, as our lives grew together, it became more difficult and daunting to even bring up the subject with her. With more at stake, I became increasingly reluctant to disclose my evolving desires – as well as my fears. I tried to convince myself that I didn't need more.

I didn't succeed.

Chapter Five
Undiscovery

I often say that I feel like the luckiest person I know. Does my life look easy from the outside? I don't know. I *feel* blessed, and I feel like I have – materially, emotionally, spiritually – everything I need.

But do I have everything I *want*?

No, I don't.

And I'm not talking about trivial things (someone to wash my car for free), or impractical things (a beautiful pair of shoes that I'd be afraid to get dirty), or things that are conceptually beyond my individual existence (world peace, humanitarian political leadership).

I'm talking about something deeply personal, something missing, that I've learned to be happy without. About my female self being not just accepted, but embraced and celebrated, by everyone important to me.

My wife does not want to meet Meredith.

Undiscovery

I've been publicly open about being dual-gender for years now. People like me seem to be extremely rare: I know transgender people who have fully transitioned, and I know non-binary people who have distanced themselves from one gender without embracing another. Living in two genders seems to be an idea that doesn't get much consideration.[2] I do know some people who have different male and female presentations, but their male and female selves keep separate company and appear in separate contexts: this anonymity can be necessary for safety and privacy, and such arrangements may persist for years, as a way to satisfy otherwise incompatible needs, desires, and obligations.

For me, the latter situation was true for a long time. I had an alter ego who was known only to a select, trusted set of people in my life. Eventually, however, I grew weary of the mental and emotional effort required to maintain a secret identity. So I allowed the line between my male and female lives to soften and blur.

Now, my friends know both of me. My workplace knows both of me. My children, my family—

Except: my wife does not know Meredith. She knows *of* Meredith, obviously, but her knowledge is limited to what gets filtered through Derek.

A good friend once asked me: "Do you keep Derek around only to preserve your marriage?"

No. I love Lisa and I love the life we have together, even though I wish Meredith could be a part of it. But for me, adding Meredith would be a bonus, and being Derek feels in no way like a sacrifice. I'm happy as Derek, and I am comfortable as Derek. *Sacrifice* would be losing the freedom and ability to be Meredith.

* * *

---

[2] The only public figure I am aware of who is similarly open about being two genders is the entertainer Courtney Act / Shane Jenek.

November 2011

I pick the dress out of the washing basket and hold it up. It's a vibrant red, full length gown with silver highlights, and will be very conspicuous on the drying rack unless I find something large to hang in front of it to obscure it. There's no way to pretend that any of my garments belong to Lisa; we are clearly different sizes and I am partial to some styles that she would never wear.

I've got no idea if my children, or any of our frequent visitors from Lisa's extended family, ever notice what's hanging up to dry on the racks in the spare room. Lisa is adamant about keeping Meredith secret, but I don't know that she's ever considered how much mental effort it takes, ensuring that all of the little details are covered. It's probably unnecessary to be as vigilant as I am, but I don't want to take any chances and be inadvertently found out, and then have Lisa blame me for the fallout.

It would be so much easier if I didn't have to expend the energy always covering my tracks so thoroughly.

It makes me resentful. Lisa has been clear: waiting until the kids are adults to tell them about Meredith is non-negotiable. Even though research shows that young children adapt to these situations easily, and the younger the better. Even though I am weary after years of sneaking around, always thinking about how to conceal any evidence, making sure my children don't inadvertently stumble upon something they might have questions about. Even though it seems like I will have to endure this arrangement for the next five, ten, fifteen years.

The dress is beautiful. It exists to be worn proudly, to be seen in. I silently rage at the pointless injustice of it all. *Why do I have to hide this?*

* * *

Undiscovery

April 2016

My best friend is visiting from Adelaide and we're out and about, enjoying the sights and sounds of Melbourne's laneway café culture. I'm Meredith for the day, which makes it more fun. There is something about two women best friends – an intangible energy that surrounds and accompanies them – that I rarely sense around a pair of male or mixed-gender friends. I often feel its presence when I observe two women together in a shop or a café, and I feel it with Bellie when I am Meredith (it's still there when I am Derek, but it is definitely more muted).

I treasure our time together; Bellie and I rarely see each other in person, communicating mostly online over chat messages. We mark this occasion, as we usually do, with a selfie when we stop for coffee and lunch. It's a cute photo of us and I happily post it on my Facebook wall.

Except I forget whose account I'm currently using on my phone, and I post it on Derek's wall.

There are a whole lot of people on Derek's Facebook friend list who don't know about Meredith.

There are a few people on Derek's Facebook friend list who *aren't supposed to know* about Meredith. Like my son. A few of my nieces and nephews. And some of Lisa's friends.

I don't know why I suddenly think to double-check which account I used, but I'm relieved that I've caught it right away.

I quickly try to delete the post. But I can't. The interface doesn't give me the option to delete. I can edit, tag, share, but "Delete" is completely missing from the list.

What the hell? I've been able to delete posts before. Why not now?

I refresh the screen. Nothing.

I try to edit the post. I can change the text caption, but it won't let me remove or change the photo. Fuck!

A full minute passes as I fumble with the controls to no avail.

I force myself to think through my panic. I'm using a mobile browser instead of the Facebook app; maybe it's caching without refreshing properly. I close the browser and re-open it and navigate back to my account page.

Still no Delete option. God damn it! This stupid thing keeps its cache persistent even when I close it![3]

Exasperated, I restart my phone entirely. It takes ages to reboot and reconnect before I can bring up Facebook again.

Finally! I delete the post without any further trouble.

But it was up for a full five minutes. And other people aren't going to be explicitly forcing their devices to refresh right now – why would they? So if my post showed up on someone's feed during that five minutes, it will almost certainly stay there long enough for them to notice it.

There's nothing I can do about that. So I just hope for the best. Bellie gives me a big hug and we try to carry on with our fun day together.

A little over an hour later, I get a text message from Lisa.

Did you see Marie's message in the family group chat?

I hadn't looked at that chat – a group containing Lisa's siblings and a few of our nieces – since the morning. I text back: *No, why?*

Lisa replies: *Marie asked why you posted a photo of Meredith on Derek's facebook.*

Oh no. No no no. I'd feared the caching delay would cause a problem, but I hoped it would be limited to one or two individuals. The family group chat would be much more difficult to contain, particularly if it wasn't made clear that my post was a mistake, and that it wasn't intended to be something for people to discuss openly. Even though most of the adults in that group chat have been told about Meredith's existence, there are a few younger relatives who – quite intentionally at Lisa's request – have not.

---

[3] Caching is a programming technique aimed at improving efficiency. Caches are supposed to be unobtrusive but they can occasionally interfere with the user experience.

More from Lisa: *She meant to ask me directly but she accidentally put it in the group chat. She's deleted it now but it was there for an hour.*

Oh, you HAVE to be kidding me. An hour??? So now, any number of things can be possible. In my mind, the family is already gossiping and asking questions amongst themselves.

Did anyone reply? I ask.

Not that I know of. But why did you post it? A mistake? I looked but it's not there now.

Yes, a mistake. I realised right away, but Marie must have seen it while I was trying to delete it. It took ages because fucking facebook made it a pain in the arse.

I hope to God that Lisa isn't angry with me about making that mistake.

I can't even be upset with Marie about the chat message, because it was exactly the same mistake I made. Wrong browser, wrong chat, same thing. What are the chances that our blunders would dovetail so perfectly together?

I spend the rest of the afternoon with a knot in my stomach, expecting some kind of fallout, while Bellie tries her best to comfort me. But anxiety isn't the only thing I'm feeling. I can't ignore the resentment I feel that this situation would never have happened if I was allowed to be open about Meredith in the first place. That this anxiety is pointless and unnecessary and only a product of arbitrary rules that I follow just to keep Lisa happy.

Nothing further ever came of the incident, which was a relief. If anyone else saw the mis-posted photo, or Marie's message, they never asked about either one.

It's somewhat telling that Lisa had completely forgotten about the whole thing until I wrote this. It's a reminder that people can assign vastly different levels of significance to the same event or experience, and it illustrates just how taxing it can be to maintain hyper-vigilance all the time. The energy spent keeping a secret can be a real burden, even if the actual chances of discovery and consequence are much smaller than our anxiety reflects.

* * *

July 2019

My phone rings just as my friend arrives at the café. Lisa is calling, which means it's going to be awkward for me. When I am Meredith my voice changes and it takes a nontrivial amount of effort (with some accompanying cognitive dissonance) to use the "wrong" voice for my current presentation. But Lisa doesn't want to hear Meredith, she wants to hear Derek.

I nod a greeting to my friend and gesture at my phone as I pick it up to answer. "Hello?"

"Can you come home? I've broken my leg."

"What?"

Lisa's voice is weak and distant. "I've broken my leg. Alani's here but she can't move me. Can you come home?"

"I'm Merri right now. How much of –"

She cuts me off. "Nevermind. We'll call an ambulance."

I'd always wondered how Lisa would handle a situation like this. I guess I have my answer.

But it's an emergency. As if I am not going to want to come home. I try to ignore the previous exchange and ask, "Where are you? What happened?"

Lisa's words are slurring and shaky. "I'm in the bathroom. I fell over. I have to hang up and call the ambulance now. Meet us at the hospital."

As I apologise to my friend for bailing on our date, I hurriedly pay for my coffee and gather my things to leave. I'm in shock, struggling to think of all the implications of this situation. Lisa is disabled from a genetic bone condition, and walks using crutches. She has limited strength and mobility.

If Lisa has a fall there is no way she can get up on her own, even without a broken leg. I don't think I would be able to lift her, and our fourteen-year-old daughter Alani is much smaller than I am.

I would have said to call an ambulance anyway, but knowing that is the sensible action doesn't ease the burning feeling in my heart. Even though I end up changing and making it home before the ambulance arrives, it still stings.

That day was quite a few years ago now. Lisa's recovery was complicated and uncertain and involved multiple long-term stays in hospital. Her mobility has been permanently affected: she uses a wheelchair now for a large percentage of her daily activities. As for me? The knot in my heart never really went away. In spite of the fact that I can be Meredith whenever I want to, in spite of the wonderful acceptance I've had from family, friends, community – the feeling from that incident still echoes painfully: even if it meant not having me there in an emergency, my wife didn't want to see Meredith.

In the process of reviewing and editing this, I have learned from Lisa that her concern that day was not actually about Meredith. She was delirious from pain and may not have known or remembered where I was and what I was doing before calling me. When she realised that I couldn't reach her immediately she decided to call the ambulance herself. However, knowing this now doesn't change the feelings I carried for years.

* * *

March 2022

"Derek, why aren't you dancing? You're sitting here all alone. Come dance with us." Sal holds out his hand.

I sigh. Most of Lisa's friends know not to bother. "No thanks."

Sal is unconvinced, and gently tries to pull me from my chair. "Come on."

"No."

"Aww, why not?"

I'll never understand why some people refuse to acknowledge the possibility that not everybody likes dancing.

Sal knows about Meredith but I reckon he's too drunk to pick up on the implication when I say, "I'm not dressed for it."

"Of course you are, what do you mean? Everyone's always dressed for dancing." He didn't get it.

I try another one. "You're asking the wrong person."

Too subtle. He looks confused. "Okay, you've said no, I'll respect that." He gives me a hug and goes back to the dance floor, sashaying around the small group sitting near me where Lisa is talking and laughing with some of her workmates. I hear snippets of their conversation.

"Can you imagine if we actually tried to implement that?"

"We should suggest it at the next staff meeting just to see Mikey's reaction."

Office politics, academic style. When high school teachers gather at parties it can be quite enlightening to hear them talk shop. Right now, though, I'm not really interested.

I watch the bodies bouncing and gyrating, mostly women in pretty dresses – and Sal, a slightly flamboyant gay man – and I think about how my experience at parties changes so much depending on who I am.

One of the unexpected things about becoming Meredith was the discovery that she enjoys parties much more than Derek does. If given the choice today, I almost always go to a party as Meredith. If you see Derek at a party it's probably because I've accompanied Lisa, attending mostly out of obligation.

Dancing has always felt unnatural for Derek. It's not that I'm worried about impressing anyone, or about looking silly. It just feels forced. Other things come quite freely: if the music is grooving I can play air guitar or air drums with the best of them; I can pull faces and behave like a drunken monkey for photos; but dancing? Forget it.

Meredith is a whole different experience. If Sal had asked Meredith to dance I would have been up there in a heartbeat. Actually, Sal would not have needed to ask; I would have already been dancing.

There is something about being feminine that fills me with a kind of essence, a feeling that diffuses from my being like a delicate, invisible aura. It is like being steeped in a gentle, sweet perfume that leaves a faintly sparkling trail wherever I go, and it compels me to move with an expressiveness that I don't usually feel when I'm Derek. It allows me to be present in the world in a way that feels affirming and vital. And sometimes, it makes me want to dance.

Lisa has never seen me enjoy dancing. As I watch Sal and the women out on the floor, I feel a twinge of envy and sadness. I don't dislike this party, but I'm bored, and I really wish I was a woman right now.

* * *

For the longest time, being Meredith felt like having a secret mistress that Lisa grudgingly tolerated. *The other woman.* Who happened to be me. And apart from a few sessions with a counsellor, we had to handle the situation largely on our own; for many years Lisa kept it secret from her siblings and her friends, which meant that there wasn't anyone who knew both of us and could lend an ear or a shoulder, or offer an outside perspective.

Even after I came out publicly, there hasn't been a significant change in the practical aspects of Meredith's existence. I still make an effort to keep Meredith out of Lisa's way, minimising my visibility and doing my best to ensure that our paths don't cross. Just as I always did through the years of difficult negotiations and uncertainty.

Our arrangement is stable now. But it doesn't seem fair – to either of us. Yet there is no-one to blame for the unfairness. We have had to navigate through challenging waters that simply *are*. We just didn't anticipate – or recognise – them when we pledged our commitment to each other.

I've asked Lisa – no, I've more or less included her unwittingly – into this ménage-a-trois with Derek and Meredith. Is it fair to expect Lisa to go along with it?

Lisa is entitled to decline a relationship with the other woman.

But at the same time, Lisa is really declining the full and complete experience of *me*. Half of my life, I cannot share with her. Is it fair to expect me to not feel rejected?

I was hurt and resentful for years, but eventually, as Lisa and I both grew into this journey, those feelings faded into the background. There is the occasional reminder, but I am generally happy with the life we have created. Yet one thing persists: I carry a deep, abiding sorrow at what is being lost, not just for Lisa, but for myself as well. There is a whole unexplored dimension to our relationship that we may never know.

Part Two

Chapter Six

Dolls Are For Girls

She is there on the shelf behind the toilet, in her elaborate beaded dress with its strange fat cylindrical lower half. Her golden hair is lustrous and her face is so pretty. As a young boy of roughly ten years old, I know that I am not supposed to be interested in dolls, and it feels like a transgression just picking her up, especially since there is still plenty of paper left on the current roll and the spare underneath her skirts is not needed. But I've never been able to examine, hold, and explore such an overtly feminine doll before. Not without other people around.

As I bring her closer, I am holding her so that she tilts back slightly and I realise that her eyes can close. I hold her upright, then lay her back, then upright again, and watch as her eyes open and shut. Her long lashes sweep up and down with my movements. She is of course neither alive nor sentient, but it almost feels like I can control her conscious state – sleep, awake, sleep, awake. I stare into her open eyes. She stares back at me vacantly, yet somehow… I'm not exactly sure what I'm imagining, but it stirs something inside me.

Dolls Are For Girls

Such a pretty doll, so vulnerable to the whims of whoever is playing with her. In the mind of my ten-year-old self, she is more than just a helpless object – looking into her glassy eyes, I sense that she wishes to be treated well. I can feel it. I hold her for a while. Then I carefully place her back on the shelf and leave the bathroom to rejoin the party.

I don't recall exactly what age I am in any of the following, but I would have to be less than ten years old. I am definitely a young child.

I am following my mother out of the department store. I am pretending to shoot random people, pointing at them with my hand in the classic gun shape. Bang. Bang! Bang. I don't know if anyone actually takes notice of me, but I do a double take when – Bang! – I realise that the woman I am aiming my hand-gun at is a mannequin. I forget about shooting. I stare at the mannequin for as long as I can before I have to run and catch up with my mother.

We are having dinner with some friends of the family, at their house. The friends include two other children, roughly the same age as me and my brother. The kids are all watching TV in the family room before the meal, and just as we are called to the table, the most captivating scene starts playing. A life-size mechanical girl is standing on a pedestal and singing about spinning around in circles. She moves like a clockwork automaton, and I am transfixed. I do not want to stop watching and go to dinner. Somehow I miss the name of the movie, so for the next twenty years all I have is the image of this singing, living doll to remember.

It was, of course, the music box scene in the movie *Chitty Chitty Bang Bang*, where the heroine Truly Scrumptious pretends to be a wind-up doll as part of a daring scheme to sneak into the villain's lair and rescue the other good guys. I learned this only after the Internet came along and I was able to find information about my peculiar desires. But I get ahead of myself.

There is a girl in my third grade class. Katie. We are in the back of the school bus, playing "freeze" – me, another boy, and Katie. Katie is very good at staying still. She really doesn't seem to mind that she is the one who keeps getting told to freeze. I don't mind either. I could watch Katie stay still for hours. Unfortunately the bus ride is much shorter than that.

One of those beauty pageant shows is on TV – Miss America, or Miss USA, or something (I've spent hours searching the Internet and have been unable to find the footage I so vividly remember). The opening number is unusual – instead of a song and dance by the entire ensemble, there is one male singer and the female contestants are all frozen like statues, posed on pedestals that move slowly along a track in the stage. A parade of perfect, smiling, real-life dolls on display, and it is the most beautiful thing I have ever seen. I want to dive into the TV, to drink it all in, let it wash over my very being... and I get called away to dinner again.

A kid who lives across the street, a few years older than me, is an avid comic book collector. In the late 1970s there is a toy franchise called "Micronauts" and an accompanying Marvel comic book series. One of the characters is called Marionette because her real name is Princess Mari, she is a fugitive, and she just happens to evade detection by posing as a literal marionette – a life-size[4] doll who dances as her strings are pulled by her puppeteer, who is actually her loyal robotic servant. My neighbour has the comic books, and the scene where Marionette is introduced features some of the sexiest drawings of a girl I have ever encountered – although I have not yet reached puberty, and I cannot understand why she fascinates me so. I cannot stop looking at her. Nearly forty years later, I still remember the dialogue from that scene well enough to find scans of the original comic pages on the Internet.

Those are some of my earliest memories of my fascination with dolls – or rather, a particular doll aesthetic, both visually and behaviourally. Having had a lifetime to ponder this, I have some idea of where this comes from: a

---

[4] Life-size compared to the other Micronauts. All of them were tiny compared to Earth humans.

desire for control in an uncertain world, or at the very least a removal of ambiguity – a doll has no choice but to accept her circumstances, and this can be oddly reassuring. However, as a child, all I knew was this intense affinity for any representation of a human female who was almost convincing enough to be real, but with obvious markers that made it clear she was artificial: a wind-up key, puppet strings, being frozen in place.

I knew enough to understand that this was a weirdly specific fascination, so I kept it to myself. And because boys were not supposed to play with dolls in the first place (thanks, patriarchy!), I was always extra careful to hide my curiosity whenever anything potentially interesting caught my eye.

Dolls were for girls. And I wasn't one. Well, I was only a young child, and hadn't yet considered that I might be.

"That's ambiguous", you say. Doll, or girl?

Yes.

Chapter Seven
Paper Dolls

By the time puberty descended upon me, I had become well aware of the effect that a suitably presented doll could have on my mental and physical state. In fact, while I did find conventional representations of attractive girls to be pleasing, they only became truly erotic when I added in the missing doll characteristics with my imagination.

Back then, the weekend newspapers came stuffed with junk mail advertising. I began secretly collecting cuttings from the women's fashion catalogues and pamphlets – the way the models posed for a typical photo, it wasn't much of a stretch to imagine that they were made of actual plastic. Nothing a few carefully drawn lines on wrists and shoulders couldn't sort out. I would turn the models into *models* – I loved the fact that the word could also mean "a (presumably artificial) representation of the real thing". I was delighted to learn that the French word for fashion model was *mannequin,* which confirmed my suspicion that living dolls really did exist for those who truly appreciated them. I fantasised that when the models weren't doing photoshoots or runway shows, they were kept enchanted, frozen in plastic poses, perhaps on display in a showroom somewhere.

The kinds of images that a teenage boy was supposed to get off on – think movies with beach babes in wet t-shirts and Playboy-style centrefolds – never really did much for me. Sure, the women were attractive, but there was something too obvious about this kind of representation of sexiness. It was much more satisfying to use my imagination. I preferred to fantasise over a modestly dressed catalogue model, captured with a faraway look in her eyes, suggesting to me that she was caught unaware, dreamily, helplessly frozen in place. A giant wind-up key drawn in her back could be the perfect finishing touch.

There were exceptions of course. What I wouldn't give, back then or even now, to be able to experience firsthand the scene at the end of the video for David Lee Roth's cover of The Beach Boys' *California Girls!* A couple dozen beauties suggestively posed and arranged like a collection of life-size Barbies, as Diamond Dave sings and dances his way through and around them – oh, if only the camera would linger on the girls a bit more! The fast-cut, short-attention-span style of video editing popularised by MTV would become an endless source of frustration in my search for video content that was actually worth the time and effort to find.

Then there was that 80s classic – ludicrously, wonderfully bad – movie, *Mannequin*. The one where a department store dummy comes to life in the form of a very young and pretty Kim Cattrall (I've always wondered what *Sex and the City's* Samantha would have to say about this setup). It's hammy and over the top, but never mind – it was (and is) one of my perfect fantasies: a beautiful girl who gets transformed from living flesh to plastic doll and back again, helpless to control where or when it happens. This makes an otherwise dreadful movie worth repeated viewings (only just).

I had learned, due to my doll-radar being acutely honed from a very young age, that there wasn't much to be found in mainstream TV and movies where the woman-as-doll was treated explicitly as an object of desire. Fembots were killing machines with no personality. Wind-up dolls were children's toys. The mannequin or statue – the Pygmalion myth of bringing a sculpture to life – had a definite romantic overtone to it which I found appealing, but the goal always seemed to be the creation of a permanently flesh-and-blood woman, not the continued existence of woman and doll being one and the same.

Alas, what I really wanted to see was not going to be found in any of the places I knew or had access to as a teenager. If my fantasies were so unusual that depictions of them didn't exist, then I was just going to have to create some myself.

Damn it. I erase my sixth attempt at drawing lips that look appropriately doll-like to me. My perfectionism is a burden I can manage to leave behind sometimes, but here it is non-negotiable: if the result doesn't look attractive to me, there is no point. Unfortunately the repeated erasures are abrading the paper to the point where it isn't possible to draw cleanly anymore; I'm using standard 8½ by 11 inch paper, and in order to fit an entire body onto the page, I have to draw at a scale where facial details need to be finely rendered with a very sharp pencil. The roughed-up fibres where I've been working and re-working are making the necessary precision impossible.

I sigh and swear as I abandon this attempt, which is disappointing because I'd managed to draw some really beautiful eyes above those stubbornly uncooperative lips. With sadness I erase everything and flip the paper over to try again on the undisturbed side.

As always, I start with the eyes. I draw them large and expressive, as befitting a proper doll. I picture the lids as shutters and draw the open eyes as segmented polygons – the lids, with their luscious long lashes, would be hinged on pivots at the outer vertices. The irises are round, but I imagine the pupils inside them as cross-hatched hexagons. At this scale, however,

I'm lucky enough to get a vaguely circular dot happening, centred correctly in the surrounding iris.

My attempt at drawing a mouth is more successful this time. Like the eyes, the lips are stylised to look as if they are a mechanical attempt to mimic a natural shape, done finely enough to pass as a worthy substitute rather than just an approximation. More than worthy – to me, their clearly artificial nature makes them highly desirable.

I lightly sketch a facial outline and a few waves of hair, and the doll begins to come to life in my imagination. Her eyes and her sweetly demure smile are exactly the kind of look I am striving for: expressive, happy, yet yearning – pleading to the observer for a connection, perhaps to be made real somehow. A doll's existence to be acknowledged, embraced, and celebrated. I lose myself in these thoughts, contemplating her beautiful face, and try to decide how I want to draw the rest of her body, what kind of pose and outfit will suit her.

They say that to be an artist you have to have a good eye and a keen sense of observation. I've spent pretty much my entire life noticing the things that, to me at least, make an attractive doll: an inviting tilt of her head, expressive hands with their delicately outstretched fingers, a contrived yet enticing pose, hinting at something delightful hidden behind her motionless presentation. A shapely figure adorned in lace and frills. Most of all, the vulnerability of her sweetly innocent face. And sexy legs. I've always had a thing for sexy legs.

It turns out that compared to faces, legs are easy.

This is how I spent a large portion of my free time as a teenager and young man. For several hours a week I would sit in my room with the door closed, pencil to paper, slowly figuring out how to recreate those attributes and manners that signified the perfect doll to me. Painstakingly learning through trial and error how to translate the detail of my fantasies onto the page.

Drawing dolls turned out to be a lifelong hobby: after hundreds of hours I became pretty adept at portraying my visions, and after thousands of hours I had developed a definite style of my own – one that would be instantly recognisable, if it weren't for the fact that I kept this all secret and well-hidden from curious eyes or would-be critics. I was too embarrassed by the peculiar nature of my fetish to disclose it to anyone. I hid my drawings well, although I constantly worried that they'd be accidentally discovered.

I stood disbelieving at the open box. Had I left the lid up like that? Surely not. I was always so careful to conceal everything. I would never leave the box open. Yet there it was, lid hinged back, folds of paper clearly visible inside.

Had the papers been examined? I couldn't tell. They were folded up the same way I'd left them but there was nothing special about my folding technique; it was the most obvious method (half, half again, then half again) and would be easy enough for anyone to do. I hadn't taken note of their orientation inside the box so I had no way of knowing if they'd been disturbed.

I shut the box lid and stepped away from the closet, sliding the door closed. Maybe I had actually left the box open earlier. The only other person with any reason to go into my closet was my mother, because there were some seldom-used household items on the upper shelves. Why would she have looked in the little wooden box amongst all the other junk that a fourteen-year-old boy kept on the middle shelf of his closet?

I wasn't about to ask, because then of course I'd have to explain why I cared.

Nothing ever came of that incident. There have been a few other close calls over the years, but up to now, people have only learned about my drawings through my own intentions. If anyone in my family ever did find them, they mercifully declined to tell me.

I became even more careful after that, making sure that my hiding place was more concealed and less likely to be accidentally discovered. I took pains to gather my eraser crumbs into bunched-up tissues so there wouldn't be an obvious pile at the bottom of the rubbish bin in my room. When I needed to dispose of drawings I no longer wanted, I burned them in the fireplace when nobody else was home. When I discovered that the resulting ashes often maintained the original shape of the paper, indicating that *something* was burned recently, I made sure to break the ashes up and scatter them around the fireplace. Occasionally I would crumple the unwanted drawings up into my pocket and find a rubbish bin somewhere outside the house, but I always imagined someone spying on me to later retrieve what I'd discarded and find out what it was.

I really don't know what I would have done if my drawings had been discovered. Sex was not something we ever discussed openly in our family, and I have no idea if my parents were even aware of the existence of fetishes – the more stereotypical ones, let alone bizarre ones like mine. I had certainly never heard of anyone else who had the kind of fantasies that I did, not until the Internet came along. So I kept it all to myself, concealing my growing collection of drawings for years, as hundreds of dolls came and went and I tried to avoid thinking about what this strange kink of mine actually meant.

You see, as I grew into young adulthood and became more and more aware of how the world worked, it had not escaped me that the highly objectifying nature of my fetish was quite at odds with my growing understanding and feelings about the way society treated women. I was becoming a feminist and it was making me feel guilty about finding dolls sexy.

Furthermore, although I hadn't yet consciously realised it, the most significant part of any fantasy was always how I imagined it from the doll's perspective. Yes, the visual aspect was external, but the pleasure in my narrative always centred around the feelings and sensations being experienced by the doll herself.

The first of these realisations was a conundrum that I would wrestle with for a number of years, never finding an actual resolution, but mostly coming to terms with its implications by paying careful attention to the nuances of my imagined scenarios. The apparent misogyny of my fantasies, on top of their unusual nature, made it that much scarier to think of disclosing them to anyone.

The second consideration – that of the doll's own experience – was much slower in working its way into my psyche, but it proved to be much more influential in shaping the way my world evolved. For years – for my entire life – I'd known that I had a thing for dolls. I assumed this meant that I wanted a doll in my life. My very own doll to admire, covet, and lavish affection on. That would be fantastic, but it wasn't until I was living on my own as a young adult – with the privacy and opportunity to explore further – that it dawned on me: perhaps I might also want to *be* the doll.

Chapter Eight

Jon

"That's so lame."

I don't remember what prompted this proclamation, but I remember the delivery, the judgement, the casual dismissiveness of his tone. I also remember that this was a recurring scene. Me and my older brother Jon, observing or investigating something, me about to get excited until my brother quashed my enthusiasm with his sneering wet blanket. The subject of his derision was always something that I expressed a preference for, or an attraction to.

My portrayal of Jon here may be somewhat unfair. I remember how he made me feel, but I cannot actually remember a specific example of the scene I've just described. The template for this interaction has simply embedded itself in my memory: if I liked something, my brother would immediately proclaim it to be uncool.

I know this dynamic is often a normal part of sibling relationships. And it wasn't so overbearing that it pushed aside every other memory about our childhood as brothers. I do remember sometimes playing together and enjoying ourselves in common pursuits, where Jon was kind, or at least indifferent, to my ideas and interests. But I mostly remember being wary, and afraid, and I'm starting to question why his opinions affected me so deeply as to colour my memories in a negative light.

Perhaps Jon's behaviour mirrored the tendency of social groups, especially children and young teenagers, to mock any individual who didn't conform closely enough. It could be that, as keenly as I felt the judgement, I was oblivious to the reasons why Jon treated me this way. Looking back, I did (and still do) have a tendency to hyper-focus on things with a level of enthusiasm that would be unexpected from a "normal" – today we would say *neurotypical* – individual. I recognise now that my behaviour is common amongst people on the ADHD and ASD spectrums, but that is a discussion for another time.

I really can't say whether Jon's behaviour towards me – at least as I remember it – stemmed from his reaction to some aspect of my own personality, or from something innate within himself. He would eventually be diagnosed with bipolar disorder in his late teens, but the mood swings and bizarre antics that characterised those later years don't really feel connected to how I remember him treating me in the years before his illness became apparent.

Regardless of the reasons, or of the actual prevalence of those condescending moments, I remember Jon being unkind enough that I learned to withdraw, to protect myself. I learned not to share too openly the things I loved. I learned to be careful about showing my most important, treasured feelings.

I pick up the eraser. One more adjustment to the gentle sweep of her calves, flowing into the reverse curve of her ankles where they meet the backs of her perfectly shaped, exquisitely sexy heels. So delicate yet so commanding, rendering her pose enticing and expressive even in her frozen state. It's taken me hours of practice and dozens of drawings to reach this point, being able to render legs and feet in high heeled shoes the way I want, stylised and proportioned to give the impression that the body is plausibly realistic, yet clearly artificial. I am very pleased with my efforts today. Not bad for a fourteen-year-old kid who's only been drawing dolls for a year.

Click! The sound of the bedroom door handle startles me and I can't shove my drawing under the bed fast enough. I am kneeling on the floor, using a large hardcover book on my bed as a desk, and as I look up it's obvious that my brother saw me hiding something. The expression on my face would give it away even if he hadn't seen my movements.

Fuck.

There is no way in hell that I would ever reveal my secret fantasies to him. Jon wants to know everything that I do, just so he can make fun of me for it. Drawing sexy girls as mannequins and mechanical wind-up dolls? I would be too embarrassed to even tell my closest friends, let alone anyone in my family. My brother? Oh my God no. If he found out, it would be the worst thing ever.

I am tense, anticipating.

"What is that? What did you just hide under there?" He looks excited and accusing at the same time.

"Nothing."

"What is it? Show me."

"No." My drawing is unsecured, protected only by the presence of my bed obscuring his line of sight. I am scared. Anxious. Vulnerable. Jon is three years older than me, taller and stronger than I am, and can physically push me around to get what he wants. I move my hands under the bed to cover the paper.

"Why not? What are you doing?"

"Go away."

"Come on." He approaches and starts to lean down to peer under the bed.

"NO." I don't even have time to think as my hands crumple up my beautiful doll. I hold her tightly wadded in my fist. Jon will have to physically assault me if he wants to see what's left of my drawing.

"Aww, come on. What was that?"

"Leave me alone!" I am exasperated now. All that hard work, ruined. Why does he have to be such a jerk?

"Fine. Whatever." He looks amused and rolls his eyes as he turns to go.

I have to get up and close the door after he leaves. I am shaken, and angry that I can't be free with my expressions and my desires. Angry that I have no guarantee of privacy. I uncrumple my drawing, wary of the fact that Jon might burst in again anytime. I berate myself for not being more vigilant.

I contemplate the folded, kinked lines of the once-smooth doll and know that I will draw another one – dozens, hundreds more. But each one is special in her own way. This doll had a flirty, mischievous charm that I'd only managed to capture once or twice before. Now, with the crumple lines across her face, she just looks sad. I carefully fold her paper up and place it in the box where I keep my discarded attempts until I have a chance to carefully, secretly, dispose of them.

I replace the book on my bed and start on my biology homework instead of another drawing.

Even with the anxiety that came from anticipating his reactions, I probably can't hold my brother completely responsible for my introversion. Our family was never very open about sharing feelings in the first place. There didn't need to be any expectation of negative consequences; it was simply awkward and foreign to the way we interacted. And of course there was the prevailing social attitude that shamed boys and men for showing any signs of softness.

Jon

My tendency to focus inward and keep to myself served me well, I think, in protecting me from the direct trauma surrounding my brother's final years. Indirectly, of course, the effects are probably still with me, to what extent I am not really sure (and may never know, in spite of being consciously willing to unpack them when, and however, they manifest).

Jon didn't live long enough to see the emergence of the part of me that would eventually become Meredith. In the years when I was discovering and exploring my emotional landscape, he was fighting with demons of his own that I don't think I'll ever fully appreciate. He had started university at Stanford, but dropped out in his second year, and in the years that followed he struggled to find happiness and stability.[5] His troubles took up a lot of my parents' time and energy, so I tried to keep to myself and stay out of the way. I don't actually know if this was a conscious decision on my part – after all, I was already disinclined to be too loud or take up too much space.

Jon's previous tendency to belittle me did abate during those years. We had only sporadic contact – he was living in Sacramento, an hour away from our family home in Cupertino, and I ended up moving even farther away to San Diego when I started university – but when I did see him, there was a softness and even vulnerability that I rarely noticed when we were younger. The tender moments that I remembered from our childhood were usually centred around animals, and in Sacramento he adopted a couple of kittens who seemed to bring him some joy and contentment. He also took to keeping tropical fish, and it was apparent how much time and care he put into their well-being as he proudly showed off his fish tank.

I even found out that he could be kind towards my own emotional vulnerability. He was visiting the family home one day when I was still in high school, and he had been rummaging through the record cabinet

---

[5] I am intentionally omitting the details of my brother's struggles here, not because I think they are unimportant, but because his story deserves to be told in its own right, and this memoir is about my own journey.

looking for one of his old albums. Since he hadn't been living there for over two years, and our parents never used the stereo, I had more or less assumed ownership of the space in that cabinet.

And I had left the folder containing some original poetry in there. Lyrics, really – my first attempts at putting my feelings to words, a whole album's worth of verses to go with the songs I heard in my heart. Absolutely cringeworthy, looking back now, but they were the earnest and genuine confessions of a lovesick teenage boy. Pining over a girl who hardly knew me, but who stirred something in my emotions more significant than I realised at the time. What would my brother make of it all?

I was afraid to ask.

But I needed to know if he had seen anything. Unsure if I actually wanted a whole conversation, I waited until he was passing the open door of my room.

"Hey. I had a folder in that cabinet, you didn't happen to look in...?"

Jon smiled. "I read it. It's beautiful."

I didn't know what to say to that.

He didn't say anything else either, and kept walking past.

Jon took his own life on the American holiday of Thanksgiving, in late November 1994.

When I think about my brother's life, and his death, I feel somewhat detached, as if it happened in a story I once read. I know that grief has no rules or time limits, but I occasionally wish that I could feel it more viscerally, in the way that the other important events and connections in my life have affected me. I like to think that Jon and I would have developed a good relationship, one where we could open up to each other without fear of ridicule or rejection. Brothers who have each other's backs when it counts. But when he was alive, I was still too wary of him, of our history, and of his unpredictable nature.

How would he have regarded me as Meredith? I don't know. As a teenager he was outwardly homophobic, not just using the word "gay" as a slur (to be fair, back then we all did), but also making unsolicited derogatory comments about other people's perceived homosexual tendencies. How would this have manifested in his reaction to any transgender person, let alone his brother?

It's hard to say. In those days there were hardly any trans people in the public eye, and certainly nobody we'd ever met. But Jon had a brilliant mind, and he was certainly capable of comprehending a wide diversity of human existence. I like to think that he would have grown, as I have, as much of the world has. If only his illness, and the arbitrary, indifferent Universe, had allowed him to.

Part Three

Chapter Nine

Jennifer

Student apartments, University of California, San Diego (UCSD)
January 1990

She is fiercely beautiful. Defiant. Standing atop the rocky cliff she faces the storm, challenging the wind, breathing it in, letting it flow through her body like quicksilver, leaving ripples behind in the furls and flutters of her billowing skirts and ribbons of dancing tresses. The spray of the ocean waves, crashing far below, leaves a mist rising in windswept trails around her. She stands proud, commanding, at one with the elements.

The roar of the wind becomes my own music as I imagine this scene, at once both inside and outside of me, taking me away from the incessant, pounding drudgery of my immediate surroundings. Doof-doof, aggressively sing-song dance music, drinking, annoying shouts and loud laughter about gossip and things that I find inane and banal. My best friend Amy has other friends that I simply cannot relate to, and it frustrates me that she thinks I would enjoy myself at this party.

Jennifer

I sigh audibly. "Jennifer..." Whispering her name out loud brings me comfort. My guardian angel, the catalyst and constant encouragement, the reason behind my search for all things beautiful. Her music provides me with an escape from the chaos and noise of this place. This is far from the first or last time she will carry me through a difficult or unpleasant experience – she is part of every moment of my life, no matter whether trivial or profound, fleeting or enduring. Or painful, or joyous.

* * *

Del Mar, California
April 1990

The sun ducks behind the thin band of clouds just above the horizon, unsuccessfully trying to hide its brilliance. The burnt sky around the bright spot stretches all the way from the line of the ocean, through the wispy remains of more cloud bands, to the scattered jet contrails directly overhead, leaving everything in the sky with a fiery orange underglow.

Jennifer is here, too, in the last rays of daylight, in the quiet salt air, in the silhouettes of the seagulls wheeling offshore in front of the setting sun. She sings to me in the sublime passages of the music playing on my car stereo, the haunting, lyrical tones of Andy Latimer's guitar merging with the breeze as it brushes my face through the open window. She is present in every moment of beauty, in each instant where my heart feels alive, in every exquisite vibration of those delicate strings inside.

Amy would call it God. I know she struggles to understand and accept Jennifer, but Amy and I are two very different people – who happen to be best friends, open to learning from each other. I think that both of us are surprised at our friendship, but somehow it just fell into place, and Amy is the first person with whom I've ever felt so comfortable sharing something this personal.

I grew up unafraid of my emotions. I may not have shown them to others, but I embraced the way I responded to the world, unashamed and unwilling to believe that boys don't cry. I was blessed with the circumstances and the wisdom to simply hide away when I needed to, rather than be bullied, or mistakenly try to fit in and reject who I knew myself to be.

My feelings were overwhelming. They were so important, so beautiful, that I gave them a name.

Jennifer.

* * *

Cupertino, California
1986

I have no idea why my heart picked Jennifer to be the one. I barely knew her, and we spoke maybe half a dozen times, never about anything meaningful. She was just someone in my history class from the previous term, and not even present in my timetable this year. Why her, and not Lesley from my dream of the previous year? I don't know; maybe because in real life, Lesley never caught my eye the way Jennifer did. Were it not for the strength of that dream, Lesley would just be another random classmate. The *feeling* of that dream is what I remember.

Jennifer, however, was a dream come true. In my conscious imagination, anyway.

How much did she know? In my mind she was always present, taking up such a large amount of my attention that it was hard to have any realistic perspective on how she perceived my actions. Perhaps she hardly cared, dismissing the time I actually asked her to a school dance as an amusing, awkward moment (she said she'd get back to me and she never did). Or maybe she understood the depth of my obsession and spent an entire year dreading every encounter. If so, I am truly sorry. I had only just begun learning what my feelings were capable of.

Jennifer

I took notice of her movements in the hallways between classes, and carefully planned my own in the hopes of a brief smile or hello, not necessarily taking the most obvious paths to my locker or to my next class. I endlessly scanned the quad during lunch, always lingering on the corner where she and her friends were most likely to be sitting. I even learned where she lived, the car she drove, the way her household was listed in the phone book. I had become a stalker. It never would have occurred to me to do anything harmful or dangerous, but looking back I realise how unnerving it could have been for her.

My fantasy was pure – I regarded Jennifer as a creature somehow separate from the girls who stirred my physical teenage hormones. Even as I was exploring and developing my peculiar doll fetish, I never allowed myself to objectify her like that. To do so would be... unfair in some way, I suppose, though I would not have been able to articulate this, or the reasons why. I didn't dream of doing anything physical beyond maybe a kiss, holding hands, gazing into her eyes. I wanted an emotional companion, not a sexual one.

I'd like to think that she would at least be happy that she inspired something so beautiful inside another being, even if its gestation required her to endure the unwanted attention of an awkward, nerdy boy who had no idea how farfetched such a pairing would be.

The thing is, I *did* know how impossible it was. But I didn't care. Maybe I spun this fantasy out of a desperate need to *feel*. I wanted to be a hopeless romantic, and with Jennifer there wasn't any risk of actually having my dreams come true. She was part of the popular crowd, and I was one of the geeky weird kids. It could have been as painful and pathetic as the worst teenage movie. But she seemed genuinely nice, and she never made me feel small during our brief interactions.

In my messy, jumbled, *yearning* adolescent heart and mind, Jennifer became a safe place. My struggles, my fears, my hopes – about things familiar to any teenager, undoubtedly – all of life's *impact* was made bearable by her presence in my imagination. Even the pain of knowing how futile, in reality, my longing for her was – this too was transformed into something that I could appreciate, even relish. How soothing it was to imagine her by my side: intimate, safe, *knowing*.

I gazed for hours upon her yearbook photo, in flickering candlelight, with sweeping movie soundtracks painting pictures in my head.

I wrote terrible high school poetry, lyrics to would-be songs, setting my feelings down where I could see them, hold them, and cherish them.

I whispered her name out loud in moments of beauty, times of need, scenes where my heart transcended the limitations of my world.

Jennifer.

It took a very long time for me to understand that the things I felt for Jennifer were more about myself than they were about her. In hindsight, it makes sense: I never really got to know her – the Jennifer of my high school infatuation – but the *Jennifer* of my inner world, well, she was always going to be with me. Long after the last hallway encounter, after time and distance ended my stalking ways, all of the awareness of my feelings and the inspiration inside me remained.

And so, then, did her name. *Jennifer* had become meaningful in a timeless way that transcended the identity of the girl I'd hardly known. Jennifer, my spiritual companion, a projection and manifestation of my most cherished emotions. I've never had the words to adequately convey the depth and power of her presence; sharing these things with Amy, and others in the years that followed – even to this day – the closest I've come is the term *guardian angel*.

Throughout the heady days of my early twenties, as I threw myself headlong into the new experiences life offered, Jennifer was there with me. Moving out of home to a new city; starting University in a demanding engineering course; learning to live with three strangers I had never met;

not quite cast adrift in the world, but certainly leaving behind the comfortable, predictable life I had lived, I set out to face the unknown.

With Jennifer beside me.

Through the years that followed, as I grew to actively embrace the unknown, as my fortunate life led me across oceans and into adventures, Jennifer was there. There, at midnight on a dormitory rooftop in the middle of Tokyo; there, in a busy café watching the world go by on a drizzly morning in Melbourne; there, with my vulnerable heart as I opened myself up to someone. Always there, weaving a thread around my experiences, building bridges of emotional understanding, gently teaching me to see what was already there in my soul.

And when I would forget – when I let the world get to me, when I ignored what my heart was saying, when I would lose myself inside my own anger and frustration, Jennifer would quietly leave. At these times, I would know things weren't right because there would be emptiness in her place. Nothing. No reassurance. No feeling at all. Jennifer was not a magical fix to be relied upon whenever life became difficult; if I was detached from my centre, she would have nothing to manifest for me.

Not until I reconnected with *understanding* – my sense of who I actually wanted to be – would she return. It wouldn't be noticeable; I would simply realise at some point that she was back, and that I was once again able to feel the things that made me thankful for my existence.

I don't know if any of this actually makes sense. As I've already said, I have never been able to find words that adequately explain who and what Jennifer is, and how her presence colours my world. My understanding has grown and evolved over the years; and will continue to do so as long as I am paying attention to my feelings and my soul.

Jennifer is just a girl from my past, someone to whom I would apologise for my naïve and clumsy actions… but *Jennifer* is her gift to me, and I am eternally indebted to her. In writing this, I could have changed her name, as I have done with others from my past, but her name is too important. It is not just symbolic; Jennifer is intrinsically linked to everything I feel.

And as I would eventually learn – discover – decide? – she is much more than just my guardian angel.

Chapter Ten

Amy

Student apartments, University of California, San Diego (UCSD)
October 1989

"What are you listening to?" Amy had phoned to ask my roommate Daniel about a recipe he'd promised to share. They'd met during the previous summer at a community cooking class and discovered they were both students here at UCSD. Daniel wasn't home just now, but Amy was a friendly and chatty person, and in our small talk I'd mentioned that I was procrastinating from an assignment by playing an album I hadn't heard in a few years.

"It's not something you'd hear on the radio. It's from 1974 and it's... four twenty-minute-long songs, on a double album." I tried to think of way to actually describe the music, and came up empty. "It's a band called Yes and the album is called *Tales from Topographic Oceans*. It's a concept album based on some ancient Indian scriptures. Really weird stuff."

"That sounds really interesting actually! I'd like to hear it sometime."

"Really?" I wasn't expecting that. Most people just dismissed my musical tastes as bizarre and uncool. "Maybe we could get Daniel to cook dinner for us sometime."

"Yes! That would be awesome!"

I was a little taken aback at Amy's bubbly enthusiasm, but since coming to UCSD I'd met a fair number of people who would have been well outside my high school circle of middle-class, mostly white male nerds who tried not to stand out too much lest we get picked on. I was just starting to appreciate some diversity in my social interactions.

Daniel laughed when I told him about Amy's call and her reaction to my weird music.

"Is she always that excited?" I looked at the CD case in my hand, wondering what Amy would think about the otherworldly cover art that was as much a part of 1970s Yes as the music.

"She usually is. Did she mention that she's a Christian?" Daniel raised an eyebrow at me and smiled.

"No, why? Uh-oh. Should I be worried?" I had mentioned the Indian scriptures that inspired *Topographic Oceans* and suddenly realised that maybe Amy wanted to talk about God and tell me that my music was leading me down the path to damnation.

"Nah, she's fine. She won't try to convert you. But she gets very enthusiastic about God. And everything else."

"I see."

Daniel laughed again. "If she can be friends with me, knowing I'm an atheist, you'll be fine. But yeah, she can be a bit…" A mischievous twitch crossed his face. "Hi! I'm Amy! I love God!! Do you??! Well if you don't then He loves you anyway!!! Isn't that great?!"

Oh dear. Was I going to have to share dinner with this girl?

Amy

I thought that hanging around with Amy was going to annoy the hell out of me. Occasionally her exuberance did get on my nerves, but I found myself unexpectedly open to learning and appreciating her joyous, unreserved take on the world. An attitude so far removed from the moody, reflective quietness that I cultivated in myself.

What surprised me about Amy was her thoughtfulness. It was easy for me to dismiss someone so bouncy and upbeat as a person who never bothered to slow down and examine their life, especially when they followed a religion that – as it seemed to me – laid out all the rules for you. But Amy didn't take everything at face value. She could have just as easily dismissed me as a boring, fun-avoiding party pooper. But she didn't. She took the time to look more closely, and to listen.

Amy opened up my heart and mind to the possibility that people very different from myself might be worth knowing. We became the most unlikely of friends.

She came into my room just as the chorus of the song began. *Jigsaw*, by Marillion. An angry, poetically charged plea to a relationship shattering in pieces, daring the leaver to show honesty in place of avoidance: say goodbye like you mean it, and spare me the excuses.

A soaring, searing, brutally poignant guitar solo trailed after Fish's tortured vocals. Steve Rothery playing as raw and honest as he ever had. I turned up the volume and leaned against the wall, breathing it in. It was a breakup song, yes, and even though it didn't speak to any personal experience of mine, it was still immensely powerful.

When it finished, Amy nearly had tears in her eyes. "That was amazing! I can't imagine… if someone had written that song for me I would be an absolute wreck!"

"Did you like it?"

She was hesitant. "I – I don't think it's something I would listen to often. It's… it's too much. Is it always like this?"

I thought for a bit. "Actually, yeah, Marillion is not... not exactly happy music."

"It makes me wonder what he's like, is he ever happy?"

"Who, the singer? The music is written by the whole band. The lyrics, though – I've heard an interview where Fish says he never writes when he's happy. I think that's probably true for a lot of writers."

"I guess. It makes me sad to think of somebody always so depressed though."

Music. The soundtrack to my life; she was genuinely interested. I did have friends who shared similar tastes, but Amy was the first person to show any curiosity who was new to all of it. I played everything for her – the grandiose prog-rock symphonies that transported me to other worlds, the jazz fusion licks that set my soul alight on the ocean breeze, the exquisite, lyrical guitar solos that always tore my heart out – she listened, and asked for more, even if it was all strange and foreign to her.

I played songs with words that meant something significant, secret, personal – something more than I could possibly explain, and I wondered if maybe she understood a little, if maybe she could catch a glimpse of how the songs touched me. For the first time in my life I felt safe to freely show my messy, squishy, emotional inner self. Amy was so different from any of my other friends, so unexpected, so giving of her time and her care.

What would she think about Jennifer?

I didn't want Amy to be my girlfriend. Other people made assumptions, given the heteronormative expectations around a young man and young woman seen frequently in each other's company. But I explicitly told Amy that I wasn't after anything more than friendship. I thought she was attractive, but if her ever-present enthusiasm wasn't enough to be too much, the God thing certainly was. To her credit she never preached to me or tried to convert me. I actually found it fascinating to consider the parallels between the things Amy attributed to God and the things I would ascribe to Jennifer – my guardian angel, after all.

Amy helped me to understand the nature, and value, of belief. Not just in a higher being. Belief, ultimately, in one's own self-worth.

I don't remember exactly how or when I told Amy about Jennifer. Maybe I've forgotten because she didn't really give me a reaction to remember. I suppose that it might have been a foreign concept to her, and confronting even to consider that I'd invented a spirituality that wasn't clearly related to religion or informed by any sacred text. But she was kind. As my friend, she wasn't going to denounce me and claim that I was misguided, not in the moment of my vulnerability in sharing this with her.

But I knew from the fact that she didn't really say anything that she couldn't bring herself to accept it.

"I'm so sorry I'm late!" Amy arrived looking exasperated, but she was laughing. My annoyance at having waited for nearly an hour eased a little, but not enough to make me smile.

"Mmm hmm." I didn't want to say "that's okay" because I wasn't feeling like it was. I'd become used to Amy being unreliable with plans, and even though I accepted it as a part of being her friend, my graciousness about it largely depended on my mood at the time.

"Tammy came over and she's having issues with her boyfriend and I couldn't just make her leave of course so then I was trying to find something in my car for her and I ended up locking my keys in the trunk and then I had to wait for my brother to help me break into my car and then he noticed that I had a flat tire and thank God he put the spare on for me and oh my gosh what a morning. How are you?" She rolled her eyes and giggled.

Amy's boisterousness occasionally rubbed me the wrong way. And I was baffled by her seeming inability to take things seriously. My own reaction to such mishaps would have been to get extremely agitated and stressed out. Having someone treat the situation like it was funny would annoy me and make me angry.

I tried not to let my uneasiness show. I knew that Amy never got too worried or anxious about adverse circumstances because, as she had told me, she trusted God to sort things out. I thought perhaps that she could be a little more proactive in trying to prevent mishaps in the first place. It was hard for me not to see a chronic lack of foresight as a character flaw.

At the same time, I was aware that some people would consider *me* to be uptight and inflexible, and likewise call these things character flaws, but I thought those people were wrong.

Little by little, though, Amy was teaching me to become more accepting, less judgemental. Even if I didn't realise it.

"I'm ok, I guess. I'm glad midterms are over. Now I can think about doing stuff that I've been putting off. You've just reminded me that my car needs new tires, and an oil change. Should we order?" I motioned towards the café's service counter.

Amy smiled. "See? God's helping me make sure your car stays safe."

I knew better than to disagree out loud, but it was hard to refrain from rolling my eyes.

She continued. "I know you don't believe it, but I think it's amazing. Like how I was able to help Tammy this morning, the CD I gave her, I only got it last week but it's so perfect for her and what she's going through. God does wonderful things if you pay attention."

"God created coffee. I'm going to get some." I stood up.

Amy laughed. "Well, yes, that too."

We ordered our coffee, and as we sat back down I realised what didn't sit right with me in Amy's earlier remarks. "Don't you think that some of what you do for people… is your own doing? Don't you want to take credit for anything?"

She looked at me with an expression I couldn't quite read clearly. Was it empathy? Pity? Together with something else. Almost like gratitude, and relief. "I take credit for recognising that God works through me. I believe that without God we are nothing. We are born wicked through original sin and it's only through the grace of God and the sacrifice of His son Jesus that we are saved. All the good that we do comes from the love of God." She smiled.

I tried not to furrow my brow too obviously. "What about someone who doesn't believe in God but still does good deeds?"

"God is still working through them, even if they don't realise it. God is showing them how they can be saved."

It was a convenient and reasonable explanation on the surface. Still, there was something fundamental here that troubled me. "Okay, but... do you really believe that you are nothing? Don't you think that's a little harsh?" Did Amy's religion discourage her from developing her self-esteem? Surely she didn't go around thinking to herself *I am worthless*. I tried to think of a way to phrase it that wasn't quite so starkly personal. "God created you, right? So isn't it... I don't know... rude?... to call yourself 'wicked' and 'nothing'? Aren't you being disrespectful to God's creation? If I was God I might be insulted by that!"

Amy just smiled, with that same mixed expression. "It's what I believe. We are so lucky. God loves us unconditionally. I am nothing, but I am saved by God and I am a better person because of it."

I thought about Jennifer, my guardian angel, the closest thing I had to the idea of God. Had Jennifer saved me from being wicked? Of course not: I didn't believe I was wicked in the first place. But did she save me somehow, nonetheless? I don't know. Yes, she loved me unconditionally; that was the same. Was I a better person for it? Possibly. Probably. What did I feel about that? It filled me with hope, and a sense of beauty. Is that what Amy's face revealed?

Sadness. Was that it? Did I see sadness in Amy's smile?

If my all-powerful loving God told me that I was nothing without Him, I'd probably be sad. Maybe I was projecting, and interpreting Amy's expression through my own feelings.

That conversation stayed with me for a long time. I started to see how Amy's beliefs aligned with, and reinforced, her inclination to be a people-pleaser. The usual result was that people were thankful, but I wondered about the hidden cost.

It was hard not to think that Amy's behaviour was driven at least partly by a lack of self-worth. It seemed like she kept herself busy spreading God's love, constantly surrounding herself with people so that she wouldn't have to be alone with her own thoughts. This was of course my own interpretation, but whether it was true or not I think it played a large part in my own long journey (an endless one, as I am periodically reminded) towards recognising and understanding the inherent worth of every person. Including myself.

After all, I had initially dismissed Amy as someone I wouldn't like very much – and as luck would have it (or perhaps it was God!) she ended up being my best friend, who had a lot to teach me about acceptance.

For the next five years Amy and I shared in each other's life adventures as best friends do – studying overseas in different countries in Europe, travelling great distances to see each other for a weekend, writing long letters (by hand – this was before the Internet). In Japan, I kept a photo of Amy on my desk in my tiny room, anchoring me to the love and trust of our friendship as I navigated through the storms of what would become the most important year of discovery in my life. Given the effort we went through, other people naturally assumed we were romantic partners, and I proudly defended our friendship as valid and real, to dispel the Hollywood-like notion that a man and a woman in our situation must end up as lovers.

Amy

There were periods when the letters and long-distance phone calls were scarce, when we were too busy with other obligations and the mundane details of life to reach out. There were misunderstandings, too – as two very different people we occasionally came at a situation with definitions and assumptions that were foreign to each other, without realising it. But we learned from each other, and we were thankful.

The fact that we had to work for our friendship made me treasure it more than I would have if things were always easy. Proving ourselves against the expectations of the world was important to me – I wanted to be different, I wanted to feel subversive.

When it finally ended, the disappointment I felt was not so much because we had ultimately failed, but because I felt that Amy had stopped trying.

* * *

Mira Mesa, San Diego, California
October 1994

"I'm getting married!!!" Amy's voice sounded sparkly and bubbly, like it was percolating down the phone line.

What? The bubbles hardly touched me as they went past.

Married?

I didn't feel the impact of her excitement because I was struggling to make sense of my reaction. Married to whom? I didn't even know there was a boyfriend. Is that why she hadn't written back in so long?

To be fair, I hadn't made a huge effort either. But nothing particularly exciting had happened in my life for months. Before the Internet, communicating long-distance took time and money; people usually didn't bother reporting trivialities.

Of course, if I'd found a girlfriend, I would have wanted Amy to know. That would be kind of a big deal.

Amy, though, had waited until she was already engaged to reveal the news.

I wanted to say I couldn't believe it, but somehow I *could*.

Why was I only a little bit surprised?

I thought back to the moment when I first felt doubt over how she viewed our friendship. We had been at the café, talking about the future.

I wanted to do something unusual, something that would be meaningful not just to Amy and myself, but to the world around us. I told her, "When – if – I ever get married… I want you to be my best man."

Amy looked confused. "But I'm not a man. Shouldn't your best man be a man?"

Before I'd become friends with Amy, I had attended a delightful wedding where the maid of honour was not a woman. He was a man – the bride's best friend. He had been amused by the label *maid of honor* and had proudly worn it, along with a man's suit. It was memorable and added depth to the ceremony. Even though it didn't resonate with me personally at the time, with Amy I could imagine doing something similar. Why couldn't my *best man* be a woman in a dress? "So what? You could still wear a dress. It's just a position title."

"I don't know. It… seems weird to me. Won't people think it's strange? Why wouldn't you pick Daniel? Or maybe your brother?"

My brother? I had never been close with my brother. In fact, I would never dream of being vulnerable enough with him to foster a relationship where we could get to that point, where I'd even consider asking him to be my best man.

I shook my head. Amy might have been super close with her siblings, but not every family was like hers. I rarely spoke about my brother – surely that fact in itself would be a clue about our relationship. "I hardly ever talk to my brother. I suppose I could ask Daniel, but we don't share that much with each other. I'd rather have you."

Amy

Amy looked away. "I guess. I don't know, I'd have to think about it. I mean, I'm honoured, of course, but… it's unexpected."

I gave her a weak smile. "It's all theoretical anyway. I've never even had a girlfriend!"

What had I been trying to say in that moment? I was telling Amy how much she meant to me, how much I treasured our friendship: *You're my best friend, and I want you there for the most meaningful moments in my life.*

And now… three years later, here I was, feeling like an outsider.

I was glad that my face wasn't visible over the phone call. "Married? When did you get a boyfriend?"

"We met six months ago. You'll love him. He's wonderful, his name is James."

James. Six months. Amy's last letter was what – eight, nine months ago? I tried not to let the hurt show in my voice, and I felt guilty for letting my disappointment prevent me from being excited for her. "I guess I've missed a lot, huh."

"I know, I know, it's a long story." She sighed. "It's been such a whirlwind… I was so confused for a while that I didn't tell anyone about him. My family didn't even know until two weeks ago when he proposed."

I felt something shift. In the awkward painfulness of that moment I didn't really want to acknowledge it, but something inside me went *ppffft* and disappeared.

I had written songs for Amy before. Simple ones, when I was first experimenting with my creativity and getting used to the sound of my voice. She had appreciated them, but I knew they weren't as lyrically or musically inspired as they could have been. After that phone call I knew there had to be one more, and this one would be the real thing. Everything I could never say before, for what did it matter now?

When I think back to the discoveries we made
I wonder what kind of miracle brought us together
we gave of each other for so many years
across oceans of trouble
through endless sunsets
looming storm clouds in the distance
but we missed the lightning didn't we
I wanted you to feel everything
and I tried but when it came time
I felt locked out I expected more I got
nothing

- from "Miracles"

I can't say for sure how or where our next conversation took place. I remember sitting once more in the café, but I also remember another awkward phone call. The years have blurred my memories into an impressionist painting: emotions and specific moments of dialogue are scattered spots of colour in a larger picture that only takes shape when viewed from a distance.

I remember feeling like I had to acknowledge the end.

"I... I don't really know how to say this..." I hesitated, wondering how my next words were going to land. "I just don't feel like there's anything left. Something... something happened over the last six months. I just can't imagine making the effort anymore." Ouch. That sounded like I was trying to dump her. But wasn't she the one who dumped me with that phone call?

That was exactly it. It felt like she didn't think I was worth it anymore. I thought she was my best friend, but I could no longer be sure how she regarded me. I wanted to tell her everything, but during the last year, as her life was going through a momentous change, she hardly told me anything.

Indeed, when I had asked Amy if she would be best man at my own future wedding, her first thought was: *Isn't it inappropriate for a woman to be your best man?* It was only one of many times she hurt me without realising it. Asking her to be my best man was so much more poetic, meaningful, than simply saying: *You're my best friend. You mean the world to me.* It was saying: *You are the sister I never had.* And she didn't get it.

"Derek, I want you to know that you'll always be special to me, no matter what happens." This was the truth, I knew, because I still felt the same way. I wouldn't have given back my friendship with Amy for the world. But I couldn't ignore the fact that it was gone now.

I had to know if she felt that there was anything left.

"What would you say if I didn't come to the wedding?"

She was silent for a while. "I don't know. Of course I want you there, but if you can't make it then I'll understand."

What was that supposed to mean? "Please, Amy, be completely honest. How important is it to you that I be there?"

I couldn't tell if she was hurt by that. "Derek, I want you to come only if you want to. If you're not there, I'll always remember that you couldn't be there, but I'll understand."

Six months before this, before that phone call, if she had told me that she wasn't coming to my wedding, I would have been devastated.

"I'm sorry, Amy. I can't. I just… I'm sorry."

* * *

Friendships can run their natural course, and sometimes the end remains painfully unspoken. With Amy I failed to recognise that the effort required was ultimately hurting me too much. It took me years to understand but looking back I can see that it was probably a bit one-sided. I called Amy my best friend but I don't actually remember her ever saying the same about me. She tried to be close with *everybody*. Any time she had ever let me down, it was inevitably because she had overstretched herself trying to be a good friend to somebody else.

When James came along, I wasn't the only one who didn't know about him until the engagement. Perhaps it was too overwhelming for Amy to consider telling every one of us, family and all of the friends she considered important, the details of what she was going through.

And then, I never even thought to find out why. I suppose I knew that asking her about my absence from the wedding was testing her to see how she felt, but I was less interested in her reasons than I was in confirming what I already suspected: that our friendship was no longer what I once thought it was.

Perhaps it never had been.

Through writing this I finally understand how much I was hurting. I had been disappointed, continually, without admitting it. But how much pain was due to the distance that had been growing between us, and the introduction of James, and how much had I actually carried all along – knowing that Amy would never accept or try to understand Jennifer? In hindsight, my need to have Jennifer recognised was more important than I knew. The fact that my closest friend was unable to do so left me with a sense of longing that I wasn't quite aware of, and likely wouldn't have been able to understand.

I wasn't intentionally being selfish. I know now that what I'd found in Amy was the possibility of being *seen,* and I instinctively wanted to know how it felt. I needed the affirmation that Jennifer was valid, and real, and beautiful. And, though I hadn't yet come to realise it, fundamentally part of me.

But I didn't have the maturity to recognise that maybe Amy also wanted and needed things that I wasn't giving her. And Amy, busy trying to be there for everyone else, would never have asked.

In the end, I am grateful. Not just all these years later, but even as we parted without really saying goodbye. Even in the pain and disappointment of losing her, I was thankful that we'd been friends, and as our lives

Amy

diverged into unexpected paths I carried my gratitude consciously and with respect for who Amy was – the enthusiastic, bubbly, frustratingly upbeat girl who had been best friends with me despite myself.

Even if Amy never really knew Jennifer, even though we both stopped trying, the importance of what she taught me will always remain. Amy was the first person to make me really consider the sacred value of each human being: we are inherently worthy – all of us. And without affirmation, whether from inside or outside, we suffer at a spiritual level.

And sometimes, we don't even know that we're denying it.

Chapter Eleven

Lauren

"I can't be the kind of friend you want me to be. I'm sorry." Her words seemed reluctant. Or was that just my wishful thinking?

It didn't matter in the end, because she'd already been the friend I needed.

Tokyo, July 1992

She catches my eye from across the common room. The first thing I notice is her hair. Dark blonde, gathered to the side and gently flowing over her shoulder. Long and silky, falling halfway to her waist. It looks like something out of a shampoo commercial. Her face is small, and she is wearing slightly oversized glasses that, coupled with her slight build and quiet presence, make her look reserved and bookish.

Lauren. The quiet one. Quiet, guarded and aloof. Not unfriendly, but clearly distanced from the rest of our small group of nine foreign exchange students. There is something about her that intrigues me. She doesn't strike me as plain or unremarkable. The way she politely keeps to herself, observing without seeming arrogant; the intelligence she reveals when she answers questions in class; her softly-spoken manner; all these things only make me want to look deeper. How would she respond to a nerdy Chinese-American boy trying to get to know her?

We're at the beginning of an eight-week intensive language program that will take us from now – the middle of July – through the Japanese summer to the beginning of fall when the academic year begins. At that point we will part ways; there are many universities participating in this exchange and we all have different academic circumstances. Until then, however, we will see each other nearly every day.

Lauren's seeming unwillingness to let anyone get to know her better is just about to kill my interest in her when, one day, she inexplicably opens up a bit. We are out of the classroom, wandering around a pleasantly relaxed corner of one of Tokyo's large city parks. It's a nice spot to do our language homework: we've been paired up and instructed to practise interactions with native Japanese speakers – asking directions, asking for the time, getting our photo taken. In between our stumbling efforts to engage the population of Tokyo's Ueno Park, Lauren's diffidence relaxes to a point where conversation between us is easy.

"So why did you come to Japan? Are you studying something specific?" She loosens her scrunchie, brushes her hands through her long hair, and re-ties it up in a ponytail. In this heat, all that hair must be troublesome. She doesn't seem to mind.

I shrug. "I'm studying mechanical engineering and I'm going to spend the year as a research student in a lab, but that's not really why I'm here. It's mostly an excuse to live overseas for a year. I spent my Junior year in England and wanted to do it again somewhere else."

"Why Japan? You're not Japanese, right? Your last name doesn't sound Japanese." Lauren impresses me by not assuming anything based upon my appearance.

"Yeah, I'm not. I'm Chinese but really I think I'm more American than Chinese. My parents were both born in the States. I don't know, I just find Japan interesting. My minor is in Sociology and it's fascinating how different other cultures can be."

Lauren looks a bit puzzled. "Sociology? That's... really different from engineering."

I smile. "I'm also minoring in music – you know, in case I wasn't doing enough." I laugh.[6] "I don't really play anything though, it's mostly just theory and appreciation."

This is kind of untrue, actually. I'm holding myself to an arbitrary standard of skill and dedication when I say I don't play anything. If I sat down in front of a piano I could make sounds that definitely count as music, and I've even written and recorded a few songs – very roughly produced using a 1980s boom box and a cheap microphone. But the idea of playing for an audience scares me, and my skills are very basic; I struggle with anything more than simple chord progressions.

Lauren brightens up at my statement. "Hey, you know what? My sister's boyfriend is a musician. He's actually Japanese and lives here – his band is playing in Yokohama on the weekend. You should come!"

My heart flutters a little. How could I say no?

The trip to the club in Yokohama was not what I'd hoped. I had expected to travel there with Lauren and was looking forward to spending more time together. Instead, she simply gave me directions and the gig details and said

---

[6] Note for readers not familiar with U.S. academic terms: the four years of study, in both high school and University, are given the names *Freshman, Sophomore, Junior, and Senior*. At University, your primary course of study is called your *major*, and sometimes people will choose a smaller additional specialisation in another subject, called a *minor*.

Some science and technology majors commonly take more than four years to complete. Officially, engineering can be done in four years, but the heavy workload typically requires abstinence from all extracurricular activities, including paid employment; not realistic for many students. This year in Japan is actually my fifth year; I will also decide to convert my Sociology minor into a second major when I return to California, resulting in an additional two years of study.

she'd meet me there, since she would be travelling with her sister's boyfriend Tomoki and the band.

After only a week in the country, barely speaking the language and able to read only a smattering of train station names and navigational signs (and years before mobile phones gave us the ability to look things up or communicate last-minute plan changes), I somehow managed to find my way to a nondescript looking block of a building in the middle of Yokohama, some ninety minutes and two train changes from where I'd started.

Lauren was nowhere to be found. I had kind of expected this, since there were five different bands on the lineup and Tomoki's band was number three. They wouldn't need to arrive for at least another hour. So I bought my ticket and found a lonely table inside the stark, dimly lit, somewhat inhospitable feeling space.

I don't remember much about the first two bands. I spent the time waiting for Lauren, not really able to listen properly, hoping I wouldn't regret coming. As the first two sets dragged on, I sat there alone, finding myself growing more and more depressed at how the evening was unfolding, compared to what I'd spent the previous few days hoping for.

Finally. Lauren appeared at my table looking slightly apologetic as Tomoki and his band took the stage. We barely had time to say hello and establish that yes, I managed to find my way here without getting lost, before the band started and the music made it too difficult to really converse properly.

So all I remember about the next forty-five minutes is sitting there immersed in loud, forgettable music, bored, barely speaking to Lauren who didn't seem particularly interested anyway, thinking *this sucks*.

When the set finished, I had a brief moment of hope when I imagined us leaving the club together, going somewhere for a drink and a bite to eat, and maybe turning this wretched experience into something worthwhile.

Lauren stood up. "Umm. I'm gonna go with the band now." Again, she seemed slightly apologetic. "Thanks for coming."

I thought *are you fucking serious?*

I can't remember if I actually said anything as she left. I just sat there for a while, stunned, wondering what the hell had happened. Wondering why Lauren had invited me to this God-forsaken place to listen to unremarkable Japanese indie-rock, if she wasn't even going to make an effort to spend time with me. Wondering what it was about her that intrigued me so much, when all I'd gotten so far was disappointment.

Well, after tonight I wasn't going to bother any more. After all, I hadn't come to Japan to get involved with a frustrating American girl, chasing after some idea of who I hoped she'd be. Better to focus on the reality of being in this country, and on the things I could actually see, and do, and appreciate.

I didn't need to be friends – or anything more – with Lauren. I was lonely of course, but I'd spent much of my life feeling lonely and I rarely let it affect how I felt about myself. Loneliness might colour my experiences but it would not stop me from appreciating them. I had trust in my feelings, and in the beauty of an inner spirit who understood the leaps and twists and flutters of my heart. A spirit I'd discovered – created, invented, recognised – because my feelings could manifest so tangibly that I gave them a name.

Jennifer.

Jennifer, always with me whenever I needed her: my guardian angel who kept the spark of hope and beauty alight inside me when the world offered nothing.

All the Laurens in the world could never replace Jennifer.

We spread ourselves down the centre of the train carriage, placing our luggage in the special bays provided, and found ourselves mostly pairing up in the unclaimed seats, two to a side. I had boarded behind the others, and by the time I'd stowed my bag there was only one pair of seats left unoccupied. And one other person still standing. Just my luck.

I didn't really want to be stuck with Lauren, but there we were. It would be awkward to make a point of taking the nearest empty single seat, five rows back. Just as awkward, but less rude, to spend the next two-and-a-half hours sitting next to this inscrutable creature who – to my frustration – still sparked my curiosity. What went on inside that head of hers? And why did I care?

I tried not to care. I tried to imagine a wall between us as I grudgingly acknowledged the small talk that we had to engage in to make this situation feel bearable. It was going to be a long ride up to the mountains and the city of Nagano, where we would be spending six weeks living in homestays and experiencing life in the Japanese countryside.

After Lauren and I had exhausted the limited variety of things we could say to each other without venturing into uncomfortable territory, I thought to hell with restraint and decided to clear the air.

"So, what was the deal at the club last weekend?"

Lauren gave me her now-familiar apologetic look. "I'm really sorry about that. I had to just follow along with whatever the band was doing. I felt bad leaving you there but… you know the Japanese group thing…"

I knew what she meant. Individual desires always defer to the group dynamic in Japanese society. You don't make waves. Even though, as a foreigner, you are granted a certain amount of room to make cultural mistakes, if you make a noticeable attempt to learn the ropes then the Japanese appreciate it.

Still, Lauren could have anticipated all of this and considered what might happen. I was still annoyed. "Yeah, I know," I grunted.

She tried to appease me. "Did you stay for the rest of the bands? Were they any good?"

I had stayed, actually. Partly because I had been too stunned to get up and partly because the music got better. "The last guy was like an Elvis impersonator. He had screaming teenage fans and everything. He wasn't bad. It was pretty funny."

Lauren ran her hands through her hair. "Oh, that's cool. My boyfriend loves Elvis, he would have liked to see that."

Oh, she had a boyfriend. Just as well, since I wasn't interested in her anymore.

Was I?

Regardless, I wasn't in the habit of making other people's romantic situations complicated. "Is your boyfriend Japanese?"

She brightened a little at my question. "No, he's back in Santa Barbara. This is the first time we've really been apart. We're really missing each other but we can't afford the overseas phone calls more than once a week."

I didn't really have anything more to say at this. I just smiled wanly and leaned back in my seat, thinking about the year ahead and how it felt to be on my own in a new country. Free. Unrestrained. Not beholden to anyone here, or back home; free to explore without having to navigate other people's preconceived ideas of who I was supposed to be.

* * *

Nagano, August 1992

"I'm very proud to be American. But I don't pretend that there aren't a lot of things that need fixing about America." She pulled her *waribashi* apart and rubbed each chopstick briskly along the length of the other one, ensuring no splinters remained.

Lauren and I were having lunch following our morning Japanese language lesson. I was still trying to figure out why I was drawn to her. She wasn't so detached from the rest of us anymore, but she hadn't really opened up either. At least she was present enough to make it feasible to spend time together. I wondered what we had in common besides our introversion and our shared sense of wonder at discovering little details about life in Japan.

"You certainly notice stuff that needs fixing when you see how other countries do things." This wasn't my first time living outside of the United States, and the year I'd spent in England, coinciding with the first Gulf War during 1990-1991, had left me very critical of the parochialism and cultural arrogance of Americans in general. I certainly wasn't proud to be American, but I didn't mention this. "Although it goes the other way too. I wouldn't want to be a Japanese *salaryman* and work myself to death."

Lauren nodded. "Or what about a Japanese housewife? I'm a feminist and the sexism in this country really bothers me." She stabbed at a piece of chicken katsu with her chopsticks. "I get angry if I think about it too much." A lock of hair hung close to her food and she absent-mindedly flicked it back over her shoulder so it wouldn't get in the way as she ate.

There it was. A glimpse into Lauren's inner fire. There was feeling there, behind the subtle and shy presentation. More than just a pretty head of hair. How much more was she?

Feminism. This was a welcome revelation. I leaned forward. "I took a class on the sociology of gender last year. I really like thinking about this stuff, and yeah it's frustrating, how much society assumes – or tells people – how they should be. But a lot of people don't want to talk about it. They think feminism means you hate men."

"Most guys don't want to hear about it." Lauren looked thoughtful. "My boyfriend gets it. I think I'm pretty lucky – Eddie's always been supportive. A lot of guys seem nice but then you find out... the way they behave around other guys, they don't respect women at all."

"Ugh. I've never liked hanging around with... like, frat boy types. Or party animals." I thought of my friends back home. I was starting to miss them, being so far away. "Most of my friends are actually girls. Or geeks. Or both."

"Quiet girls with glasses?" She raised an eyebrow at me.

Indeed.

Maybe I'd found Lauren after all.

I was recounting what I'd done that day as I sat with my host family on the tatami mat around the low dining table.

"Where did you go for lunch?" My host mother was good at asking me simple things, to help me develop my Japanese language skills.

"A katsudon restaurant in Gondo Street. With Lauren."

She smiled at this. *"Same as yesterday. Always Lauren? Someone special?"*

I knew what she was hinting at. "Gaarufurendo de wa arimasen." *Not my girlfriend.*

She nodded, but there was a twinkle in her eye. Mothers think they know things, regardless of what country they come from.

Well, maybe in another timeline. In this one, I didn't have the insight or ability to articulate exactly what Lauren was to me, even in English, let alone Japanese.

I'm listening to the rain outside my window as I read the little paperback that Lauren has lent to me. *The Tao of Pooh,* by Benjamin Hoff – a cute little exploration of how Winnie-the-Pooh and his friends can teach us some important existential truths.

The passage in front of me talks about *Wu Wei:* using intuition to know when the time is right, rather than brute-forcing your way through the world. Not necessarily performing any actions at all. Awareness of oneself and one's surroundings. Listening. Being *Sensitive to Circumstances.*

I've been known to struggle with circumstances.

I'm excited, and more than a little anxious, because in return for borrowing this book, I've let Lauren borrow the cassette containing the songs I'd recorded over the previous year – my very first attempts at making my own music. I'd even sung on some tracks, lyrics I'd written myself, and very few people in my life are privy to this side of me. I feel vulnerable opening up to Lauren and I'm hoping I won't regret it. But she seems interested in my creative inner life so I'm giving it a chance.

Reading *The Tao of Pooh*, I try to pay heed to the lessons it presents. I think of how difficult it was to begin a friendship with Lauren, and how it ended up being possible only when I stopped trying. Listening to my own intuition would have been easier if I could actually understand what it was telling me.

And what about now? What do I imagine she is doing – listening intently to my music, eyes closed, headphones on? Or busy doing something else, my cassette sitting temporarily forgotten at the bottom of her bag? Why do I imagine this is a possibility?

The little book in my hands doesn't offer any insight. It's not so much that I'm trying too hard – I can't actually *do* anything to change this situation. All I can do is wait until I see Lauren again. It's all well and good to just be like Pooh and walk simply through life, letting things happen as they come, but what am I supposed to make of the anxiety I feel while I'm waiting for those things to happen?

The Tao of Pooh summarises *Wu Wei* as "without doing, causing, or making". With Lauren I guess I don't really have any other option. Our schedules this week don't allow time for lunch together, and over the next several days I only see Lauren briefly at language class. She never mentions the cassette or my music. I wrestle with the urge to ask her directly if she's listened to it but I want more than a casual answer; this is not something to bring up as we're heading in different directions after being dismissed from class.

Has she gone cold again? Why is she doing this again? She could at least give me a hint – does she like the music? Is she going to have questions? I thought I'd found Lauren, but now that I've reached out with something so deeply personal, it's like she hardly acknowledges that we know each other outside of class.

Or is my anxiety simply distorting my perception? I can't tell if I'm being unreasonable – with Lauren, with myself – who knows?

All I know is that this feels awful.

The rain drizzles outside. There is no meaning or intent behind the weather; it just *is*. I try to let it soothe me.

I had to wait a week, but thankfully I wasn't disappointed when Lauren finally found time to give me her thoughts on my music. Actually, "not disappointed" is understating my experience quite a bit.

She liked it.

One song, in particular, she *really* liked. Loved.

It was a song I'd produced in one magical, singularly-focused afternoon-into-evening-into-late night, where I hadn't planned it, where I had just started by noodling around on my keyboard. *Swept Away*. She'd played it over and over.

'Cause I know
When the sun comes out
And the road shines forever's way
Across oceans love sweet sapphire bay
You sail the dreams of every day
When the wind blows all the years away
In a picture frame you see today
Your love from dreams of yesterday
Always just a horizon away
When the tide comes in so once again
You're swept away

You sing there your love and every time I'm
Swept away

You know how, when you're young and impressionable and full of emotion and things can overwhelm you and then you hear a song and it just opens a flood of feelings and speaks to you like it's your very own?

My song did that for Lauren.

"It made me think about Eddie. It's like you wrote it for us. It's amazing."

More than amazing.

Up until now, the few people who had heard my music had responded with polite acknowledgement, or at most, some appreciation of my compositional attempts and how they reflected the influences of my favourite bands.

This was different.

It took me a minute to process the significance of what this meant, and then it was like the doors had been thrown open. In front of me was a landscape that I'd always been vaguely aware of, one that real artists got to walk through, but one that I'd never seriously considered trying to reach. A landscape of unlimited colours and feelings. Possibilities.

Right there, and now I was part of it.

I'd connected with somebody through my music, in the most meaningful way. I had experienced this from the receiving end, but this time I was the one giving. The one being heard.

And there was more.

My inspiration for *Swept Away* had come from a place so close to me that it felt like laying my soul bare to put it down in a song. Lauren's reaction was like hearing proof that Heaven was real.

An angel. My muse. My very heart.

Swept Away was, of course, a love song I'd written for Jennifer.

The next few weeks were simultaneously a blur and a slow-motion dream that left me gasping from its intensity. Lauren finally seemed to be *present* – engaging, interested, connecting. I showed her who I was, and I felt seen. I absorbed every moment, and she mostly listened, and asked questions, as I dove off the delicate bridge I was building between us. I wanted Lauren to join me in exploring the water, to see how deep it went, to see if we would get lost, or risk drowning. I jumped on and off the end as the bridge grew, testing it with every new addition, wanting to make it strong, to know her equally, to fortify our connection with parts of both of us. While she sat dipping her toes in the water, I leapt all around her, looking for the occasional flash when she revealed something beneath her quiet reserve.

We spent our last week in Nagano together almost every day after class. I'm sure the woman who ran the *katsudon* restaurant thought we were young lovers.

"I can't believe you've never had a girlfriend. You're so in tune with your feelings. You could give so much to someone."

Well, wasn't I doing that now? Except this particular girl already had someone else. At what point did our intimacy become too close? All we ever did was talk.

As present as she was for me, I didn't feel like Lauren freely allowed me to reciprocate.

"One day you'll meet someone who you want to give everything to." She paused, looking into the distance. "Well… not everything."

Was she the same with her boyfriend Eddie?

Little by little, I was learning to accept things. Lauren rewarded my efforts and interest only when I relaxed and didn't try.

She was suddenly sharp, direct. "If you've never had a girlfriend, then where did the song come from? *Swept Away*, it feels so *real*."

I smiled at this.

She looked momentarily alarmed. "Where did it come from? Please tell me you didn't just make it up."

I sighed inside, with a mixture of happiness and familiar longing. Her name in my thoughts, as it so often made itself present. *"Jennifer…"*

Lauren

* * *

Tokyo to Kyoto, September 1992

And so as we departed Nagano, our little cohort of exchange students merged with a dozen more from another language program, on a nine-day bus tour heading west across Japan's main island from Tokyo to Osaka and Kyoto, I told Lauren the story of Jennifer.

We sat at the front of the bus together, spending the hours quietly talking and listening, as the Japanese countryside rolled past. As the bus driver deftly guided our oversized vehicle through narrow village lanes and over twisting mountain roads, we explored the possibilities hidden around every new corner that our conversations revealed. As each day unfolded, we were greeted with new gardens to wander through, our tour taking us to visit a dozen temples and shrines and castles, their beautiful surroundings all blending together to become a single backdrop, an idyllic impressionist painting through which we gratefully, reverently moved.

I'm sure the other students on our bus thought we were young lovers.

At night, we stayed in *ryokan,* Japanese inns, sometimes sleeping in communal rooms separated by gender. I hated being stuck with the other male students, most of whom behaved in ways that today we would call "toxic masculinity" – boasting, strutting, speaking suggestively about the female students, and generally carrying on trying to prove who was top dog amongst us. Dickheads. I tried to ignore them. If they said anything about Lauren and myself, I didn't hear them. I longed for the peaceful daytimes I had with Lauren, and felt alone as I kept my distance from the group.

This wasn't the first time I'd felt like I didn't belong amongst other men. But I hadn't yet become aware of just why, and how, I felt different. I think I subconsciously sensed – and still believe – that if given the chance, each one of those jerks would gladly drop the act, relaxing the social front they'd been taught they needed to project, and allow themselves to be more fully human.

I didn't imagine that each one of them had his own Jennifer, though. I *was* different. And I didn't care whether it made me wrong, or special, or better, or less worthy. I resented the way the world didn't seem to appreciate me, but I wasn't about to stop *being* me. I would protect and nurture the beautiful flame burning inside. I would be defiant in my tenderness, and build bridges for people who bothered to take notice.

On the final night of our tour, we stayed in a hotel in Kyoto where each of us had our own room. Late at night, not wanting to sleep, not wanting this time to end, I found myself once again with Lauren. She wanted to read some of the song lyrics I'd written, songs mostly yet to find their music, but which still, through words alone, reflected and revealed the fire and beauty I held in my heart. Songs that lived handwritten in the pages of a folder I kept with me wherever my adventures took me.

Leaning against the wall, sitting together on Lauren's bed at one o'clock in the morning, we immersed ourselves in my lyrics.

> *Just a figure in a lighted doorway*
> *evening comes as clouds burst*
> *night begins and the city lights*
> *nearer the heart of you to find first*
> *inside the pictures play their games*
> *far away time and no words to mean*
> *everything everywhere every time it was there*
> *raining skies will remember your dream*

There are some conversations that I will remember forever. Maybe not word for word but enough to script a pivotal scene in the movie of my life.

I have written many things inspired by Jennifer, not just the song that spoke so dearly to Lauren. Each lyric is special to me in its own way, as a record of the journey I have travelled in search of, and recognition of, my guardian angel.

Lauren

I remember gesturing vaguely into the air, attempting to illustrate Jennifer's presence.

"But why do you externalize it like that?" Lauren asked. "I think she's just... you."

What an odd thing to say, I thought.

Lauren and I eventually drifted apart. In the end, she decided to turn back, leaving the bridge I'd built open ended, halfway out over the water. Water that eventually flowed past, taking with it the magic and the heartbreak of that time in Japan, leaving me with fading memories but also bringing me the sense that, even if our time was fleeting, I'd been given an amazing, miraculous, beautiful gift.

> *When the days turn*
> *I see the shadow fall*
> *And suddenly you're a thousand miles away*
> *And the silence yearns*
> *To hear the music call*
> *But the feeling always waits another day*
> *And I could never understand*
> *So I'll just let it be*
>
> *And remember this bridge will always be here*
> *And I'll always meet you there halfway*
>
> *Across a bridge*
> *I lay a line*
> *And where the patterns cross*
> *The laurel grows*

* * *

Double Exposure

Tokyo, October 1992

Her voice was quiet over the phone line. My little dorm room in Tokyo felt like it might as well be on another continent, another planet, not just a few suburbs away from where Lauren was. There wouldn't be any more long lunches or idyllic garden walks. The summer was over; real life had started, and there were new challenges and experiences awaiting us, not to mention some important academic concerns to attend to. I could commute to the engineering lab on the other side of the city, but I couldn't go to see Lauren. Physical location was irrelevant; the distance between us was insurmountable.

"I can't be the kind of friend you want me to be. I'm sorry." Her words seemed reluctant. Or was that just my wishful thinking?

I'll never know for sure.

It was over.

I saw Lauren a couple of times during the year, when our original group of students got back together, but we both acted like the summer had never happened.

Except that it had, and it stayed with me forever.

I think she's just... you.

I lost touch with Lauren after returning to California, but if I could tell her now, I would recite that line to her with all the thanks that 30 years of understanding can foster.

Part Four

Chapter Twelve
Chrysalis

The year is 1997 and the world is going online. Slowly. The Internet is allowing people to discover and explore interests that would be embarrassing, awkward, or shameful if they were not hidden behind closed doors. It is also allowing private, isolated souls to discover there are others like them. Like me.

I listen to the scratchy sound of the modem connecting and wait patiently for the status message that says I can begin "surfing". Back then the buzzwords made the Internet sound so hip and cool, when in reality the cool people were probably out partying while the surfing was being done by lonely nerds in their bedrooms. Again, like me.

My first stop is *www.asfr.com*, a website serving as the de facto hub for the online "technosexual" community. I've discovered this group of like-minded people by using Lycos and AltaVista (pre-Google search engines) to look for things like "female robot" and "sexy mannequin". "ASFR" stands for *alt.sex.fetish.robots*, which is the address originally given to the specific interest channel for this topic on Usenet – the early Internet's most comprehensive information sharing service (kind of like modern social media with discussion and comment threads, but decentralised, non-commercial, and largely confined to nerdy technical circles).

By the late 1990s, when I am living by myself in Melbourne, online in my one-bedroom flat and eagerly discovering all things ASFR, technology has progressed enough that Usenet is becoming obsolete. There is a new way of presenting and distributing content that is flashier and more user-friendly: early websites. The legacy of the Usenet ASFR acronym lives on, however, in the language used by the technosexual community and in the names of our websites.

Each ASFR site has its own particular bent within the broader scope of the fetish; there are three main areas, with robots being the most obvious. The other two – mannequins and statues – don't appear at first to have a lot in common with robots, but there is considerable overlap in the themes of transformation, domination and control. Not to mention the outright objectification of the female character. There are nuances present, and the fantasies are imaginary, but the overall themes have caused me a fair amount of soul-searching in light of my otherwise feminist convictions. I also fear that people will judge me on a simplistic reading of these things, and I have rarely disclosed my fantasies to others.

A lot of ASFR content consists of erotic fiction, in wildly varying levels of quality. Tonight, I try my luck and click on one of the many stories I haven't yet looked at. The title suggests it's a piece about a woman who willingly gets turned into a robot – something definitely in line with my doll fetish (non-consensual scenarios also appear in ASFR, but I try not to judge the fantasies of other people and instead concentrate on the things that do interest me).

The plot is a familiar one: Girl has desire for eternal beauty; some technology conveniently exists to facilitate robot transformation where physical appearance is duplicated and enhanced; the question of cost, ethics, identity and self are completely ignored; girl becomes robot; girl discovers that sex as a robot is a thousand times more pleasurable than it was as a flesh-and-blood human; girl presumably spends eternity being a sexual object and is completely fulfilled.

The writing isn't bad and there are no conspicuous spelling or grammar mistakes. More importantly, I find the story enjoyable. The author does a reasonable job of conveying the girl's perspective as she gets transformed and lives through her experiences as a robot, and this treatment of her inner feelings definitely appeals to me. It's nice to read about an attractive woman in an erotic situation, but when the writing makes her experience feel genuine to me – then there is something else it touches on, something I can't quite identify. Yet.

It is notable that in the ASFR world there is virtually no objectification of male characters. The community doesn't feel particularly *un*welcoming to members who vary from the (presumably) cisgender, heterosexual male majority; there is an awareness that we are all a bit weird here, and to exclude anyone would go against something innate and unspoken within us. But a suggestion to create a space for male robot content, while received with a general feeling of "sure, why not", has proven to be something of a non-starter, with little to no traffic or activity to show for it.

It is also notable that – in these early days of the online ASFR community – out of a few dozen active members, only three of them present as female.[7] The first is openly transgender and wishes she was actually a subservient, unthinking robot. The second hasn't revealed much about herself, but seems to be interested in the same female-as-object type of content as most of the community. The third is someone who uses a feminine-sounding name, a drawing of a female doll as their profile picture, and has written a couple of stories about a girl-turned-windup-doll that, in

---

[7] On the Internet, of course, one can never be absolutely sure of anyone else's true gender, age, sexuality, etc.

the opinion of the previous member, could only have come from the heart and mind of another woman.

This third member is actually a transgender woman but hasn't realised it yet. Give her another few years.

*** * * ***

Sometime in 1998

It's Saturday lunchtime and the restaurant is full, the large round tables crowded with people busily eating and conversing. The noise is like a background tapestry – colourful and slightly too blurry to make out the details. Most of the voices I can single out are speaking Chinese.

My friends John and David have invited me out to yum cha, which I grew up knowing as *dim sum*. *Yum cha* is the term used in Australia – I prefer it, actually, because it's one of my favourite kinds of meal, and the play on words, well... it's yum.

John and David are a gay couple and the first such couple I've met who live openly without fear or shame (I have had a very sheltered life up to this point in my late twenties). They live in a trendy inner-city converted-warehouse flat and seem to collect stray friends from the LGBTQIA+ community on a regular basis, often providing them with lodging, care, and found family. I count myself among these friends, in spite of the fact that I am the first straight boy[8] they have adopted in this manner. I met them through David's irrepressible Auntie Ling, a gregarious extrovert of a woman who befriended me on a backpackers bus tour during my first week in Australia.

Today, John's friend Marty has joined us and has brought a companion with him. Robyn is a transgender woman, and she is gorgeous. Tall, with

---

[8] I am nowhere near an expert regarding the language used to describe people in the gay community, but my friends would certainly call me a "straight boy" in this context. In transgender terms, at this point I was still an "egg" – someone who had not yet emerged and was still unaware of their true nature.

long blonde hair and softly sensitive eyes, she is immaculately made up, poised and graceful. She embodies a carefully crafted feminine demeanour that stops just short of spilling over into caricature. Perhaps she is trying too hard, but I don't care, because I am fascinated. My eyes follow her hand as she lifts her cup to take a drink, her perfectly manicured nails reflecting the pink shade of the scarf draped around her neck.

I have no idea why I take such notice of Robyn. I assume it is because I have never met a transgender person before, but this obvious explanation obscures the deeper reasons I haven't come to understand yet. With large hands and a firm jawline, Robyn is probably well aware that she attracts undue attention – I try to be careful not to stare too much. Also, I am still quite shy in social situations and I worry that I will be tongue-tied or say something unwise, so instead I just listen.

Looking back, I realise that I had questions to ask that I didn't even know how to formulate.

A few months later, we went out to lunch again. I was chatting with John about something – I don't remember really, it could have been anything – not necessarily related to the topics of gender or my perpetually single, dateless, sexless, yet seemingly happy existence that endlessly amused and befuddled my friend.

Across the room an attractive young woman caught my eye as she stood up from her seat. There was nothing particularly distinctive about her – a dark-haired white woman in a plain blue dress – but she struck me as graceful and softly feminine in her appearance and movements.

In that short moment I saw her, it hit me.

I wanted to be her.

Why couldn't I be her?

I didn't know the word *transition* yet. *Sex change* is what I knew to be involved regarding men who became women, and it was drastic, and unquestionably medical, and it seemed so severe, so disruptive, so final. Through the magic mirror into a new life, never to return.

As quickly as these things entered my mind, I relegated them to the same mental compartment where I put all of my silly and impractical ideas, but not without some sadness and resentment.

I honestly can't remember if the following exchange took place, but I have a vague feeling that it might have:

Me: "I should have been born female."

John: "You could be a girl. Why not?"

* * *

I put my pencil down and lean back, holding the paper at arms' length. I take a long look at the drawing and make it real in my head: a beautiful mannequin wearing a lacy, revealing dress, vibrant and sexy, alive but captured, suspended, frozen in place. She stands with her legs slightly apart, feet firmly set in her skyscraper heels, one hand on her hip and the other gracefully held out slightly by her side. There is a support pole between her legs, fixing her to the pedestal she stands on inside her glass case.

A living doll on display.

I look over at the corner of the room. In my imagination, she is there, waiting patiently, illuminated by artfully positioned gallery lights reflecting glimmers in the curves of her shiny plastic body. She is so alluring, so beautifully vulnerable, yet so unreachable.

I close my eyes and hold the scene in my mind. I visualise her face up close, frozen yet so full of life behind her softly expressive gaze. What is she thinking? What is she feeling inside?

What is it like to be her?

I've drawn hundreds of dolls, and even though my drawings are objectifying from an external perspective, I've always found it appealing to imagine the doll's inner thoughts and experience.

But today, I finally realise – admitting to myself – that I want to be the doll. I want to feel beautiful and sexy… and feminine.

I open my eyes and the corner is empty, save for my backpack and an umbrella leaning against the wall. There is no feature lighting to showcase such mundane items.

I close my eyes again and imagine myself, wearing something soft and pretty, standing in tall, sharply delicate heels, on a pedestal in the corner.

International shipping is exorbitant. And that's if I can even find somewhere that ships to Australia. The Internet is touted as being a global information superhighway, but at this point in history, online shopping is a new concept for the masses and anything I can find is inevitably US-centric.

After spending a few days hesitating over both the cost and the fear of being discovered, I place an order for some high heeled pumps from a site based in Ohio. I am nervous about using my real name but the order acknowledgement email, written by a real person, is perfectly professional and shows no hint of mockery or judgement.

It takes weeks, but when the shoes arrive I am breathless with anticipation as I collect the parcel from the post office. I can't wait until I get home; I open the box inside the car after checking carefully to see that nobody in the carpark is near enough to see in through the windows.

The shoes are beautiful. I've always drawn classically-styled heels on my dolls – no chunky platforms or bizarre heel shapes. My new pumps are a bit shorter than the ones in my pictures but they have nice clean lines and the graceful, tapered stiletto heels that I love.

And they fit well enough. I am so happy.

But I want – I need – more than shoes.

Sexy lingerie. If you want sexy lingerie, you can find it online. Everyday clothes? Not so much. In the late 1990s nobody is using the Internet for "normal" purchases yet (printed mail-order catalogues still exist, but unfortunately I don't know about any Australian ones).

The anonymity afforded by the Internet means that the earliest viable online merchants are mostly from industries where the customers find a tangible benefit from not having to enter the shops in person. Customers like me: single men living alone who have no socially acceptable reason to purchase "female" items.

More careful selection, hesitation, re-selection, and eventual submission. The premium I pay for privacy is a steep one – I could save a lot of money by simply going to the nearest department store – but it's worth it. My new satin nightgowns are luxurious and make me feel pretty, even if I don't have the curves to fill them out the way I'd like to.

I also learn that I prefer standard bikini cut underwear. G-strings are… everything I expected them to be.

The air feels thick around me, like I am immersed in some kind of invisible molasses, only there is no smell or stickiness. Just a notable, frustrating refusal of my limbs to move any faster than the painfully slow motion of this dream predicament.

For it is a dream I find myself in, one which will recur multiple times in different variations over the next few years. I am wearing my lingerie and heels, and I am walking outside, feeling exposed and vulnerable. There is nobody in my immediate vicinity, but I know the street will become busy soon, and I am trying to get home before I am caught in public wearing my skimpy, inappropriate outfit.

Whenever I have this dream I always wake up before I make it home. I find myself in my bed, my body sweating from the panic and exertion. My feet hurt from the high heeled shoes: I am wearing them in bed, along with my nightgown. In spite of my recurring dream ordeal, I often sleep dressed this way because I need to feel feminine and pretty – even if I haven't quite realised or admitted to myself why.

Whatever it is that compels me to explore this part of my psyche, it doesn't stop. My secret stash of women's clothes and accessories keeps growing until I begin to worry about having enough hiding space, and how to conceal everything if I ever have to move residence.

In the meantime, I am living a life I consider not particularly remarkable. I go to work every day, I do the grocery shopping, I see my friends and go out to eat on the weekends. I spend a lot of time drawing, which I suppose is a hobby just like any other regular pastime.

My real hobby keeps taking up more and more room, however, not just in my apartment and in my free time, but crucially, in my head.

Chapter Thirteen
Duality

I often worry about how to reconcile my doll fetish with my feminist convictions. With depressing regularity, I find my online feed full of women's rage in the aftermath of news around some high-profile man's rape allegation and the noncommittal responses to it by other powerful men who *could* hold him accountable but frustratingly, excruciatingly, never do. It's exhausting reading the endless comments from women rightfully angry about their own lived experiences, the misogynistic media culture, and the frequently apologist nature of mainstream discourse around sexual assault. Interspersed between the accounts of rage and solidarity are posts from men (and the occasional woman) arguing the old chestnuts of "reason" and "logic" regarding evidence and due process, and attempting to derail the conversation by bringing up statistics of violence against men (the term coined for this tactic is "whataboutism").

I struggle with the male/female dichotomy when it comes to addressing these issues. Gender should not come into play when we talk about how humans treat one another, yet society has well and truly made sure that gender matters. In addition, non-binary and genderfluid people are either ignored, or else they get put in a very odd position when these discussions happen. In truth, non-binary and genderfluid people are likely to suffer discrimination and abuse, including sexual assault, not only from the usual suspects who target women, but also from anyone who feels threatened by gender nonconformity and ambiguity.

As a dual-gender person I can identify with the rage and despair that women feel, as well as with the anxiety that men have about the possibility they will say or do the wrong thing – or worse, be unfairly accused of a serious crime. I am a man, and I am well aware of the privilege that men have. I am also a woman, and I am well aware that the real danger for women vastly outweighs the real danger for men here: not just in the frequency of these incidents, but also from the effects of them. The fallout from sexual assault is so much more severe and life-changing for female survivors than it is for male perpetrators. How many high-profile men accused of rape actually end up with their lives and careers significantly impacted? Very few, if any. Women who speak up about being sexually assaulted, however, can expect to have their entire existence dragged over the coals, often in public with the complicity of the media.

On the surface, my fantasies are easy to dismiss as unenlightened and straight-up misogynist: women as literal dolls. This interpretation renders my publicly stated value system null and void; I am a fraud. It is for this reason that I have, to date, been careful about disclosing my fetish to anyone outside a select group of trusted friends. Yet as I come to realise how closely it is connected with my female identity, I have no choice but to address it as I write about becoming Meredith.

There's a recurring conversation in my head that surfaces whenever I think about the paradox I find myself in:

"Your doll fetish is sexist. You're reducing women to objects. You're fantasising about a literal living sex doll." My accuser is firm in their conviction.

My female side steps up first. She identifies with the doll. "It's consensual. The doll wants this. And it's reversible at any time."

I am fully aware of how convenient this argument is.

My accuser is having none of it. "Once the doll has been frozen, she can't indicate otherwise. She loses the ability to say no. Consent isn't valid if she can't change her mind."

I start to enjoy the thought of a helpless, frozen doll. And of course the ever-present guilt gets brushed aside. "The doll never gets mistreated. It's a fantasy. Nobody is actually getting hurt. It's not like I can go and create a sentient mechanical woman for real, or enchant someone and turn her into a plastic mannequin, even if she did want me to." Why do I imagine my male self saying this? Have I been conditioned by years of the pop culture idea of this relationship dynamic?

But it's clear this is a tenuous position. *It's problematic, therefore I'll make it a fantasy. It's a fantasy, therefore it's okay.* Truth be told – if I *was* able to make this fantasy real, would I be able to resist?

"You'd do it, wouldn't you?" My accuser looks at me knowingly.

My female side is unapologetic. "Is it so wrong to want to be taken care of, to be vulnerable and trusting? I wouldn't be a helpless doll for just anyone, but for the right person it would make me so happy." I imagine the joy of being frozen on a pedestal, enchanted for a tender, considerate lover. Alluringly feminine and radiating my beauty.

It sounds so regressive. Women are supposed to be independent, resourceful and self-actualised these days, and I agree with this. My fantasy feels like a betrayal of my values. Yet it is the tension between the independent woman and the helpless doll that tantalises me so much. Or rather, it is the independent woman *rendered* helpless that does it. The woman and the doll are one and the same. A vibrant, vital spirit, captured –

by her own choice, or through impartial circumstance, but never through the coercive actions of another person.

There is a strong element of "rescuing the damsel in distress" here. I very rarely talk about the more extreme aspects of my fantasies because it is very easy to interpret them in an unfavourable way. Indeed, many years ago my first psychiatrist sent me off to a specialist after I disclosed these things to her, for what I later realised was an assessment to see if I presented any danger to women (the conclusion was that I was safe). This was after I showed her some of my drawings of broken wind-up dolls and disassembled mannequins, their shapely body parts displayed in revealing, carefully arranged poses. These images appeal to me not because I wish to harm women or enjoy imagining their pain; in fact it is critical to my fantasy that the experience is *never* unpleasant for the doll. The attraction for me is the heightened objectification. She is a living doll, bound inside the sheer physicality of her body, which is accentuated by the presence of exposed joints, springs, gears and loose wires. The setting is clean and inviting. There is no blood or leaking oil or messy trauma. There might be sparks, or an aura of frisson around her assembly seams; the extent of her distress is the sharp tingling of unattainable desire. The expression on her face is one of wistful longing, or perhaps one of unexpected pleasure, captured and frozen in mid-surprise. A helpless mechanical woman in pieces, awaiting the attentions of someone who can put her back together, repair her beautiful body, make her whole and bring her to life. To me, it's not just sexy; it's intensely and delightfully romantic.

In the meantime, she is placed on display – a literal model of a woman. Her dollsbody is exposed in all its glory, whether wholly intact or in need of attention from more than just an observer. Occasionally nude, but usually dressed in a strategically flirty outfit that reveals her true nature – even when fully assembled, she has visible seams; a hex socket fastener flush with the smooth skin of her hip and thigh; a small display readout on her neck; a misaligned shoulder pivot; a deactivation switch. Her body is designed to remind her lover, and herself, that she is forever an object, at the mercy of the limitations imposed by her construction. An object to be displayed, admired and coveted: under a glass case in a gallery, in a shopfront window, on a pedestal under a spotlight in the corner of a busy nightclub. More objectification, this time of the kind that everyone is familiar with: the commodification of female bodies.

My accuser knows I struggle with the fact that my desires align with this exploitation. "It's not just how you treat the doll privately. You fantasise about her being frozen in a department store window. You want to put women on display for consumption by men. You're perpetuating the glorification of the male gaze."

Well, it's not *just* the male gaze. I do know women, including myself, who like to ogle a nicely-shaped woman as much as any man does. But my accuser isn't exactly wrong, either. Evidence that the male gaze has shaped our society is everywhere, and I willingly indulge in it. Like I asked myself before, how much of this is informed by the culture I grew up in and still live in?

I don't know. My affinity for dolls started at such a young age, and is so deep-seated within me that I don't think it's possible to find the answer. I am both the subject *and* the object in my fantasies, and when my dreams play out there is no exploitation of either side. There is only beauty and pleasure and joy.

I don't have a reply for my accuser. I can never have the last word, because we just end up just going round in circles. I have learned to live with the conflict.

Part Five

Chapter Fourteen

Lisa

To: Lisa
From: Derek
Date: Oct 8, 1999 7:16 pm

Hi Lisa,

I hope you'll take time to read this amongst the dozens of responses you're probably receiving from your personal ad. I liked what I read in it (it's very rare for someone to not equate fun with nightclubbing, it seems).

I'm a transplanted American, of Chinese descent, who came to Melbourne four years ago and didn't leave (permanent residency application under way as I type this). I've lived in a few places around the world, studied a couple of very different things (engineering and sociology) and ended up settling in a place nobody expected (Australia).

I have a pretty liberal (little ell) view of the world, but a somewhat conservative approach... meaning that I am not offended by much, and respect differences, even (occasionally) celebrating diversity, but don't often shout my views at the top of my lungs, or dress wacky, or dye my hair chartreuse (that's the conservative part, although I do have long hair). Most of my friends are gay men or straight women and I have always been interested in the great gender divide, and the differences between what we *are* and what we *like* (and whether they are really linked). I'm not out to redefine what a "straight male" should be, but I have found that just by being myself I ended up where I am now (wondering, like a lot of nice men, what the deal is with the attractive nasty ones). Yes, I do try to keep the cynicism at bay... but what is a romantic idealist to do?

Oh yeah, the usual stuff, if it matters to you: 29 yrs, 5'8", slim, Chinese-American, long hair, glasses, Virgo (western), Dog (Chinese), and wouldn't you know I love cats and dislike dogs. One of my gay friends said I'd make a good lesbian. It's a provocative thought to say the least.

Derek

===============

From: Lisa
To: Derek
Date: Oct 13, 1999 4:40 pm

Dear Derek,

Let me first say that I am very sorry for not replying sooner, but my modem has been playing up and being very very naughty. I am usually much much quicker at replying.

I did enjoy your letter. The first thing though which disturbed me was your dislike of dogs... ouch!! My best friend is my dog... sad but true. I am sure though that you don't mean dogs like her, as she's a precious thing. I hate (big H) cats, as they make me sneeze. Hmmmm...

I am not sure what you know about me already really, so I think
I might need some questions from you. I know that's a bit daggy,
but I could ramble for hours otherwise. I am probably a little
conservative at work, but I can be quite wild at times... always
within safe boundaries though. I am 34... yes... an older
woman... Taurus, born in the year of the snake. I'm not really
sure about the Chinese horoscope, but I know I am a fairly
typical Taurean. I have five sisters and one brother, so I
always have someone to hang out with. It's funny how when you
grow up (????) you actually can get to like your siblings, and
put aside all the childish squabbles.

I think you'd probably know I am a teacher. At the moment I am
eagerly waiting for the Year 12 students to leave. I have them
for English, and they are driving me crazy. Only five more
school days for them. Yippee!!!

I hope I have given you some information. Please let me know if
there is anything in particular you want to know.

Take care.

Lisa

I met Lisa through a now-long-forgotten dating website, one of many that dotted the online landscape before a handful of monolithic businesses eventually took over everything.[9] The website was one where it was free to sign up and create a profile, but where you had to pay a monthly fee (five dollars) for the ability to send messages to potential partners – if you were male! Women were allowed to send messages for free. I don't know if this strategy ever attracted a significant number of women users, but apparently

---

[9] The early Internet was full of sites that were basically copies of existing ideas from the offline world. Long before the invention of Tinder and "swiping" to indicate interest (a concept which makes no sense in an offline context, although it would make a hilarious comedy sketch), there were sites like OKCupid and RSVP.com.au, more sophisticated and successful versions of the early dating sites like the one where I found Lisa. And those sites were themselves just copies of the lonely hearts page of the physical newspaper, where people could post personal ads looking for dates.

the male users of our dating site weren't very good at writing. Lisa told me that my first message stood out simply by being readable!

Lisa was (and still is) a high school English teacher. Given how discourse on the Internet has (d)evolved, I'm thankful we met online when we did – a few more years and I doubt she would have bothered.

For years, people were surprised to learn how we'd met. Back then, there was a perception in society that the Internet was full of weirdos, which was probably true (and I would say this hasn't really changed – neither the perception nor the reality!). Obviously the dangers of online dating haven't changed between then and now, but meeting a partner online is common today. I suppose people have just learned to manage the risks and put up with them.

I do feel a slight sense of pride in being a successful early adopter, though. I hope Lisa feels the same – she definitely found herself a weirdo.

```
From: Derek
To: Lisa
Date: Oct 14, 1999 8:23 pm

Hi Lisa,

Don't worry about the delay in replying. I'm not always punctual
with these things myself. I figure that most women who put ads
on the internet will get swamped with replies anyway. And I know
from working with computers that they always break when it's
important. :)

It's too bad you Hate cats, but I guess I can forgive you. If
you'll forgive my dislike of dogs. Depends on the dog - quiet
ones that don't slobber everywhere are OK (can you see why I'm a
cat person?) :)

On siblings and growing up - there's nothing like growing up to
teach you just how much growing up you have to do. My only
sibling, an older brother, died in 1994. He was manic depressive
```

and took his own life (it wasn't a surprise when it happened). Unfortunately, during his life he ended up alienating almost everyone at one time or another. We were never that close, and I mourn the loss of that potential as much as I mourn the loss of his life. It's like I knew him but didn't know him. Perhaps because he was usually judgemental towards me when we were growing up, I tend to end up with caring, sympathetic, close friends who I normally see one-on-one - maybe looking for a close sibling I never had.

I like that you're an English teacher. Year 12 English was my favourite class in high school by far. I had the most wonderful teacher who taught me how much literature can speak about the human condition, something your average high school student tries not to think about too much. It was because of him that I thought I might end up being a teacher myself. Those plans only got bypassed, really, when I ended up staying in Australia.

Got any questions or rambling things to say at me? :)

Derek

===============

From: Lisa
To: Derek
Date: Oct 15, 1999 7:36 am

Dear Derek,

Well, you could say that I have been swamped with replies, but very few actually snare my interest that much. I am not interested in a Neanderthal really, so I like people who can string a sentence together. Might sound harsh, but I am entitled I figure.

I'm sorry to hear about your brother. My husband died of cancer two years ago... so whilst I cant identify with exactly the same thing as you, I can certainly empathise.

Lisa

You'll be glad to know that my baby (my dog Ricki) doesn't slobber everywhere... but quiet she's not. She tends to be quite vocal when anyone comes or leaves... and she's not too fond of men. I think she's a feminist.

I'm late for work now... so I haven't got questions for you at the moment... but I'll try to think of some. :)

Lisa

===============

From: Derek
To: Lisa
Date: Oct 15, 1999 7:10 pm

Gronk put sentence together. Gronk be college graduate!

I've actually had this silly ambition to write a novel for about five years now. But somehow it keeps getting postponed. A few years ago I wrote a couple of short stories that I think came out decently.

I like that Ricki is a feminist. I am too. Of course then you can start arguing over what feminism really is.

I'm sorry to hear about your husband. I suppose I don't know what it is like to lose someone who is very close.

By the way, I'm impressed that you get up early to answer e-mail... that's dedication... :) Actually you don't want to know what time I usually get up for work. The idea is that I can then leave early. Sometimes this succeeds.

cya!
Derek

Over the next few weeks we emailed back and forth quite regularly. We didn't discuss my brother, or Lisa's first husband, any more for a while.

Perhaps those things would have been a bit too heavy to get into at this point. And it certainly would have felt weird for me, as a potential partner, to ask about a previous lover who wasn't actually an ex. I don't think we were uncomfortably ignoring the subjects; it was just that we needed more time to get to know each other.

Much of our conversation involved learning about each other's daily life and habits. A few things stood out that might be potential issues, but we both tried to avoid making quick judgements or assumptions about them. I confessed to being something of a petrolhead, which set off some alarm bells, but I was quick to reassure Lisa that I wasn't antisocial about it – I was mostly just a car nerd, and didn't drive a loud V8 or do burnouts everywhere. I also mentioned my weekly volleyball night, which of course involved exercising (even though that was mostly just a side effect; I played simply because it was fun). In her reply Lisa revealed that she had a disability that prevented her from doing a lot of physical activities.

```
From: Lisa
To: Derek
Date: Oct 19, 1999 2:39 pm

[excerpt]
I have very bad knees as a result of a calcium problem, so three
hours of volleyball would definitely not be for me. In fact I am
not allowed to do any weight bearing exercises at all... It
really shits me at times, but I try to take a philosophical view
on things like this, as I believe there are always people who
are worse off. I also mostly have to use crutches to walk... not
because of pain or anything, but to reduce the pressure of bone
on bone in my knees. This is another area that bothers me too.
It is amazing how many people cannot see beyond the crutches, as
if the entire person is somehow defective. I can't believe I
have told you this already. You must inspire trust in me for
some reason... must be because you're a petrol head and fitness
freak?!
```

I had never considered whether or not a disability would affect my interest in someone. I didn't have a reaction to Lisa's disclosure other than curiosity, so I figured I might as well find out. Things like volleyball and cycling (I still rode occasionally at that point) were simply fun things to do – I didn't arrange my entire life around them. It might be nice to have my partner alongside me, but I never imagined it as inevitable.

```
From: Derek
To: Lisa
Date: Oct 20, 1999 10:45 pm

[excerpt]
Well the freak part is probably accurate :)

I actually don't know many people who have chronic disabilities
(if that's the term) so if I say anything stupid it's not on
purpose (feel free to tell me off, though).

I'm glad you are comfortable enough to tell me about it. You do
have to be careful about meeting people on the net. I have had
some good and not-so-good luck with this medium.
```

My correspondence with Lisa headed into the deep and philosophical. We shared our thoughts on relationships, the frustrations of navigating the dating world, and happiness in general. And of course, the stereotypes and expectations placed upon men and women. It seemed to me that even if romance didn't happen, I'd found a really interesting person to be friends with.

Chapter Fifteen
Soapboxes

Lisa and I continued writing to each other for a few weeks. I don't know why we didn't move to phone calls sooner, but we both seemed to be quite content to use email. This was probably because writing allows for reflection and editing when discussing complex and nuanced ideas. Indeed, we would return to this method of communication during some difficult times in the years that followed.

I had spent the preceding decade exploring the apparently rare phenomenon (to my observations at least) of close non-sexual male-female friendships. My own experiences with Amy and Lauren had given me a heightened awareness of society's expectations, particularly the ever-present assumption that two such friends would inevitably become romantically involved (I was disappointed by the ending of the movie *When Harry Met Sally*, which I felt lacked the courage to follow through with the subversion it hinted at). Having learned that I preferred the company of women over men, I was curious to find out Lisa's take on mixed-gender friendships.

Soapboxes

```
To: Lisa
From: Derek
Date: Oct 25, 1999 1:58 pm

[excerpt]
Question: are most of your good friends male or female? For some
reason, over the years, I have noticed that I tend to become
good friends with women who tend to become good friends with men
(who tend to become good friends with women (who tend etc. etc.
etc.))  And for the most part, we all complain to each other
about how awful it is trying to meet someone decent! Hmmm... my
life is NOT a movie. My life is NOT a movie. Repeat.

===============

To: Derek
From: Lisa
Date: Oct 25, 6:41 pm

[excerpt]
A lot of my good friends are male... so your theory was correct.
And we do lament the lack of suitable partners around. And how
much we hate the meat markets etc etc etc. I don't mind my life
being a soap opera though... really I don't!
```

So what would Lisa think about me if I disclosed that I'd reached the age of twenty-nine without ever having a girlfriend? The world was constantly giving me signs that this was something I should feel ashamed about. I tried to ignore that, but I worried a potential partner might see that as a reason to avoid me.

This wasn't actually a problem; I had to remind myself that I wouldn't want to be partners with someone who thought that my lack of experience was a deal-breaker. So far, Lisa didn't seem like the type of person who would judge me for it, but if my impression was wrong, I figured it was better to find out sooner than later.

Double Exposure

To: Lisa
From: Derek
Date: Oct 26, 1999 2:19 pm

[excerpts]
You might also be interested to know that at age 29 I've never had a steady girlfriend, or even an unsteady one at that. Add up the fact that I've had quite a few close female friends, and quite a few gay friends, and it's not surprising that my mother once asked me if I was gay. I don't know if she really suspected anything, but I thought it was highly amusing.

Sometimes I wonder if women, in spite of what they say, still want "traditional" (i.e. macho, manly) men... which I definitely am not. But I'm not going to change who I am or the way I relate to people. I just end up getting cynical if I'm not careful.

Most of the time I am pretty optimistic... I have learned to be happy on my own, and the biggest reason I haven't done anything desperate or stupid to get involved with someone is because I *am* happy on my own, and am not looking for someone to fix anything.

Of course, all my experience with romantic relationships is purely vicarious, so I may not know what I'm talking about...

I guess I better stop before I end up on a soapbox, huh.

================

To: Derek
From: Lisa
Date: Oct 27, 1999 9:33 pm

[excerpts]
I'm glad you thought it was funny and not offensive when your mother asked if you were gay! I think it's good for kids to keep their parents on their toes. My parents never quite know what

Soapboxes

I'm going to do next. I love shocking mine with my tattoos and especially my nose ring. I have to think of something new to shock them with soon...

I am surprised you haven't been inundated with girlfriends. We women like sensitive, intelligent men who aren't yobbos... well I speak for myself I guess, but I'm sure I'm not alone. The problem with most SNAGs (Sensitive New Age Guys), is that they all seem to be gay... which puts them out of the relationship stakes, but they're great for friends.

And I would have to say you should never ever change who you are simply to fit into someone else's idea of what they want. Mind you, compromises are part of all relationships... not that I am an expert by any means... but you can't expect to go into a situation with another person and not expect to have to give on some things. Just so long as you keep the things that are intrinsically you.

Anyway... now it's my turn to get off the soap box, with just this thought. I think the most important thing I've learnt in the last few years is that we, as people, are never static... we are ever-changing and developing.

Indeed. If only we could have foreseen the developments that would actually happen in our shared future. But for now, the sentiment was largely theoretical. I have this image of the two of us standing on soapboxes in a town square, courting each other with philosophical thoughts and questions pitched across the plaza over the heads of unsuspecting passersby. Return volleys eagerly anticipated and rich with ideas and clues to each other's inner character. It was exciting and engaging in a shared, intimate way, regardless of the fact that we couldn't physically see or hear each other.

```
To: Lisa
From: Derek
Date: Oct 28, 1999 3:42 pm
```

[excerpts]
Nose ring? Tattoos? Ouch! Glad it's your skin and not mine. I hate needles. Anyway do you get complaints from parents about your nose ring (bad example for the kids, etc.) or do you not wear it at work?

There are plenty of SNAGs out there who aren't gay. Most of my straight male friends fall into this category. Probably all of them! I do believe that sexuality (and gender identity, which I think is a separate issue) is a very fluid thing and most people might surprise themselves if they really asked themselves some deep questions. Unfortunately, we're usually brought up to believe that there are only two possibilities.

Life is messy and complicated. People are complex. If everything was simple enough to be mapped out, I bet you that the great explorers wouldn't bother exploring. Sometimes searching is worthwhile just so that you can come up with more questions.

As far as things that are central to your being... well if those were at issue, then the person wouldn't be right for you. I think that a fit is determined largely by the connection of those bits inside people. And of course they change too, and perhaps the longevity of a relationship is determined by how well two people can change together.

Lest you think I'm trying to be profound, I realise how cliched the above paragraph is. But I still think it's true.

I'm curious... has the fact that your husband died been a problem for men you have met since then?

I didn't know how to ask that last question without being abrupt. It didn't really fit anywhere in our discussion but it had been in the back of my mind the whole time, and I was pretty sure by now that Lisa wouldn't be offended by it.

I had to wait nearly a week for Lisa's reply because she went on an interstate holiday with her best friend. She sent me short emails every couple of days to let me know she hadn't disappeared, and I opened each one with eager anticipation only to be slightly disappointed she was too busy having fun to write back. Not that I really expected her to interrupt her holiday, but it was hard to be patient.

When Lisa finally replied properly, it was like we'd never paused our conversation.

```
To: Derek
From: Lisa
Date: Nov 3, 1999 10:34 am

[excerpts]
I do know that there are SNAGs who are not gay. I would just
like to meet them!

I would argue that whether I have tattoos or rings everywhere or
whatever has very little bearing on my abilities as an educator.
I do however understand that some people may have a problem with
it. I haven't had any complaints yet... I guess I do things like
that to express the slightly 'wild' side I have.

I have 3 tattoos... but none that can be seen.... unless you
know me pretty well. I got my first one when I was 29. My
husband and I both got each other's names in hearts and flowers
on our hips. In retrospect... I would do it again I guess with
him, as had he not died we would have been together for as far
as I could see.

The nose ring I only got a few months ago. My sister who lives
in Brisbane has one and I quite liked hers... so I copied. I
just have a small diamond in it... so it is not obtrusive or
anything.

You asked if my husband's death had been a problem with men
since then. I'm not exactly sure what you mean? The people I
have been involved with since have of course known about him,
and all that happened, but its not like I am bitter and twisted,
or that I am pining for Pat to come back. I don't compare people
```

> either... that certainly would not be productive. I am a firm believer that all our experiences shape us... so for anyone to be with me they have to know what Pat meant to me... and the things we went through, and the things I went through, as these are profound things in my life which have shaped who I am now.
>
> Sometimes you have to take chances with relationships. There are no guarantees ever as I have learnt, so if you are expecting one, then you'll never take the risk. I think that living with regret of chances not taken and the wondering of what if, would be far worse than taking a chance.
>
> In terms of changing for a partner... I think we shouldn't change who we are intrinsically. Though sometimes there are things we do change, and they are often things we would have considered ourselves to be set in. We surprise ourselves with how well we can adapt when we want to. But some things are too important to the bigger self... like philosophies etc... so these shouldn't be changed for another person to accept us. So far so good. We agree on this.

I really appreciated Lisa's thoughtfulness and willingness to engage with the kind of ideas we were discussing. It felt kind of weird, like we were writing in circles around the question of "will we get together", but it was also tantalising and exciting. It had been a long time since I'd had the opportunity to connect with someone in this way.

I also appreciated the fact that Lisa didn't make a big deal out of our relative experience levels. She could have tried to school me in relationships, given that I'd disclosed how much of a novice I was, but instead she engaged me as an equal. She took my ideas and observations and helped validate them, addressing them using her own real experiences.

As it turns out, our words also hinted at how things would actually unfold in the years to come. Our ideas and convictions about change within a relationship would come to be thoroughly and severely tested, along with our beliefs about honesty and trust.

Chapter Sixteen

Prescience

Reading the emails I sent to Lisa, I am amused at the (now obvious) signs hinting at Meredith's eventual emergence. Signs which actually predated the emails themselves: while we were telling each other about the experiences we'd had meeting people on the Internet, I sent her a short story I'd written several years earlier, about an online chatroom encounter with a man who assumed I was female.

> To: Lisa
> From: Derek
> Date: Oct 26, 1999 2:19 pm
>
> [excerpt]
> Did you figure out that the story I sent you is partly autobiographical? And then you have to figure out what part I played!
>
> It's not too hard when you think about it, although a few of my friends guessed wrong. But I realised that honesty was a big

issue there, and it really made me stop and think about how this
internet thing really affects people.

===============

To: Derek
From: Lisa
Date: Oct 27, 1999 9:33 pm

[excerpt]
It would be presumptuous of me to say who is you, since I don't
know you that well... but if I had to guess, I would say Leah!

Lisa was perceptive. I liked that. And she didn't seem put off by the fact that I'd "pretended" to be a woman online – although maybe that's because I was upfront about it, addressing the moral implications and consequences of my choice in the story itself. I don't know if Lisa suspected anything deeper. I certainly didn't, at least not consciously. I've included the story, *Stones Unturned*, at the end of this book because I think it provides an amazing example of foreshadowing that only becomes obvious in hindsight.[10]

It's hard to believe that I didn't connect the experience behind that story, along with my ever-present thoughts about men and women, to the possibility that I myself might be transgender. But I was simply trying to make sense of a world I had never quite fit into. And instead of concluding that I was the misfit, questioning why my feelings about gender didn't seem to match what society taught me, I questioned why there were arbitrary rules in the first place.

---

[10] The story is based on an experience I had in late 1995, when I presented in a chatroom as an intentionally (and clearly stated) fictional character, who was the protagonist of a novel I intended to write. And who also happened to be female. Surprise! (I never did get around to writing the novel, but I think this memoir is a worthy substitute.)

Prescience

At the time, I had already started experimenting with wearing women's clothes in private, but I hadn't yet figured out its real significance. I didn't know what it meant to be transgender, nor did I think to question whether I'd ever have (or need) the courage to come out. I thought I was just philosophising with my musings and my writing. Trying to imagine how a woman's perspective might feel. And of course I was doing this with the very limited knowledge around gender diversity that was available in mainstream discourse at the time (which is to say, hardly any).

Reading these emails now, I am amazed at how willing I was to reveal my thoughts to Lisa. I guess I figured I might as well go for broke, since my strange ideas about gender would eventually become apparent anyway. I didn't go as far as disclosing my habit of wearing women's clothing, but if Lisa didn't run a mile upon learning the things I did reveal, then I could appreciate that she was someone really special.

```
From: Derek
To: Lisa
Date: Nov 04, 1999 11:30 pm

[excerpts]
If you really want to meet a SNAG who isn't gay, I might be able
to arrange something :)


I say I am straight because I have only ever been attracted to
women. But I often joke about identifying more with women than
men... to be honest I think that I chose, in some prior
spiritual world, to live this life as a male so I could meet
some sort of challenge I set myself. I do suspect that I would
have been very happy born female. Not that I am unhappy as a
male (lest you think I am contemplating a sex change or
something!). But the whole dualistic nature of the male-female
difference seems somehow too restricting. I feel as if I could
fall on either "side" equally comfortably.
```

Normally, people who don't know me very well start edging away at this point, so I tend not to talk too openly about this stuff. But my close friends are all aware of the joke about me being a "pre-operative transsexual lesbian"...

Confused? Well if you're still reading this and still plan on replying, I'd say you're doing better than a lot of people would.

===============

From: Lisa
To: Derek
Date: Nov 06, 1999 00:04 am

[excerpts]
The question of male/female stereotyping and roles within society is one I consider often. I have never been attracted to women... but I can honestly say, the idea does not repulse me... and I can certainly understand why women are more comfortable with other women. So the concept is one that interests me.

As for edging away because of your honesty and your reflective capacities... well... I don't know what to say. I am very interested in your emails, and look forward to them.

As for your considerations of sexuality and gender roles, I think this is way more healthy than assuming the role society has set for you without a second thought. My first ever boyfriend was always very sensitive and 'soft' I guess you could say, and we broke up because he realised he was gay. At the time it freaked me out, as I thought I had turned him gay (I was only young!) but I know that I am definitely attracted to men who have a feminine side and who aren't afraid to be sensitive and not 'macho'.

So you can help me meet a SNAG who is not gay... tell me more. I am interested in this idea! :)

===============

Prescience

From: Derek
To: Lisa
Date: Nov 07, 1999 02:13 am

[excerpts]
I'm glad you are open to this discussion... I definitely have a strong feminine side... hey, I just had a thought that maybe I never got together with any of my women friends because they all assumed I was gay and I just hadn't admitted it yet! That is really quite funny.

So there's this SNAG who isn't gay... if you wanna meet him, you just have to suggest a time and place... :)

Chapter Seventeen
Dating

November 1999

I'm five minutes early, but Lisa is waiting for me at the restaurant when I arrive. She's cute, like her photo. I'm nervous and hope that my voice doesn't shake too much when I say hello.

She accepts my handshake as I sit down. It's brief, and feels too formal and businesslike for the situation. But I don't know what's expected here: I would feel ridiculous trying to do the back-of-the-hand-kiss like some kind of Victorian-era suitor, and a hug seems too presumptuously intimate since we've only just met. Besides, she didn't stand up – which also means I don't have to worry about attempting the alternating-kiss-on-the-cheek thing, which some of my friends like to do.

Lisa already knows that I am new to this dating thing. I wonder if she expects me to be awkward in person, even though I've been (I hope) confidently articulate in my emails. I try not to think about my body language too much – I learned many years ago that trying to impress people by worrying about and calculating my behaviour just ends up making me feel uncomfortable – and even more insecure than before I'd tried.

I notice she already has a drink, and her hand trembles slightly as she lifts her glass for a sip. Good to know I'm not the only nervous one. I order a glass of wine and we peruse the menu, and then settle in after the server takes our order.

We make a bit of small talk at first. Even though we've spent weeks having thoughtful discussions over email, it feels odd to jump straight into a deep and meaningful conversation when meeting in person for the first time.

Our nervousness doesn't last long. It quickly becomes apparent to both of us that the person sitting across the table is true to the words we've been reading on-screen. Oddly though, we don't really get into the kind of conversation that we've been having in our emails. Maybe it's a nice change from the intensity of our written communication. We share a light, pleasant evening, enjoying our dinner together with a sustained interest in each other and no red flags.

I'm thinking about whether to order dessert when Lisa's phone rings. She looks at the number and excuses herself.

"I'm sorry, I need to answer this. It's my best friend. He wouldn't be ringing me while I'm on a date unless he really needed something."

I'm glad that Lisa is comfortable with the idea that a man and a woman can be best friends. Given that nearly all of my closest friends throughout my life have been female, I would have a difficult time dating a woman who might be jealous or anxious at the idea that my best friend might want to "steal" me from her.

Lisa puts the phone down after a couple of minutes. She looks concerned, and a little disappointed.

"My best friend's grandma just died. He needs someone there with him right now."

I don't know what to say, so I just mumble, "Oh... I'm sorry to hear that." I'm disappointed at the timing, of course, but I'm not going to protest. At least I'd had a chance to finish my meal. I would feel a bit pathetic sitting here eating by myself after we'd already started our date.

So that decides the question of dessert. We ask for the bill, which we split evenly, and as we stand up I notice how short Lisa is. It makes her cuter.

I can't help blurting out, "Wow, you really ARE short."

Lisa smiles. "I told you!"

She must get this a lot. I feel foolish.

I also notice her crutches, which are impossible to miss, but I don't say anything since I already know about her disability from our emails.

We briefly hug outside the restaurant before heading to our separate cars.

On the way home, I receive a text message.

Hi, I wanted to let you know that I really enjoyed the evening and I didn't want to leave. My best friend is in a difficult place and he really needed someone to be with him tonight. I hope that you don't think I was bailing on our date.

I am so inexperienced – it hadn't even crossed my mind that someone might collude with a friend to create an excuse to leave a date. Now I feel even more foolish for being so naïve, but I am relieved I wasn't actually subject to such a tactic.

For our second date I suggest a restaurant near my place, since our first date was in Lisa's neighbourhood. It would be inconvenient taking separate cars into the busy streets around the restaurant, so Lisa meets me at my place first. I show her my humble one-bedroom flat, hoping that she approves of how I live, and then I drive us to dinner.

The evening passes without any interruptions, and it seems to go too quickly. We linger for a while after eating, until we notice that the restaurant has emptied and the staff look like they're waiting for us to leave so they can clean up and go home. It's pretty apparent that this might be the start of something. Neither one of us brings up the question, though – it is only our second date, after all.

Back at my place, I invite Lisa inside, not with any ulterior motive, but simply because it would feel awkward not to. I offer her something to drink and we sit and chat until it gets late enough that I start to worry she might want to stay the night – I'm not prepared for that yet.

I don't know if she expects, or hopes, me to offer, but luckily she excuses herself without any awkwardness. I walk her to her car and we stop for a hug next to the road.

I bend down to embrace her, and before I can register what's happening, Lisa is stretching up and kissing me on the lips. And it's an unquestionable cliché, but there is a spark.

The next thing I know, she's in her car, driving away.

Wait, I think.

I stand there dumbfounded. What just happened?

Hey...

That was really nice. I liked that.

Come back?

I feel like a kid who has just discovered chocolate.

Chapter Eighteen

Together

We're lying on the couch together after dessert. It's our third date. Lisa invited me over for dinner and it's been a lovely evening, if a bit unseasonably warm for so early in summer. The air conditioner struggles to keep the open-plan kitchen-dining-living room area cool, and lying next to Lisa I am too warm to be comfortable. I don't complain though; this is a long-awaited event I want to experience without letting something circumstantial like the weather ruin it.

Intimacy with a woman. I am 29 years old, a virgin, and though I've hugged a lot and occasionally snuggled together with my female friends once or twice, I've never been this close to someone in this way – with mutual *intent*.

"If I spend the night here, does that mean we're going to make this a thing? Us?" Perhaps I'm being old-fashioned, as plenty of people have casual sex or friends-with-benefits, but I want to be sure there is no misunderstanding about each other's intentions.

Lisa looks at me with hope and kindness in her eyes. And... gratitude, and is that a hint of sadness? "I want you to understand that nothing is ever certain in life."

I know exactly what she means. There are photos of her late husband on the shelf. If he hadn't been taken by cancer, I wouldn't be here.

I nod. "If you want to give this a go, I'm willing."

She smiles. "Yes."

With that, I have to tell her. "There's something you need to know about me before we do this."

"What is it?" Her smile doesn't disappear, but it turns curious.

The decision to inform Lisa about my strange interest is easy to make. I don't want to start a relationship hiding it and then have her freak out upon discovering it down the track.

Actually telling her is slightly more difficult. "I, um... like to... um. Wear women's clothes."

She doesn't look shocked. Thoughtful, maybe, but she doesn't seem disturbed by my revelation. "Like what? Dresses? Underwear?"

"Dresses and skirts and shoes. Underwear I guess. Just at home, in private."

"You don't go out then."

"No."

"Okay then."

I spent the next two years learning how to be in a relationship. Navigating wants and needs and discovering that some of the things I previously expected to be important turned out to be inconsequential, at least when it came to reasons for loving someone. Lisa and I might not have shared many interests (and still don't), but we have learned to appreciate each other's enthusiasm for things that we might not have otherwise noticed. The qualities that we do consider important in a partner should exist independently of any external characteristics or activities anyway. Qualities like empathy and open-mindedness. Thoughtfulness. Self-awareness.

And cheekiness. I never realised how much I would enjoy having someone to bounce mischief back and forth with. This wasn't an immediate discovery; I was raised in an environment where family relationships were carefully managed and mischief was discouraged. Where communication was filtered and drama was avoided if at all possible, especially if it would be visible to outsiders. It was a culture shock meeting Lisa's family: seven boisterous, strong-willed siblings who can speak their minds and actually get along with each other. Raised by strong, complicated, principled (and flawed, like all of us) parents, Lisa and her siblings are all very forthright, caring and generous (with their time and with their opinions!). It's unsurprising that they all ended up in careers that serve the community in some way, such as nursing and teaching.

And they are frequently, fondly, and humorously calling out each other's quirks and foibles. The love they have for each other is very apparent, and although I found it difficult at first, I gradually got used to the chaos of family gatherings and grew to appreciate the candour and the humour of their interactions. I'm glad Lisa was patient with me when I became overwhelmed and cranky at times.

With Lisa at my side, I slowly loosened up. As I did, I also learned to embrace my shy, hesitant inner child. Lisa is unashamedly enthusiastic about many cute "childish" things (particularly Winnie-the-Pooh and Hello Kitty) and my newly-empowered inner child was happy to go along with it. We quickly became one of those insufferably precious romantic couples who can often be seen provoking the disdain of bitter and cynical people.

I put up a small whiteboard (Winnie-the-Pooh themed of course) on the wall next to our bedroom door, with an erasable marker hanging next to it so that we could leave little notes for each other. Occasionally they were practical reminders like grocery items or appointments, but more often they were sweet little declarations of love, just because we wanted to make each other smile.

One day I verbally called Lisa "punkin", emphasising the childish pronunciation, and the following day she left a note on the whiteboard that said "punkin loves toodle bottom."[11] I changed it to "toodle loves punkin bottom" because the phrase "punkin bottom" tickles my brain in a delightful way. Ever since then we have playfully argued over whether Lisa actually is, or is not, a punkin bottom. She insists she is not. I disagree. To this day I address my cards and gifts to her with "P.B." and even though she claims she doesn't know who they're for, she still opens and accepts them. I rest my case.

Lisa's siblings found this nickname, and all of our cute little habits, fairly ridiculous, over-the-top and sickly sweet. Upon encountering one of our frequent displays of affection they would often joke about needing a bucket to throw up in. But it was obvious they didn't harbour any mean or nasty sentiments, and I think their complaints were given with loving admiration. As if they should be so lucky. They were happy to see Lisa with someone who made her happy, after she had experienced the trauma of losing her first husband. As a close-knit family they had also lost a much-loved brother-in-law, and they welcomed me with open arms.

As loving and accepting as her siblings were, however, Lisa didn't want them knowing anything about my crossdressing. This seemed reasonable, since I only wore my dresses and heels around the house, but it also posed a slight problem: three of Lisa's siblings lived close enough to us that they habitually dropped in without warning. So while I was thankful that Lisa didn't have a problem with me wearing women's clothes, I was still anxious about being discovered whenever I did.

I was never caught out by anyone. And for a couple of years, my attention was largely focused elsewhere: I had applied for permanent

---

[11] Childishness means that farts are always funny. This seems to be an immutable law of the universe.

residency in Australia a few months before meeting Lisa, and because my education and work experience were in different fields, it turned out to be a long and complicated process. Dealing with the Immigration Department's bureaucratic hurdles took a lot of time and energy. On top of that, Lisa and I decided to get married.[12]

---

12 If I had known I was going to have so much trouble getting permanent residency, and also known that I would marry Lisa, I would have simply waited and obtained it through marriage.

Chapter Nineteen

Party

"Eeek! That feels so weird! Arggh! Stop!" It felt like Lisa was trying to tickle me in the eye with a chopstick.

"Hold still. I can't draw straight if you keep flinching."

I steeled myself and suffered through the rest of the mini ordeal that is having someone else apply eyeliner pencil to your eyelids.

"Women do this all the time. Stop being such a baby."

Easy to say when you're not the one having the pointy thing held two millimetres from your eyeball by someone not known for her fine dexterity.

Eyeshadow wasn't much better. Seriously, it felt like she was trying to push my eyeballs back into my head through my eyelids. It didn't help that the lighting in our bathroom was weak and uneven, so I had to keep moving and tilting my head around, changing Lisa's point of reference each time.

I can't remember if I insisted on applying my own mascara. I don't recall being stuck in the eye with the bristles so I probably did it myself, even though I had never done it before.

Looking in the mirror after my face was done, I wasn't sure what to think. Was I pretty? Did I look like a man wearing make-up? Was it confronting to see myself like this? I needed time to process what I was looking at.

Did I feel any different? I couldn't really tell where my expectations ended and my actual experience began. It almost felt like I should interact with the world differently, somehow, but if you'd asked me to identify and articulate what that meant, I wouldn't have been able to. Would people expect me to prance around like a drag queen? That would feel unnatural, like putting on an act. My outfit, my made-up face – they didn't *feel* like a costume.

So if I wasn't playing dress-ups or hiding behind this get-up, then, what was my purpose in doing this?

Looking back, I realise that I was actually nervous about it being too *revealing*.

I undid my ponytail and let my dark hair fall around my face. Lisa's foundation was several shades too light for my skin, so I looked like a ghost. A ghost in a little black dress. With great legs and a flat chest.

"We can call you Shadow," said Lisa.

It was the year 2002 or 2003 – a few years before it became clear just how deeply I felt my femininity. Meredith wasn't discernible yet, let alone identifiable with a name; at that point, all I did was wear some dresses and heels now and then. I'd never worn make-up, and it seemed far-fetched to imagine having the chance to try it.

Until now. A Mardi Gras party being thrown by a friend of Lisa's, and our back garden was the venue. What better chance to get completely done up *en femme* and see how it felt? I nearly didn't ask, because whilst Lisa seemed comfortable with Derek-in-a-dress, I'd always taken care to keep anyone else from seeing me. Derek-in-a-dress-and-make-up-in-front-of-Lisa's-friends was an entirely different level of gender nonconformity, even if others did think I was doing it on a lark for a party. I knew it was more than that – I didn't yet realise just how much more – but I'm not sure Lisa had considered this. At any rate, she was quite willing to do my make-up.

With a few butterflies in my stomach, I followed Lisa out the door into the backyard where a number of guests, mostly Lisa's work colleagues, had already gathered.

"Oh my God, you look better than I do!"

Wolf whistles.

"I'd kill for legs like that!"

"And you can walk in those heels! That's not fair!"

I was worried about revealing too much of myself, but of course the first thing people noticed was, in fact, the costume.

When you see a man in drag at a Mardi Gras party, your first thought is probably not going to be "Is this person transgender?" The context of the situation provided me plenty of cover for my insecurities. Still, I remember explicitly trying not to act feminine, and even pretending to be slightly awkward in my four-inch stilettos because I didn't want to appear too well-practised with my walking.

It was a nice feeling, being admired for something that otherwise might be cause for ridicule. I could definitely get used to this. The problem was having to find a suitable excuse to dress up. Even if this party became a regular thing, it wasn't going to happen more than once a year.

There were no questions afterwards, of course. No rumours, no assumptions about my inclinations. Mardi Gras allowed me to hide in plain sight, and besides that, there had been other men dressed in drag present that evening. Cisgender and heterosexual men, which is what everyone assumed me to be as well.

We never had another party like that. Lisa's friend moved overseas and nobody else in our circles ever brought up the idea again. I would have considered organising one but as I only had infrequent contact with my friends in the gay and lesbian community (and didn't know a single transgender person) it made very little sense for me to be the person making the effort.

I had previously told Lisa I wasn't interested in going out dressed as a woman, but this was no longer true. After the Mardi Gras party, I realised that I wanted to be seen by people. And this desire grew stronger every time I remembered how it felt to be accepted that night, even under the fabricated assumptions of the circumstances.

At the same time, I was terrified at the idea. Not because I was afraid of anything specific, such as being laughed at, or even violently abused. I think it was more of a general fear of what it meant in the long term, and a fear of admitting to myself that I understood this.

Sometimes, however, the compulsion to act is unconcerned with understanding, and is stronger than the fear of consequences.

Chapter Twenty
Prickly

It was a few months after the Mardi Gras party, and I couldn't stop thinking about how it felt to be seen publicly as female, even though I knew that other people thought it was a costume. I wanted to feel that spark inside again, that lightness and joy of my femininity, amplified by the softness and prettiness of my clothing and by the delicate nature of my demeanour, unconstrained by the bounds of my social conditioning.

Lisa was lying on the couch reading, and I had been putting away the weekly shopping, thinking about a woman who'd caught my eye in the supermarket. She was so beautiful, wearing a simple, flattering dress, moving with such understated grace. I found her attractive; but there was something else, too. Something about her very presence: her long, softly curled hair, the gentle contours of her figure under the pastel shades of her dress, the way she smiled at others when negotiating the slow, disorderly traffic of carelessly-driven shopping trolleys. All the subtlety of her unselfconscious beauty – I wanted it for myself.

It's never easy to have any conversation that starts with "We need to talk" or "There's something I want to tell you". I didn't know how to approach the subject, let alone understand these feelings well enough to articulate them. As I placed the last few items in the cupboard and gathered the empty shopping bags, I just said, "I think I want to go out dressed. I know I said before that I didn't want to, but... I think that's changed."

Lisa looked up from her book. "What do you mean, 'go out'?"

"Outside. I dunno where. And... like, with... more." I waved my hands vaguely at the front of my body.

"Like with boobs?"

"Yes."

Lisa was silent for a few seconds, comprehending what I'd said. Then, "I don't want you wearing fake boobs."

"What about make-up? You didn't mind when we had the Mardi Gras party."

"That was different. And that was just a party."

"I guess." Except for me it had been a lot more than a party.

"You said you didn't need to go outside." She looked annoyed, and at the same time, oddly validated, as if she'd been expecting me to confess this eventually.

"I know."

"How am I ever going to know whether to believe what you say? You can change your mind anytime." Her words were pointed. Prickly.

"I don't know. I don't know how to answer that." How could I bear to reveal what I couldn't even admit to myself – that I wanted to know what it was like to move through the world as a woman?

"So instead of just being 'like' a woman, you want to actually 'be' a woman."

"I... I don't know."

My reply was so useless. But what else was I going to say?

She looked directly through me. Prickly turned into sharp, purposeful, decisive. "I don't want you to. I don't want to see you in boobs and make-up. I don't want to be married to a woman."

"Okay."

I didn't want to hurt my wife. I loved her and I had to try and be happy with how things were.

But I did want to be a woman. How could I repress it?

I often wonder how I would feel if Lisa was like me, and had a male alter ego. Would I want to see him? Hang out with him? I can't even imagine what a male version of Lisa would be like, because it is so outside the bounds of reality as I know it. It's not that she's hyper-feminine or anything. She even has some "typically masculine" traits: for instance, she rarely discusses her feelings, and for most of her life she has resisted asking for help, even when doing so would save significant time and effort given her physical disability.

But it just isn't *her*. I can't picture it at all, a male version of Lisa. There is nothing – just a blank slate, devoid of anything I could possibly react to, either positively or negatively. I can't gain any insight into how Lisa feels about Meredith because I have no basis for comparison.

I'm also very conscious of how it might appear to the reader, to an outsider – why do I stay with someone who won't connect with such an important part of my identity? It would be so easy to portray Lisa as the antagonist in my journey. But of course this would be incomplete, and unfair. We love each other, we made a commitment to each other, and neither one of us is willing to give up, even in the face of an uncertain future.

It could very well be this uncertain future that sustains me. People grow, and change. And hope.

"You've been so strong," says one of my close friends as she reads a draft of this chapter.

I don't know if "strong" is the right word. Determined maybe? I know the things I want, and as far as I'm concerned they don't have to be incompatible, so I have no reason to abandon any of them. But I have to accept the uncertainty and be prepared to face the reality that eventuates.

Ironically, given her declaration at the start of our relationship, Lisa has made it clear that there are some things she is absolutely certain about. Yet her words to me that night on her couch have proven to be more prescient than she may have realised.

Part Six

Chapter Twenty-One
Click-Clack

June 2003

My pulse fills my ears, rhythmically punctuating the silence around me. I wince as the sound of my car door shutting echoes in the early morning air. I breathe. Look once up and down the street. It's still dark; the streetlights glow silently over the quiet houses and their sleepy little gardens. There's nobody else about. Good; it's extremely unlikely that I'll be seen and recognised. Impossible? No. But unthinkable, really – in terms of consequences, should it actually happen.

The incessant beat of my heart drills an admonishment into my head: *This is dodgy. What the hell are you doing?* I'd told Lisa that I would only wear these clothes inside the house, but here I am. Trying not to think about what it would mean for our lives if she found out.

If anyone does appear nearby, I have to pretend I don't care – constantly looking over my shoulder is going to appear even more suspicious than I already feel. It's unusual to be out walking at this hour in the first place. Add in my appearance and there might as well be a glowing target on my back.

Even with my long hair, I am clearly a man dressed in women's clothing. Someday I might be less anxious about presenting this way, but it's 2003 and most of society still subscribes to last century's gender norms. Anyone spotting me is going to wonder why the hell a man is teetering down their suburban street in a pencil miniskirt and stilettos at five in the morning (the outfit is a stereotype, but it's not uncommon for transgender women to start this way).

I know I am being foolish and reckless, but I don't care. I'm way past attempting to rationalise this. I am committed, having surrendered to whatever it is that compels me down this path.

Once around the block. I've looked up this neighbourhood on the map and found a route that will take me around five or ten minutes to circle in my heels, without any need to backtrack. I wouldn't want to deal with the awkwardness of encountering someone, only to run into them again just a few minutes later!

The sound and feeling of my heels striking the pavement is something I've dreamt about for so many years, and it is glorious – the sharp, delicate staccato announcing what I'd learned at a very young age and have subsequently never failed to take notice of: *Here comes a woman.* It is thrilling and exciting – the way the shoes hold my feet in their rigid, pointed posture, how the tall heels force my hips back and chest out, how they make my movements feel dainty and delicate, and so very *feminine*. Even as my feet wobble beneath my unsteady gait, even as my nervousness makes every distant car sound like it is approaching directly behind me, I drink it all in. I am outside. In the open. Even when, only halfway around the block, my feet start complaining about being forced to endure this experience, I ignore their protests and carry on, single-minded in the pursuit of my foolish, monumental, life-changing, trivial goal: to walk around the block dressed as a woman.

Ten minutes feels like an hour and also like thirty seconds.

The nerves slowly dissipate as I sink back into the driver's seat of my car and close my eyes. I've done it. For years I've wanted to know the feeling of wearing these clothes out in the open, and now I've done it. And I liked it.

Now I have to live with the knowledge that I did this without telling my wife.

Now I have to live with the knowledge that I want more.

August 2003

I've barely slept. I'm too anxious and excited about my secret little plan. Luckily, Lisa is a sound sleeper, and won't query why I was tossing and turning all night. She was still snoring gently when I crept out of the house thirty minutes earlier than usual.

I remove my glasses and massage my temples. It does little to alleviate the empty feeling in my head. My eyes are stinging from the lack of sleep, and the bright lights and cold, stark air inside the early morning train aren't helping. I miss the warmth and comfort of bed, snuggled up against my wife. But I am resolved to carry out my little adventure. A few months onward from my little sojourn around the block, but this time the risk – and the stakes – are higher.

The other passengers pay no attention to me, but I can't help feeling conspicuous. I'm nervous it looks obvious that I'm hiding something inside my awkwardly overstuffed satchel. The bag might as well be transparent, revealing my women's clothes, and my secret, to the world.

Melbourne Central Station has an exit into its adjacent shopping centre, open at this hour only to provide commuters an outlet to the street above. Yesterday I found a small, unused room in a hallway behind some renovations, accessible to anyone because the lock hasn't been installed yet.

As I enter the mall I am relieved to see only two other people heading the same way. I wait to let them pass, checking my shoelaces so they won't wonder why I've stopped. When I reach the hallway, the area is deserted. I slip into the room and close the door behind me. Oops. The lights haven't been installed yet either. Now what?

Leaving the door slightly ajar, I make use of the illumination coming through the gap, hurriedly changing into my office skirt suit and heels and stuffing my male clothes into the satchel, which doesn't quite close over my chunky men's shoes.

I release my ponytail and let my hair fall around my shoulders. Now for the real adventure. The office is a fifteen-minute walk from the shopping centre, out on the streets, amidst all the early-morning activity in the city. People heading to work, cafés opening up, garbage trucks crawling through tight alleys to empty the bins which will be full again at nightfall. Mostly-empty trams trundling past with their deep metallic rumble, punctuated by the bell and squeaking of the doors upon arriving at a stop. Everyone I see moves with some sort of purpose; nobody is idle enough to really notice me. I'm just another office worker getting an early start.

And so I click-clack in my heels along Elizabeth Street and up Little Bourke, past Hardware Lane, its trendy establishments still awakening as the morning attendants unfurl their café umbrellas over the outdoor tables. I picture myself sitting with a coffee in one of these places, dressed exactly as I am – but imagining this makes me sad, longing for what I can't have. It's an impossible fantasy. My journey doesn't extend beyond today's limited, singular focus: walk through the city to work dressed as a woman.

Round the corner to William Street and towards my office building, and there are three young men crossing the road, heading my way. Damn. We are going to come within a few metres of each other and there's no avoiding it. I keep my head straight and walk with intent, making sure not to look their way as they pass by.

Just before they move out of earshot I hear one of them speak.

"That was a man..!" A neutral statement of fact, with just a hint of surprise in his voice.

Oof. I know that without boobs and make-up, to any observers I am obviously a man wearing women's clothing. Yet the explicit acknowledgement of this still has an unexpected impact. I realise that in doing this, I want to be *seen*. But how do I *feel*, hearing a comment like that? Shame? No. Disappointment. Longing. Envy. Realistically, will I ever know what it's like to be seen as a *woman*? Am I too afraid to stop sneaking around, and actually consider the impossible?

I don't know. It's too confronting to imagine the consequences of following this path any farther than to my destination this morning. Instead, I simply try to concentrate on the last hundred metres. I can see my office building now. The surroundings are clear. I don't expect another encounter; it's earlier than my usual starting time and I'm always the first one in.

Arriving at the entrance, I stride purposefully into the building, the sound of my heels echoing against the stone tiled walls of the empty lobby. I delight in the sensation as I cross the floor. *Click-clack. Click-clack.* A sound and feeling I will never take for granted.

The lift doors open as soon as I press the call button. I step in and let myself relax as they slide closed. Success! I'm happy and excited and a little perplexed – the thoughts I've been avoiding keep sneaking back into the corners of my mind. What have I just done? And why?

In the office restroom, I pause before I change back into my male clothing. I'm relieved, but reluctant. I wish I could stay dressed like this for longer. But I have to face reality now. Men don't wear women's clothing to work. Yet... *why do I have to be a man?*

I'm not being honest with myself, let alone with my wife, and eventually I'm going to have to acknowledge all of this. I know that my high heels are going to have another outing. I am choosing these steps, but at the same time they feel somehow inevitable.

Click-Clack

If anybody asked, I would be unable to explain why I feel like I've accomplished something important here. I can't put it into words – not the nature of what I've just done, nor my reasons why. And I have no intention of telling anyone – so hearing another perspective isn't really a possibility. In fact, I won't disclose these things to anybody for nearly another twenty years.

Chapter Twenty-Two

Belonging

People are surprised when I tell them I used to be shy. I remember myself as an awkward teenager, feeling out of place in almost every social situation, instinctively seeking connection but not knowing how to find it. I didn't think there was anything wrong with me, but I certainly knew that I was different from most people.

Even amongst fellow nerds, with whom I shared interests in music, cycling, and board games, I was mostly unsatisfied with the quality of the friendships I found. I never felt like my desire for meaningful connection was reciprocated, even if there were only two of us present. And I often felt lonely even in the middle of a larger gathering, as if my friends included me out of habit, and that my presence or absence would make no difference to their experience.

The truth was probably nowhere nearly so depressing – if my friends didn't enjoy my company I would not have been able to call them friends.

But our interactions were limited to the familiar and superficial, and my attempts to forge deeper connections were met with awkward resistance.

February 1987

"What's in this folder?" I pick up the large envelope from the car seat as I climb in and sit down.

Martin backs the car out of my driveway, concentrating on the road. A year older than me, and already holding a driver's license, he's giving me a lift to school today.

"That's my Stanford essay. I need to drop it off to Mister Kalina before class. He offered to review it for me."

I'm immediately interested. The university application essay can be an intensely personal affair – its purpose is to provide applicants with a place to express themselves outside the narrow bounds of standardised test scores. I consider Martin to be my closest friend, mostly because we share a deep interest in music, but I have had somewhat limited success in discovering what Martin actually means when he says a song "really gets him". I am keen to get a closer glimpse into his inner life.

"Can I read it?" I ask.

Martin quickly shakes his head. "I'd rather you didn't."

His abrupt reply stings a little. If he'd asked me to read my Stanford essay, I'd have welcomed the chance to share it.

"Why not? I bet it's really good. I wanna read it." I know that Martin is articulate and smart and it's probably a fantastic essay.

He takes his eyes off the road and looks directly at me. "Please don't."

His brief stare conveys a clear message: *If you value our friendship you will understand that there is a boundary here. Do not betray my trust.*

Behind the message, I also sense fear.

I put the folder in the back seat and quietly concede. "Okay."

I don't know how Martin really viewed our friendship. Was there ever anything more than the music? I had a nice tape deck and he didn't, and I happily recorded all his albums onto cassette for his car stereo. Would he have gone to the same effort for me? I enjoyed most of the music and I didn't feel like he was using me, but he didn't spend hours doing things in return; maybe he felt indebted and didn't want to give me any more leverage by revealing his secrets. I'll never forget the look in his eyes. Did he actually mistrust me? Perhaps he was afraid to open up to anyone, not just to me in particular.

Clearly I wanted more from Martin than he was willing to offer. We remained friends, and kept in touch for a few years after high school, but he always stayed at arm's length. I gave up trying.

More than thirty-five years later, I write this and realise that I still feel hurt.

I knew, instinctively, that what I desired was unusual. So while I was disappointed, I wasn't all that surprised. Teenage boys weren't expected to relate to each other in the way I wanted friendship. Sharing feelings, hopes and dreams – it seemed to me that these things were supposed to be reserved for your girlfriend.

But scrawny, geeky, teenage boys like me didn't get girlfriends. So I didn't expect nor seek out emotional connections outside my friend group. Instead I became introspective, keeping my innermost thoughts and feelings to myself and just skating by on the surface of my social life.

My emotional needs went mostly unfulfilled until I left high school and entered university, where I started a series of close friendships – all with women, save for one exception – that shaped my life in my early twenties. This was years before I became aware of being transgender, so at the time I thought I was simply unusual in preferring female over male company. Looking back, however, with the knowledge that gender stereotypes haven't really changed much in thirty years, I wonder: does my affinity for emotionally intimate, one-on-one friendships indicate that I'm truly a girl? Or is it just evidence proving that I don't adhere to the male stereotype?[13]

I don't really think there is such a simplistic explanation. I am pretty sure that friendship styles are unreliable indicators of gender, and that my own experiences and observations are simply a reflection of my inherent desire for connection. Perhaps I only notice examples of women's friendship when they appear in intimate contexts like a shared afternoon coffee. People without close friends, regardless of gender, are simply not going to be visible in the same way.

There are also other dimensions to consider, particularly regarding neurodiversity (most commonly referencing autism and ADHD). Neurodivergent styles of friendship can occupy an entire book's worth of exploration; neurodiversity can affect social interaction in subtle and profound ways, and gender stereotypes, applicable or not, can strongly influence our interpretation. Women are expected to be more adept at communicating and reading social cues; men are expected to be more direct and focus on action; yet anyone of any gender can exhibit any combination of traits.

And then, how do we explain these stereotypes in light of evidence that neurodiversity and gender diversity seem to go hand in hand? My own observations of the transgender community, as well as my experiences throughout my own life, align with the research here. I don't have a formal diagnosis at the time of writing this, but as I learn more about neurodiversity I feel strongly that many of these things apply to me.[14]

---

[13] Gender stereotypes suggest that male and female friendships have different dynamics: men share activities, women share feelings. In my experience, these stereotypes are common enough that they feel like reasonable generalisations, even though I believe they are harmful. When stereotypes are common enough to seem reasonable, they become self-fulfilling: we start to project and unwittingly apply them to our subconscious biases.

[14] The psychology and neurology of gender identity is a fertile – and often politicised – topic that could span volumes. This book isn't the place to expand upon these ideas; I include them to provide context for my experiences.

Double Exposure

As a teenager and young adult I didn't think about this background at all. I simply lamented the fact that emotional intimacy was such a rare phenomenon in my life, and I resented the idea that this was normal. The actual reasons are less important than the way my feelings coloured my relationships and interactions. I suspect that other transgender women would recognise my dissatisfaction and the persistent feeling that something was missing amongst my group of male friends.

When I was thirty years old I finally found a group of friends who matched and returned my want for connection. Up until that point my close friendships had all been individual; in groups I usually found the atmosphere and conversation to be superficial and unfulfilling. I often felt somehow different from the others: slightly out of place, sometimes even like a hanger-on to be politely tolerated. Ironically, in this group I actually *was* different: I was the only man, surrounded by a dozen women.

Even more ironically, I became part of this group as a result of finding a girlfriend, who eventually became my wife.

When I say I was surrounded, I mean it in a mostly figurative sense: this was a group of women I met on the Internet. I had little doubt that they were authentically presenting themselves, though, since the context of our gathering was an online wedding forum.[15]

---

[15] This happened in late 2000, when the Internet was still a relatively new phenomenon for most people. But there was a cohort of early adopters who saw the potential for social interaction many years before social media was invented. Before Facebook and Twitter came along, even before MySpace, there were mailing lists, newsgroups, chatrooms, and forums.

Even before the World Wide Web became available, a nerd who wanted to communicate with other nerds could use a dial-up modem to connect their computer to a Bulletin Board system (BBS). This was an electronic version of a bulletin board you might find at a community centre, except the content could be more than just for-sale and want ads. Users could create discussion threads, and local communities could form around specific interests. With the technology of the day, posts were usually limited to text only, and login would be restricted to a single user at a time (automatic time limits ensured that others could take turns). Multi-line BBSes existed but they were uncommon, and the operators would have to install dedicated phone lines to handle the traffic.

Belonging

Shortly after we got engaged, Lisa discovered the forum and signed up, thinking it would be a useful resource for us as we set about planning our big day. I also joined up, mostly out of curiosity, and discovered that socialising online really appealed to me. While Lisa only logged in occasionally, I found myself checking the forum nearly every day, quickly becoming one of the most active members. I gained some notoriety as the only man in the community, and I delighted in how everyone treated me like "just one of the girls".

The forum did prove to be a good source of advice and feedback for our wedding plans, but to me its real value came from the interactions I had with other users. Over time the forum evolved beyond its primary focus on weddings – it became an online version of the corner pub or café, where people gathered just to socialise. It was about the same size, too: given its original specialisation and the relative novelty of online community spaces, there were probably about a hundred active members, with maybe a dozen users online on a typical evening. Regular members stayed active long after their own weddings had happened, and some personalities were clearly discernible through the content and style of their posts.

As with any community larger than a handful of people, the forum membership contained a wide variety of social relationships: friends, groups of friends, acquaintances, strangers. There was also the occasional drama, trivial and otherwise – online conflict existed well before Twitter and Facebook came along. Luckily, the outbreaks were usually brief and limited to a few users (often repeatedly the same ones).

One day, I was feeling ridiculous and made an absurd post which contained only the word "melon". This was noticed and commented upon

---

Forum software took the BBS concept and made it accessible to the Internet. An online forum could handle many users at once, limited only by the size of its Internet connection and server hardware. As computers and bandwidth grew in capacity, it became possible to share images and even video along with text content. For many years you could find forums online for all kinds of communities, and although they have been largely supplanted by Facebook Groups over the last decade, some forums still exist, even if they are relatively quiet now.

by some of my friends who also replied with the word "melon". There was no premeditated plan to this; it just happened spontaneously and organically, and I found it amusing to see who joined in. Of course there were some forum members who thought it was annoying and posted replies stating as much. Others were just puzzled by the randomness of it all.

Because not everyone shared my enjoyment of the absurd, the melon post caused a small amount of drama (I had a reputation for being silly, which wasn't universally appreciated). After a handful of private messages amongst my friends lamenting the uptight nature of certain members, I had the idea of creating a separate place where we could gather and be silly without annoying people. Being a longtime nerd, I already had my own Internet domain, and my webhosting account included chatroom software. So I set up a private chatroom for me and my friends.

I called it "melonworld".

Chapter Twenty-Three

Melonworld

There's nothing particularly notable about this moment. It's just a random evening sometime in the first half of 2005. Why now?

Why not?

The urge to share my female side never goes away. I simply try to live with it and ignore it. Until now, there hasn't really been anyone in my life – besides Lisa – with whom I feel comfortable talking about my strange existence. And even with Lisa, it's not that comfortable: she is accepting but not exactly enthusiastic. I do have friends in the physical world who would be receptive, and I've told a couple of them, but they have become infrequent contacts due to time and distance, and we rarely get a chance to meaningfully engage. I am, as ever, hungry for connection.

I never intended for melonworld to become anything more than just a hangout where my online friends and I could talk nonsense and generally be ridiculous, but it has become something more. It feels like we have cultivated a safe space. Perhaps it's just my imagination, or wishful thinking. But I'm going to go with it.

Telling all the melons at once seems a little reckless, though. Especially since they pop in and out of the chatroom randomly and most of them will only see the chat history later. I want to be online at the time, so I can actually have a conversation about it.

Kylie's here now, so I send her a private message.

```
[mookers] Hey
[kylie] Hi
[mookers] Whats new
[kylie] Not much. Just online while I'm doing some knitting
[mookers] Wanna know a secret
[kylie] Ooooooooh yes of course!
[mookers] I have a female alter ego
[kylie] Ooooooooh serious?
[mookers] Yes
[kylie] Like a drag persona?
[mookers] Not drag. Just me, except female
[kylie] TELL ME MORE
```

I had a hunch that Kylie would be receptive. I'm glad I was right.

```
[mookers] She's called Meredith. She's been around for a few years I guess, but I've only given her a name recently
[kylie] Meredith, like from that new show Grey's Anatomy?
[mookers] No, I picked the name first, but everyone's going to think it's because of that stupid show!
[kylie] Great timing hehe
[kylie] Does Lisa know?
```

[mookers] Yes. Sort of. Well, she knows about my clothes and doesn't mind me wearing them around the house. I haven't told her I've chosen a name yet

[kylie] Do you ever go out as Meredith?

[mookers] No. I didn't think I wanted to, but lately I'm starting to question that

[kylie] What does Lisa think?

[mookers] She doesn't know :(

[kylie] :(

[mookers] I told her I didn't need to go outside but I don't think that's true anymore

[mookers] I can't wear my girly clothes unless Alex is in his cot in his room now. He's getting old enough to notice

[kylie] What do you think Lisa would say about you going out?

[mookers] She'll say no

[mookers] She doesn't want anyone to see me

Lisa doesn't really want anyone to *know*, either. I don't think she'd try to stop me from telling my friends, but Kylie and the other melons aren't just *my* friends – Lisa was the one who signed us up to the wedding forum, after all. It probably doesn't matter that she hasn't gotten to know the melons nearly as well as I have. She does have a melonworld account but rarely logs in, preferring to do other things in her spare time.

I try not to think about the fact that I'm not going to tell Lisa about this.

[mookers] I don't have boobs or make-up anyway, so I wouldn't feel or look as feminine as I want to be

[kylie] :(

[mookers] I would love so much to get completely done up in a glamorous dress and see what I look like

[kylie] You'd be beautiful I'm sure

[mookers] as if I'd ever get the chance

```
[kylie] That must be so hard. Thank you for sharing with me
[mookers] Thank YOU.
[kylie] I would totally do your make-up for you. It would be fun
[mookers] I wish you could!
[kylie] Come visit!
```

Oh how I wish that was possible. Apart from the fact that I don't know how I would explain it to Lisa, I would feel like a selfish jerk leaving her at home with a toddler and a new baby to look after while I flew to Sydney just for a makeover.

It's not actually something I'm torn over, because the idea of indulging my desire to be Meredith is so far-fetched that it's not even a consideration. Just a pipe dream.

```
[mookers] I'd love to. Maybe someday, in my dreams...
[kylie] Yeah I understand
```

One by one, I tell a few of the melons about Meredith. Each of them seems surprised and interested. I am encouraged, but also frustrated. I want to be able to share freely and openly, and I feel guilty keeping secrets from Lisa.

I only confide in the melons I'm closest to, and it becomes troublesome remembering to keep the messages private. It's also risky, since an accidental slip up could reveal the existence of such private conversations to the entire chatroom (and, of course, to Lisa). So I create another chatroom, called "the core", and only invite the melons who know about Meredith.

Even though Lisa would never attempt to investigate, I'm uneasy with the idea of hiding my online activity. But she's already made it clear that she's not okay with any escalation of my feminine side. I don't tell her about the core. I'm convinced that she will object to the idea of sharing Meredith with people we both consider friends. Yet the outlet provided by the core quickly becomes vital to my mental well-being – the pain of repression, were I forced to shut it all back in, would make me utterly miserable. And I would resent Lisa – more than I already do – for wanting to stifle my expression, at the same time feeling guilty for causing her distress by overriding her feelings.

I am torn between my love and consideration for Lisa, and my unwavering desire to discover what womanhood could be like for me. So I attempt to satisfy both, by moving in this secret space where Lisa never thinks to look. I'm afraid of having a difficult conversation and I'm avoiding the pain of confrontation. Not to mention the fallout if Lisa makes me choose between herself and Meredith.

I also never consider the position I put the others in, making them implicit conspirators, privy to this inner world that they wouldn't feel comfortable revealing to Lisa.

In spite of any misgivings, I persist. I feel seen, and I can't go back to hiding. Over the months that follow, I find my affirmation in this group of women who accept me for who and what I am. In melonworld, and especially in the core, I am nourished by the feminine energy flowing through the ether, carried by the words of my friends. This is the tribe I have been instinctively searching for – found unexpectedly, seeking individual connection, finding it and discovering more. The core – Bellie, Di, Kylie, Aysha, Simone, Cath – these are precious friendships that sustain me, these women with whom I feel completely free to be myself, even if I'm only able to channel Meredith through my keyboard.

At the end of 2005, Simone is two months away from thirty years old, and she makes plans to throw a party with some of the Sydney melons. Even though it means I'd be away from my family, I really want to attend.

Surprisingly, Lisa agrees to let me make an overnight trip. Her sister lives near us and can help with our children in my absence.

I hatch an impossible plan.

Chapter Twenty-Four

Sydney

February 2006

It's amazing how much mental effort I expend on organising things that only a few people will ever know about.

I'm going to visit the Sydney melons and I am travelling alone. This means it is easy to give into the temptation of opportunity: without telling Lisa, I am going to let Meredith out. I feel guilty about hiding my plans, but I can't pass up this chance to know what it's like being a woman in public.

I won't be flying as Meredith. Apart from being wildly unrealistic – I'm not keen to face airport security as my very first challenge, and besides, I don't own any make-up – I want to have someone with me for support when I start interacting with the world. So I have organised things to allow a full afternoon with Di and Kylie to help me. We don't tell the other melons what we're doing, though. Safer to keep it to just the three of us.

The secret planning feels exciting, and I can hardly contain my anticipation. And my nerves. I am anxious – I can't escape the fact that I am keeping all of this concealed from Lisa. In the back of my mind, this tugs at my conscience, but my better judgement is being overwhelmed by the tantalising prospect of Meredith being free. Overwhelmed, but not drowned out; secrecy necessitates planning and the secret behind the plan is always present in the big picture. Perhaps fittingly, spending so much energy thinking about logistics is my way of coping with the guilt.

I take care to pack my bag when Lisa isn't in the room. A lace top, a pencil mini, bra, pantyhose, stiletto pumps. The small handbag I purchased one day, convinced that it was the most suspicious thing I could possibly be doing with my lunch hour.

There is a public toilet in the shopping centre just off the freeway heading out to the airport. More logistics: if I leave the house half an hour early, I will have time to stop there and change clothes – I will engage in what is known as "underdressing", sneakily layering my girly outfit underneath my T-shirt and long pants.

The morning is quiet and there are few people around as I park the car. I find the toilet unoccupied. It's a bit manky and the smell isn't great, but it's private and fully enclosed – more than just a partitioned stall in a walk-in room. Thankfully, the floor is clean enough to set things down without them getting wet or mucky. Still, it's a far cry from a proper changing room, and I feel awkward and exposed as I strip down to change everything underneath to women's garments. My heart jumps when someone rattles the locked door handle trying to get in; there's no clearly visible "occupied" indicator. By the time I've finished, it feels like I've taken an hour, even though it's only been ten minutes.

It's uncomfortable, wearing two layers of clothing. To make things worse, the weather is hot and sunny. The forecast for Sydney is forty-one degrees, which would be torture even if I went out in a singlet and shorts. But I have committed too much time and energy to this endeavour to let the heat dissuade me. Weather be damned, my efforts will not be denied.

The airport formalities and the short flight itself are routine and uneventful, but I am nervous and self-conscious anyway. I hope I don't appear suspicious. Do the other passengers notice that my clothes hang slightly oddly when I move? My T-shirt fabric doesn't slide smoothly over the lace of my girly top. Can the slight extra bulk of my skirt be seen around my hips under my chinos? Who the hell wears a miniskirt under long pants anyway?

I am fully committed to this.

Di is waiting for me as I come off the air bridge. A beautiful, solid, imposing, six foot tower of a woman who gives excellent hugs. My excitement at the afternoon to come feels like it is vibrating out my pores.

"We are going to have SO much fun today! Ever tried on a corset?" Her chipper demeanour matches my nervous energy.

I haven't, but I'm taking small steps. "I'll settle for chocolate. We're going to Colefax, right?" Di is one of the few people I know who is as much of a chocolate snob as I am. She's been raving about this chocolate place for months.

"Of course, sweetie. I wouldn't dream of skipping that."

The little red Holden Barina waiting in the carpark looks simultaneously wrong, and somehow so right, for a person like Di. Big woman, small car. It matches the quick, snappy, somewhat self-consciously cute manner of her conversation. Inside, there is an accumulation of random clutter: an umbrella, empty mint tins, dog toys. I pick up a couple of sun hats off the passenger seat and throw them in the back where they scatter a pile of receipts onto the floor. "Oops. Sorry."

Di is unconcerned. "Pffft, I don't even remember what those are. I'll sort them out later." She pulls out a tin from somewhere between the front seats. "Mint?"

I take a mint from the tin, wondering how many times *later* has come and gone for the various items in this car. I am grateful to have the support of this big-hearted, generous friend who is unashamed of showing her own mess, both literal and figurative. It makes me feel included.

We leave the airport and begin threading our way into the Sydney lunchtime traffic. It's very warm, as forecast, and I am keen to get rid of my outer shell. Fumbling around my seatbelt, I awkwardly wriggle out of my T-shirt.

"I was thinking you might be dressed already." Di knows me well.

"I couldn't help it." As if I was going to wait any longer than I had to. I remove my stilettos from my bag. They are a classic pump style, black with a four inch heel, just a simple shape with no chunky platform or superfluous adornments. I'll never tire of admiring shoes like this – the elegant sweep of the arch and heel together, the suggestion of sexual power contrasted with the vulnerability of being confined and restrained, the simultaneous embodiment of both the delicate and the severe.

"Nice shoes!" Di glances over at me as she slows for a pedestrian crossing. I feel self-conscious as I realise the man crossing in front of us can see that I'm wearing a lace top. My hair is still in its ponytail and my face is unadorned. The man gives no indication that he notices anything unusual.

We start moving again. I kick off my boring men's shoes and remove my socks. A bit more wriggling and fumbling and my legs are out, pantyhose glistening in the sun. Reaching down, I push my bunched-up chinos aside and coerce my feet into the unyielding shape of the stiletto pumps. My skirt really is provocatively short, especially now sitting with my legs splayed slightly akimbo due to the angle of my new footwear.

They say that trans women who emerge as adults go through a flirty teenage phase, reclaiming – perhaps subconsciously – an experience they were denied growing up. One day, I might be content to wear flat shoes and skirts that extend past my knees. Today is not that day.

Now that I'm dressed accordingly, I feel ready to try *being* Meredith. It's a strange place to be – examining my own movements and behaviour in real time. I'm unsure if what I want to do is merely what I *think* I should be doing as a result of my socialised expectations, or if it is something innate that I am not yet familiar expressing. I'm worried that I will be *acting*, and deluding myself into believing it's a part of who I am. It's impossible not to be self-conscious.

I let my hair down. Closing my eyes, I breathe in deeply and think: *I am Meredith*. I push myself back into the car seat and straighten my posture, holding my knees together. If I wasn't sitting in Di's car, how would I be carrying myself? Prim and proper in my sexy office miniskirt, aware that women are held to a different standard of comportment than men are? How much of the way we relate to the world is learned, and how much is natural? And is one necessarily *better* than the other? Is that even a meaningful thing to ask?

These questions will intrigue me for years, and as I write these words I still haven't come close to figuring out any answers.

Di is a big fan of opera and has taken voice lessons for some years. It's fortuitous that I am able to exercise my girly voice here.

"I've been trying out a female voice and want to know what you think."

Di nods in approval. "Well go on then."

I concentrate. "Ahem. ... Hi, I'm Meredith!" I am very self-conscious and feel slightly embarrassed for some reason. Maybe because I know that Di has some experience with voice training.

"Aha, I see what you're trying to do. You want to use your head voice, not your chest voice." Di touches her forehead. "Imagine your voice is being projected from up here."

"My head voice. Up here. How's this?" The technique I've learned, from a page on the Internet, does make it easy to imagine the actual sound coming out of my forehead. It's a strange, unfamiliar sensation.

The quality of my voice, however, reminds me of a stereotypical drag queen. "I feel a bit camp talking this way. Daaaaarling, you're faaaaabulous!"

Actually, it *does* seem natural to flick my hand dramatically and toss my hair when I say this. Maybe it's more than just the voice. Not that I am striving to present as an overly effeminate caricature, but there is something that compels me to be more expressive than usual as I experiment. I try not to think about whether this is a learned expectation. Instead, I attempt to relax and settle into this new way of being.

I am Meredith.

I am a woman.

I feel it. I am channelling, embodying, a feminine essence. A woman's heart. The richness, softness, fullness of experience, layers exposed and vulnerable. Not that I ever felt hard or brittle or incomplete in my male existence, but there is something more, something tangibly different now, allowing my female self to be explicitly present. Unexpected, but perhaps not surprising, is the feeling of my mother's embrace. It is soft and suffused with a kind of knowing – the acknowledgement of shared experience. It is immediate and vibrant, and makes me think of sanctuary. Of resilience and sacrifice. Of understanding.

We arrive at Kylie's place and park on the street outside the front garden. The house is only a short walk away but it's still a moment to consider as I leave the shelter of Di's car: I am being Meredith, out in the open, in daylight, for the first time.

I am nervous and excited as I take the steps. It's familiar and new at the same time; I have worn these heels for many hours but apart from a few, secret, pre-dawn excursions, my walking practice has been limited to indoors. Pavement and concrete footpaths feel different, plus there are stray twigs and pebbles to contend with. I pick my way carefully to the front door and enjoy the feeling of the delicate, constricted gait that the heels induce in my movements.

Kylie is a few years younger than both Di and myself, and greets us with enthusiastic hugs. It's the first time I've met Kylie in person after several years of online friendship. She's well known in our group for being a make-up fanatic, and I hope she can work some transformational magic on me this afternoon.

The three of us don't spend a lot of time catching up on news and happenings, since we see each other online nearly every day. Instead, we get right down to the project at hand: make me look like a girl. Kylie produces a box containing some "chicken fillets" – silicone cups of substantial thickness, designed to adhere to one's breasts and increase them by a full cup size. They're an enhancement device instead of proper prosthetic breast forms, but they'll do wonders for my flat, bony chest. They feel strange stuck to my skin and don't quite fill my B-cup bra completely. Still, underneath my stretchy lace top they manage to give me a vaguely defined bust shape.

Kylie is deft and quick with the make-up. The whole day is starting to feel a bit surreal, so I don't really pay close attention to what she is doing.

"Turn your head. No, the other way. Now look down." It's easy to just kind of zone out and obediently follow her instructions. She certainly knows her way around a make-up kit. I don't even know what half the brushes are for.

"This might feel a bit pokey." Here comes the eyeliner. Suddenly I have flashbacks to when Lisa did my face before the Mardi Gras party a few years ago, before she decided she didn't want to see me wearing make-up. Thankfully Kylie has a more delicate touch and my eyeballs remain largely undisturbed.

Mascara time. "Look up. Left." Prod, sweep, flick. "Look right." I try to envision myself someday doing this with such ease and familiarity. Perhaps I should be paying better attention.

"Done! Go have a look in the bathroom mirror."

Sydney

My reflection looks pleased, if a little bit pale. It's not the first time I've been made up, but I still haven't yet had the privilege of wearing a foundation to match my skin colour. I think I look okay, though, and I am ready to try my luck at being a woman out in the world.

The heat of the day has intensified as Di and I depart Kylie's place. Kylie isn't coming with us; she has a previous obligation this afternoon. We'll see her again later at Simone's party. Unfortunately by then I won't be pretty anymore. There will be too many people to keep this comfortably secret, so I will have to return to being Derek for the evening.

I dream of frocking up for a party, but at this point I don't expect to ever have the opportunity. I try not to think about what I will do if – when – I end up wanting, needing, more than this one afternoon.

Our first stop is an alternative fashion boutique in Newtown called Gallery Serpentine. It's full of exquisitely detailed Victorian and baroque apparel, all bodices and flowing skirts and lace embroidery. And corsets. I've been intrigued for years by corsets, attracted to their elaborate aesthetic and overt femininity, but I've never had the chance to inspect one up close. I run my hands over the nearest one, feeling its satin finish and fitted curves. I am surprised by just how heavy and stiff it feels, even in the sections between the boning. It's amazing that such an inherently severe device can be used to reinforce a delicate, pretty, feminine appearance. Perhaps that is part of the allure: the juxtaposition of the unyielding and the vulnerable. Armour decorated in floral trimming.

"Are you looking for something in particular?"

The voice comes from a vision I can't quite comprehend.

It could be an elf, or a fairy, or some other kind of mythical woodland creature. My eyes register an androgynous looking being with short blond hair and a strong jawline, wearing a dark green corset, black floral skirt, and green satin heels with black ribbon laces and platform soles.

"I... um... no, I'm just browsing thanks." I have to catch myself and make an effort to speak with Meredith's voice.

The attendant smiles. "No problem, just let me know if there's anything you need help with." They sashay away to the desk at the back of the shop.

For a second, I don't feel like me wearing a miniskirt and heels is particularly daring.

Di comes around the end of the display rack, holding a dark cluster of laces and stiff curves. "I'm going to try this on." She heads off in the direction the attendant went as I follow, surprised at how *normal* this all seems.

The next several minutes are fascinating to me, as I've never seen anyone don a corset before. I am familiar with the image of the lady-in-waiting hauling with all her strength on the laces as she braces against her foot planted in her mistress' back, but – fortunately or unfortunately, I'm not sure which – I don't get to see that spectacle happen here. There is a fair amount of grunting and pulling though, and Di looks amazing once they are finished.

I imagine myself in Di's place. What would it be like? Could I ever feel free enough to so boldly assert my femininity? I look at my own reflection in the shop mirror, at my trim figure and sexy legs, and think actually, yes, one day. But whatever my own feelings tell me, the fact is: I am not free, not now. This afternoon is simply a taste of what *could* be, if I did have the freedom to do this whenever I wanted. I am bending the rules today, being dishonest by omission. My wife does not want me out in public dressed as a woman, and I did not tell her of these plans.

As good as the corset looks on her, Di decides that for the money – the price is $250 – the fit isn't quite satisfactory. This does not stop me from marvelling at her magnificently-supported bust, but it does make me feel a little better about not trying one on. It's a lot of money.

Sydney

Removing a corset is much quicker and easier than squeezing into it, and involves significantly less grunting. In a couple more minutes we are heading out of the shop. As we reach the exit I stop for one last look at a beautiful, deep violet number hanging next to the door. I imagine myself buying one, but if I did it would just be an expensive collection piece for me to hold and admire, and then put away in hiding until – who knows when? For where would I go dressed in it? And who would help me to put it on?

We head from Newtown over to Haberfield to visit the Colefax chocolate shop. I am feeling slightly despondent after being reminded by the beautiful corsets just how improbable, how unattainable, a life as Meredith really is. I have today, but after this, then what? Back to dressing up in secret, stuck inside where I don't get to experience anything that would affirm my existence as a woman. Inside the house with Lisa I won't be able to wear make-up or breast forms, for she has deemed these things a step too far. So "Meredith" will be no more than Derek-in-a-dress. What's more, in a few years' time our children will be old enough to wander out of their rooms after bedtime, and there will be nowhere private left for me at all.

I try to stop lamenting my situation and concentrate instead on the present moment. If this is to be my only fleeting glimpse into a life I cannot have, then I want to experience it as fully as this one day will allow. At least then I won't be left wondering. Besides, I'm pretty sure this will end up being my only chance: I feel guilty enough keeping this from Lisa, and I am certain that if – when – she finds out about today, then things are going to get a whole lot more difficult.

We arrive at the shopping strip in Haberfield. Di finds a car park half a block away from Colefax, on the opposite side of the road, so we have to walk back and cross between moving cars to get to the entrance. It's not a particularly busy street but I am keenly aware of my attire and – living in the present moment – how it's just a little bit out of place here on a Saturday afternoon. I can't really tell if anyone passing by is looking at me, but I suppose a tailored office miniskirt, long legs and stiletto heels are useful for stopping traffic.

The shop is also a café and there are some customers sitting inside when we enter. I am extremely self-conscious now, but I try to act casual, tottering up to the counter and ordering my coffee and my chocolates using this strange girly voice coming out of my head like I do this all the time. *I am Meredith, and this is real. I am alive, and I am here, interacting with the world.*

"Can I please have a cappuccino, a mint leaf, a raspberry cup, a dark truffle, and a chilli truffle?" Easy peasy. The strangest thing about this situation is the fact that there is chilli in some of the chocolate truffles. According to Di, they are out of this world, and it's one reason why we are here.

The woman behind the counter goes along with my reality without question. "Let's see… one of those, one of those, one of these, oh yes these are delightful, good choice… is that everything? Twelve dollars fifty please." She is friendly and courteous and it is pleasantly reassuring.

I pay in cash. Touchless credit cards are still in the future, and I'd have to hand my card over for processing. The name on my card does not match my current reality and I don't want to tear an inconvenient, uncomfortable hole in the fabric of this moment.

As we look around to find an open table, my eyes sweep past two women sitting at the front window. I'd seen them look up as we walked in, and I had the feeling they were watching us from behind when we were standing at the counter. One of them looks at me and smiles warmly. I try to smile back but I'm certain I look awkward doing it. Nevertheless, being acknowledged by a stranger's smile feels validating. It's an unexpected gift that affirms my presence and the reality of the present moment.

Right now, even if only for one moment in a few short hours – I am Meredith.

Living in the moment means discarding your expectations. I wanted to accept the experience of today as it presented itself. It turns out this has been quite an easy thing to do (actually, the chilli truffles were good but I *did* have expectations they didn't quite meet). Presenting to the world as Meredith, I faced no ridicule, no abuse, no questions or demands that I explain myself. Everyone has been perfectly civil and polite to me all afternoon.

I guess if I'm honest I'd have to say I had hopes, not expectations. Hopes for an uneventful few hours, where I get to experience being perceived as just another woman going about her day. And this is exactly what the afternoon has brought. At the same time, my choice of outfit reflects something else, directly at odds with the desire to blend in: the need to be seen, to be acknowledged as feminine and attractive. Many years later I will learn to address this need with clothing that is more thoughtful and not so obviously revealing. However, today I am embracing and expressing only what I currently know. Understanding how I want to be Meredith out in the world, and what the experience means to me, will come later (and indeed will never stop evolving).

I don't know if people find my outfit noteworthy; nobody mentions it. I certainly *feel* special wearing it. I feel attractive, and feminine, and vulnerable. That I can feel all these things while going about the business of an ordinary Saturday – there's something delicious, almost naughty, about it. It's as if I've stumbled upon some delightful secret – known to all womankind, of course, but unknown to me until today. I had no expectations but the afternoon has been fulfilling in a way that I would not have been able to articulate beforehand. I never imagined that being out in the world as a woman would feel so special and yet unremarkable at the same time.

Alas, my time as a woman does come to an end as the afternoon fades. It will be some time – months, even years – before I am able to fully reflect on the day and its experiences. For now, sitting here amidst the clothes piled haphazardly upon Di's bed, I find a way to pack Meredith away, back inside the suitcase, back inside myself, and re-emerge in the comfortable, familiar existence of Derek. I try not to think about the future and the unlikelihood of ever having this chance again.

I am unexpectedly weary, although it should not surprise me. I have just spent an extraordinary day being myself in a way I have never been prepared for. The effect it has had on me cannot be characterised as simply a result of the nervousness or excitement that comes with an adventure; it is something more holistic, more encompassing of my entire state of being.

It also comes with a feeling of accomplishment and deep satisfaction.

That evening, at Simone's party, we are all sitting around relaxing and enjoying each other's company. It's nice to be able to see my friends in person after having known most of them for years only from a name and words on a computer screen.

Simone is showing us some new shoes she bought herself for her birthday. They're beautiful strappy gold heels and I am envious at the ease with which she models them. I'm back to being Derek and even though Kylie, Di, and Simone are aware of my feminine side, some of the other people present don't know yet.

I want to live vicariously through my friends. "Hey George, you should try them on," I say as Simone places her new shoes back in the box. Georgina – everyone calls her George – is a poster girl for the "practical, no-frills" style of presentation: simple cotton dress, sensible flat shoes, minimal make-up. We've all chatted about shoes online before so I know that George, Simone and I all have similar size feet. Seeing George wearing these glamorous party shoes will be amusing.

George lets out a slightly incredulous grunt. "Ha. As if." But then she looks at Simone, who smiles and hands over the shoe box. George takes the shoes, carefully manoeuvres her feet into the straps, and stands up.

"There's a mirror in the bedroom. Have a look!" Simone motions for George to follow.

"Hey, I look pretty good in these! Maybe I should dress up more."

I watch through the doorway as George turns and stands with her feet at various angles. She has nicely shaped calves, and the shoes are doing their job well. I feel a twinge of envy which doesn't dissipate even when George takes the shoes off.

"I wanna try them on." I say it before I have a chance to think twice.

Simone looks at me with a strangely concerned expression on her face, like she's trying to force an unexpectedly strong reaction into coherent words. "Um. Do you have to?"

"No, but why not?" I'm feeling a little bit bold. The shoes are beautiful. I'm surprised at Simone's reluctance. She didn't have a problem with George wearing them.

"Okay, I guess."

I try to ignore the unexpectedly weird vibe happening here and I carefully don the shoes, feeling the delicate straps, impressed at how they secure my feet using such a tiny amount of material. I don't have any strappy shoes of my own so this is a new experience.

Simone looks worried as I stand up, like I'm a big clumsy oaf who's going to break her precious new heels. I don't think that this is really her concern though – I'm clearly being careful, and I'm smaller and lighter than she is. What is it that I see on her face, then?

I look in the mirror and wish that the rest of my outfit matched the shoes. They look sexy. I make a note to find myself some strappy heels one day.

I take them off and hand them back. "Thank you."

Simone puts them away briskly, and the party continues.

I found out later why Simone acted so weird when I tried on her shoes. After the weekend of the party, she more or less stopped logging into melonworld. The few brief times I did see her online there was something awkward about it. People say that text-based communication loses the nuance of face-to-face and voice interaction, but the written word is still powerful, and when it is immediate and unfiltered and created in its own contextual moment – as happens in an online chatroom or with instant messaging – then it unquestionably captures something more than what the words on the screen would convey at first glance.

Simone and I were close friends. I had thought she was accepting and supportive of Meredith – she'd never given me any indication otherwise. The melons were my tribe. My girl gang – *girlfriends* in the sense that straight women use the term. Especially those in the core – I felt safe with them, I could open up emotionally and relate to them with my feminine side. It turns out that Simone was just going along with the idea of me being female as long as she wasn't confronted with it in person.

I could tell there was something going on. That somehow I'd ended up with a wounded friendship, and it was going to be painful to face it and give it the attention it required. After a few days of suffering anxiety over this, I sent Simone a private message.

[mookers] Hey

[simone] Hi

[mookers] I need to know

[mookers] You have a problem with Meredith, don't you

[simone] I guess so

[mookers] You never mentioned anything before

[simone] It was all theoretical in my head I guess, until my party

[mookers] Nothing's changed for me. I have high heels here too you know

Sydney

I thought about all the times in the melonworld core, where my friends were so interested and supportive of me talking about being Meredith, and wondered if anyone else knew how Simone felt about it.

> [simone] I just don't understand why you need to be Meredith
>
> [mookers] I don't understand why either, but I'm not going to reject myself for it
>
> [simone] I don't support Meredith. I'm not *rejecting* you
>
> [mookers] It sure feels like you're rejecting a huge part of me

Her words reminded me of how some Christians say they "love the sinner but hate the sin" in a leap of mental gymnastics that lets them believe they are not being bigots. As if *being* is something that a person can simply stop *doing*.

> [simone] Would it be bad to change your name?
>
> [mookers] What do you mean?
>
> [simone] I don't actually like the name Meredith
>
> [mookers] What's wrong with my name?
>
> [simone] It's a stupid name

Insulting someone's chosen name is not a great move.

> [simone] Maybe if you had a nice name - I'd be more accommodating
>
> [mookers] Oh, yes ok, I'll change my name just to suit you... as if!
>
> [mookers] Why should Meredith do anything for someone who isn't supportive of her?
>
> [simone] Don't be like that

I was starting to get angry now.

[mookers] What do you expect?

[simone] I expect you to be as tolerant and accepting of views that are not as you perhaps may *want* them to be

[mookers] You're preaching tolerance and acceptance to me?

[simone] I preach nothing

[simone] If anything, it is my *need* to protect you from ridicule from OTHERS that makes me have a degree of distance from the whole Meredith thing

Oof. Hiding behind the "concern" smokescreen. Did Simone even realise what she was saying?

[mookers] I think that's a rationalisation

[simone] I don't. I think that a lot of people feign support - when it's really mere curiosity.

[mookers] So you're saying I'm naïve and pathetic for believing my friends

[mookers] And you're doing me a favour by giving me the hard truth

[simone] Errr no

[mookers] Who is ridiculing me then?

[simone] I am generalising

[mookers] Nobody I care about is ridiculing me, and nobody I care about considers me worth ridiculing... except perhaps you?

I started to feel a little depressed, as I had fancied myself a better judge of character than this.

[mookers] Of course I want acceptance. But on the other hand I don't expect Joe on the street to care

[mookers] I *do* care what my friends think, however

[mookers] And if you think I am worthy of ridicule, then that says more about you than it does about me

[simone] Why are you *assuming* to know what I think?

[mookers] I'm not. I'm inferring your views from what you say

[mookers] Other friends of mine are happy to accompany Meredith out in public. There is no 'protection from ridicule' clause there

[simone] You almost seem to *expect* acceptance from your friends - simply because they are your friends?

[mookers] Well, yes

Was she for real here? What was her definition of *friend?*

[simone] I accept that you are a trans-gender person Derek - and all that implies. I don't however feel the need or desire to embrace how that actually manifests itself.

[mookers] So why joke about "conditions" under which it would be OK for you to "accommodate" Meredith?

[mookers] If you don't wanna see her, don't even joke about it

[simone] Do you think perhaps - that this is the end. We just part ways.

There it was. Acknowledgement of what was really happening. But I wanted her to openly admit her reasons.

[mookers] Why does it have to be?

[simone] I'm just disappointed that you seem to have dismissed me because I am not as accepting as you perhaps would like me to be

Seriously, framing it as *my* problem? I hadn't realised just how much growing up Simone still had to do.

[mookers] It's natural, I'm gonna gravitate towards those who are supportive

[simone] I'm supportive of your journey... but I cannot claim to be supportive of how that manifests itself

[mookers] That sounds like semantics

[simone] No it's not

[mookers] That's like saying "It's ok to be gay, as long as you don't sodomise other men"

Had she not ever heard, and understood, the bigotry behind these tired old conservative talking points?

[simone] I'm supportive of your experience and how it makes you *feel*. I am not supportive of hearing you gabber on about trivialities such as heels and skirts

Wow. This was rich, coming from the Handbag Queen herself, who would get endlessly excited over expensive brands of stylishly designed containers to carry your stuff around in.

[simone] And as I said above, maybe, since you naturally won't "gravitate" towards me because I can't offer you the enthusiasm you want, we just kind of let it go

[mookers] See, the fact that you are suggesting we part ways... that tells me that you really do have a problem with Meredith

[mookers] It seems to me that you have an issue just KNOWING she's there

[mookers] And, well, if that's the case, then there's nothing I can do

[simone] Well it's obviously a big enough issue for me that I can't just turn a blind eye

[simone] And no, there is nothing you can do - this is *my* issue

Maybe she did have a bit of self-awareness after all.

[mookers] Well obviously I'd love for you to accept all of me for who I am. If you feel like there is no point unless you are able to do so, then I guess you have to decide

```
[simone] And I think that you need to realise that not everyone is
gonna want to come along for the ride for you - and so be it - there
will be some casualties - I might be the first - but probably won't be
the last

[mookers] Of course I realise that

[mookers] Like I said, it's your choice

[mookers] I guess I won't be seeing you around, then

[mookers] Thanks for the good times... I mean that

[simone] yeah same - we had some fun

[mookers] nite nite

[simone] nite

simone exits from this room
```

I stared at the screen for a while. My anxiety had dissipated, as had my anger. Now there was just a lingering sadness.

    I don't know how long I sat there for. Half an hour? An hour? Eventually, I saved the chat transcript to a file, turned off the computer, and went to bed.

Chapter Twenty-Five

Reckoning

I only lasted a month before confessing to Meredith's little escapade. I guess I knew that I'd eventually have to own up, but I had been avoiding even thinking about it. At this point, no matter what I did or said, the damage was done. It simply wasn't visible until I uncovered it. And Lisa was completely blindsided by it.

I don't even remember the conversation we had. I'm sure it was uncomfortable, and probably quite brief. Lisa tends to go silent and withdraw while she processes confronting information. I can still feel the anxiety and uneasy heaviness in the air as I revisit the aftermath for this writing.

Lisa felt betrayed by everyone involved, and rightly so. I had tried not to imagine the effect it would have on her, even though I had no illusions about how much she would be hurt. I'd been selfish and irresponsible, paying no heed to the feelings of everyone else caught up in my meticulously calculated recklessness. I had no excuse for what I'd done. Yet

I'd felt so free that afternoon. I couldn't bring myself to regret it, even with the betrayal – because I couldn't imagine any other way I would have had the chance to experience being Meredith.

The following day at work, I was completely unproductive, just sitting at my desk depressed, worried, unable to focus.

I received an email from Lisa. She preferred to have discussions in writing because it gave her time to think.

```
From: Lisa
To: Derek
Subject: :(
Date: 22 March 2006 7:58 am

You have no idea how hurt and disappointed I am. And not just by
you.

The melons are your friends. If they were my friends as well,
they would have strongly suggested you tell me.

So they are not my friends really... and it just proves that I
am not a melon.

They have encouraged you... especially Di and Kylie, to deceive
me, whether explicitly or not.

I have much more to add, but I haven't the energy to do it at
the moment.

I just feel very very sad.

==========

From: Derek
To: Lisa
Subject: RE: :(
Date: 22 March 2006 8:23 am
```

I wish I could find a way to do this without hurting you. I feel so selfish but it's killing me to keep it all hidden. Who can I share it with, if not my friends?

I know I put the melons in a difficult position, but they aren't responsible for my actions. Even if they are your friends too, but you hardly ever come online so of course they know me much better. But this whole fiasco is my fault. I'm sorry.

==========

From: Lisa
To: Derek
Subject: RE: :(
Date: 22 March 2006 10:12 am

A few thoughts.

If you ask yourself why you didn't tell me before going, I think the answer would be because you didn't want me to say "don't do it". Therefore it was a very conscious decision on your part to keep it from me. You involved others in it too... by having Kylie do your make-up and Di go with you, and I assume they knew that I didn't know. I cannot imagine helping a friend of mine do something I know that their wife doesn't know about and may not like. I would not be comfortable with that.

Especially when your friends know me as well. The old cliche of the wife being the last to know. I cannot begin to tell you how much that hurts me. I feel like a fool for being so ignorant. I know you said the melons aren't responsible because they are your friends more than mine... so at least I know where I stand with them... the wife of a friend.

I am so sad. I don't know how/if I can get past you keeping such an important thing from me. You have deceived me and lied by omission to me, about something that is obviously so very very important to you. I guess it is also that by keeping this from me you have created distance, and at the same time fostered closeness with others by sharing with them. And I know you are sorry... but is that sorry for doing it (I don't think so) or sorry for upsetting me?

I don't know how to not feel sad anymore. I think damage has been done and I don't think it is going to be easy to fix it. And I know you feel bad about it all... but at the moment I can't really take your feelings on board because I am trying to deal with mine. Of course you have all your friends to talk to, and I'm sure they'll be sympathetic with you. I have no-one.

So there you have it... a few probably rambling and not very coherent thoughts I have been having.

==========

From: Derek
To: Lisa
Subject: RE: :(
Date: 22 March 2006 10:47 am

I think even if I'd told you what I was going to do, it wouldn't have mattered what you said, and I would have done it anyway. And been resentful about having to negotiate. Or else you would have felt pressured to say yes and then been resentful yourself.

I don't want to hide things from you, but I don't know how to continue hiding from everyone else. I can't explain why I feel the need to do this. I just wish you could find a way to be okay with it.

I don't know how to fix this. :(

I couldn't help feeling that if Lisa wasn't ashamed of me then she would have been able to discuss our situation with her own friends. She always insisted she wasn't ashamed, but if that were really true, then why did she keep everything to herself? If she wasn't ashamed, then why did she object so strongly to me telling others about Meredith? I loved her, but it had become unbearable to keep hiding myself to accommodate her feelings.

In hindsight I can see that Lisa was much more upset about me betraying her trust than she was about me actually going out in public. But I was so focused on the idea of exploring being Meredith and pushing for my freedom that the trust seemed like a necessary sacrifice. And my resentment at being constrained blinded me to the significance of my betrayal.

I didn't ask permission because I couldn't risk the answer being "no". The anxiety and unease between us would have just happened before my trip, rather than after. And then I would not have felt free in Sydney, even if I had gone against Lisa's wishes and been Meredith anyway. So I took the easy path and swept the fallout under my conscience until weeks later when it finally ate through my guilty resolve.

I hadn't actually considered what would happen after returning from Sydney. I suppose I always knew that it would be impossible to maintain the secret, but as with any other discussion about Meredith with Lisa, I had chosen not to think about it.

Chapter Twenty-Six
Escalating

To Lisa, my desire to be Meredith must have felt selfish and inconsiderate, but to me the line between *wanting* and *needing* was impossible to define. On any given day, my *want* to be Meredith could go harmlessly unfulfilled. But given enough of those days, and the *want* might grow strong enough to overcome common sense, as well as significant barriers of impracticality and inconvenience. At what point has it become a *need?* When I find myself tottering around the block in stiletto heels in an unfamiliar neighbourhood at five in the morning? When I organise a secret plan to spend a girly afternoon with a friend in another city?

There was an outlet I might have used instead of sneaking Meredith off to Sydney, had Lisa originally been willing to allow it. The Seahorse club, or more formally, Seahorse Victoria[16], was a Melbourne-based support group for crossdressers and transgender women that provided a safe, discreet

---

[16] The "Victoria" part of the name refers to the Australian state of Victoria. It is purely coincidence that it is also a female name (fittingly associated with elaborate women's fashions!).

space for people to express themselves. I had wanted to check it out a few years earlier but Lisa had said no.

I thought perhaps it was time to revisit the question of me attending, and I brought it up a couple evenings later. Lisa didn't say much at first. The next morning she sent me an email.

> From: Lisa
> To: Derek
> Subject: Seahorse
> Date: 25 March 2006 9:15 am
>
> My initial thought is that it will be a lose-lose, like everything else has been. If I say go ahead and do it, even though I may not be really comfortable with it, then I will end up being resentful. If I say don't do it, you will end up being resentful. The only positive solution is if I say... fine go ahead, and am happy about it... which puts all the onus and responsibility for it onto me.

I really tried to imagine myself in Lisa's position and feel sympathetic – if things were reversed, and she wanted to go and do something dangerous or irresponsible or downright evil, of course I would ask her not to. But I couldn't see why me being Meredith in a safe space like Seahorse should pose a problem for anyone else. It felt so unfair that Lisa allowed her own well-being to be affected by my self-expression. And somehow she turned it around to the idea that I was making *her* responsible for my happiness.

I couldn't figure out how to talk to her about it. Every time I wanted to ask her why she objected so strongly to me going out as Meredith, I felt like a child testing the patience of a mother who'd made up her mind and was perilously close to breaking point. It didn't help that Lisa had been raised in an environment where difficult, upsetting emotions were usually buried and avoided. This is why she preferred to have discussions via email. So even though she was my wife, I could never get a clear sense of her state of mind.

Escalating

I imagined some bogeyman following Lisa around every minute of every day, making sure I never ever tried to be a woman or else he'd make her suffer somehow. Why did this have to be a hostage situation? And then, why did it feel like *I* was the one being manipulative?

Dangerous, unfair, irresponsible – none of these external perspectives ultimately made any difference. Meredith was an intrinsic part of me and I was struggling to repress her. Yes, being visible could be dangerous, but fear was such an unjust reason to keep hiding, and I refused to be ashamed of my feminine side. Once upon a time, disabled people were hidden away too, out of shame and fear of oppression. I was always saddened by the fact that Lisa took pains to hide her crutches for photos. Imagine if I insisted that nobody in my life ever found out Lisa was disabled. I wanted to point this out but I couldn't do it without feeling spiteful.

It was clear to both of us that we needed help navigating this. Even though Lisa wasn't keen on the idea of Seahorse, we didn't know where else to start. I reached out to them.

```
To: Info@Seahorse
From: Meredith Lee
Subject: Looking for help
Date: 26 March 2006 2:03 pm
```

Hello,

I am a 35yo crossdresser, married with two small children. My wife knows about my dressing but my children do not, and I am not out to anybody else in our (large and frequently present) extended family. Some of my friends know, and have gone out in public with me dressed, but I have kept this fact hidden from my wife until recently. Unsurprisingly, when I came clean with my wife, things did not go so well.

We had discussed me joining Seahorse quite some time ago (nearly two years) and she was strongly opposed to the idea. I reluctantly gave up, thinking that perhaps I could get by with the occasional dressup at home. However, the occasions are extremely few and far between now that my son is not confined to a cot at night. I believe this is why I have recently been thinking about ways to dress elsewhere. When a weekend trip to visit my friends in Sydney by myself came up, I took the chance, and this led to the current situation with my wife.

I do not wish to keep secrets from my wife any longer, and we are considering counselling to help us work through the issues of my betrayal of her trust and her fear of my coming out. I was hoping that someone at Seahorse might be able to suggest, or point us in the direction, of a therapist or other resource to assist us.

Regards
Meredith Lee

==========

To: Meredith Lee
From: Abby@Seahorse
Subject: RE: Looking for help
Date: 26 March 2006 5:20 pm

Hi Meredith,

There are a number of professionals that do offer counselling in Melbourne. It just depends what you are looking for.

Here is one recommended psychologist:

Sarah M. XXXXXXXXX
Phone (03) 9XXX XXXX
LGBTQIA, families, coming out, transitioning. Eastern suburbs.

Otherwise I think Seahorse would provide an excellent avenue to express yourself in a non confrontational manner.

Abby
Seahorse Secretary

Escalating

Lisa found this slightly unsatisfactory.

> From: Lisa
> To: Derek
> Subject: Counselling
> Date: 26 March 2006 6:46 pm
>
> Surely our issues are not only Seahorse related since they are to do with basic trust and deception issues.
>
> I think if Seahorse recommend a therapist then I would feel a bit like it was therapy to help or make me accept the whole thing, rather than general relationship issues. I know for you it all revolves around the cross dressing, but not so for me.

I didn't know how to address the trust thing. To Lisa, it must have felt like I'd been secretly unfaithful, but to me, it felt like I was simply trying to claim the right to explore my own existence.

I think Lisa knew, at some level, that my need was genuine. I didn't yet know how far I was willing to push things – was I still "just" a crossdresser or was I actually wanting to be a woman? But Seahorse provided a space to figure it out, and there would be clear boundaries to help reassure Lisa.

> To: Abby@Seahorse
> From: Meredith Lee
> Subject: RE: Looking for help
> Date: 27 March 2006 7:50 pm
>
> Hi Abby,
>
> My wife feels that if we were to see somebody recommended by Seahorse, it might feel as if she is being pressured to "accept" the whole thing.

> I have had some further discussion with my wife and she is no
> longer opposed to the idea of me joining Seahorse, given that
> the meetings are held in a private, unadvertised location.
>
> Meredith

Attending Seahorse wasn't accompanied by any dramatic revelation or epiphany. Seahorse did eventually change my life, but things happened slowly and without much foreshadowing. At first it was awkward, and kind of anticlimactic – meetings were basically a room half-filled with people sitting around chatting quietly. But it was something, where previously I had nothing. I hoped the fact that things were largely uneventful would help to allay Lisa's fears. From the outside, it was completely mundane; in practical terms it simply meant that I went out on a Saturday night once a month.

Instead of engaging someone recommended by Seahorse, we decided to return to a counsellor we had previously seen a few times, when we needed help navigating the changes in our lives following the birth of our first child. Even though Julie had no experience with transgender clients, she was familiar to us and had an easygoing, no-nonsense approach that we both liked.

Treat it like a hobby, said Julie. Hobbies are manageable things, and don't need to be shared by both halves of a couple. Seahorse meetings were held once a month on a Saturday night. I could be out playing golf every weekend or meeting my friends for Friday night poker sessions. The practical implications would be the same – I would be away from the house during these times, leaving Lisa to look after our two small children. Lisa would similarly be entitled to her own pursuits. With a bit of consideration and give and take, it could be a perfectly reasonable arrangement.

It felt like it, for a short while. Seahorse became my outlet, a monthly reprieve where I could release Meredith from her hidden cage and allow my femininity to breathe freely. But there was something crucially different about this that couldn't be compared to a typical hobby: the persistent, profound, all-encompassing secrecy.

Chapter Twenty-Seven

Tiptoeing

May 2006

Six P.M. on a Saturday evening, and the shopping centre is quiet. It's late autumn and the twilight feels crisp; the previous day's rain has left the air clean and clear. Everyone has finished their afternoon activities, and although the restaurants are open, there's a lull before the rush of dinnertime. I've picked this place, halfway between home and the Seahorse meeting venue, because it is far removed from my normal routine – there is very little chance of encountering somebody who will recognise me. It also has a conveniently located disabled toilet near the entrance where I've parked.

I've changed in a public toilet before, but this is the first time I've done a full transformation and emerged as a woman. It's far from ideal as a place to do my make-up but at least there's a mirror and it's reasonably clean. I'm also worried that I'll be monopolising the disabled facilities for an excessively long time, but I'll just have to work as fast as I can and hope for the best.

As far as Lisa is concerned, Meredith only exists at Seahorse. The gatherings are held at a location only known to members – a community meeting space with access to a small kitchen and the restrooms. The room is reserved for Seahorse on the evenings when we meet, and the entrance is obscured from passersby so that privacy can be maintained.

But changing from Derek to Meredith and back again, all within these boundaries, feels deeply unsatisfactory. Meredith is not a character in the theatre, where she comes to life only for a few hours each time the show is presented. Nonetheless I am being asked to treat her this way. There are two separate worlds: inside the meeting venue, and outside where "real life" takes place. Derek is permitted to cross into both spaces, but Meredith is not.

It diminishes the validity of Meredith's existence if she can't walk in the door as herself.

It seems that I can't stop hiding things from Lisa.

I rationalise my decision with the fact that I don't intend to do anything after changing except drive to Seahorse. I simply want to walk into the meeting as Meredith. All of this – the planning, the scouting of an unfamiliar location, the awkwardness of briefly tiptoeing through a public space as a woman, hoping to be invisible – it's all in service of my arrival at Seahorse. And it's satisfying. Everything goes smoothly, and when I enter the meeting room it feels quietly affirming.

Before the following month's meeting, I have an idea. Maybe Lisa will be okay with me changing at a trusted friend's place before going to Seahorse. A friend who understands the difficulties of being LGBTQIA+ and having to negotiate the hurdles of society while trying to be true to yourself.

My good friend John – a gay man, one of the first people I told about my crossdressing even before I'd evolved into Meredith. He knows of my struggles, and of course he is willing to offer a place for me to change. John and his partner David also know Lisa, and they would not support me doing anything against her direct wishes.

Lisa says yes. Reluctantly.

I tell her how much I want to arrive at Seahorse as Meredith instead of as Derek, and she grudgingly concedes. I grasp at this somewhat unexpected development and dare to imagine the future. John and David's apartment is so much more than just a different place to change. Being with a friend makes it feel somehow more authentic. More *natural*. Does Meredith have a chance at life beyond the fabricated walls of a local community hall?

When the next month comes around, we've had a couple of sessions with our counsellor Julie, and Lisa has changed her mind. It turns out that doors once opened can close again.

```
To: Derek
From: Lisa
Subject: A few thoughts
Date: 08 June 2006 10:12 am
```

Ok...well here are a few thoughts I have that need to be shared. I think I like to write them for 2 reasons. One is that it lets me plan what I want to say, and the other is that I don't like to disappoint/upset you, so that's why this approach.

I think you will be disappointed by what I'm going to say.

I thought I had said at Julie's on Tuesday that I wasn't cool with/comfortable with you getting 'dressed' with other people, i.e. your friends. I know I had previously said OK to going to John's, but I believe that was because I felt powerless to say "No...I'm not happy with that". Our sessions with Julie have made it clear to me that I am not helpless, and that I can say... I am NOT cool with that. Sometimes I think you choose not to hear me, so I will say it really clearly: I am not cool with you getting ready for Seahorse at John's. Then it is up to you what you do with that knowledge.

In terms of the 'deal' Julie talks about that we need to have in terms of Meredith... my limit is Seahorse. Nothing public at all. If I ever change my mind about it I will tell you.

Then it becomes up to you what you can 'live with'.

I am sorry that I am not more cool with it. I really am. I hate to disappoint you, or to impose limits, but in this case I guess I have to, for my own happiness. You are right when you say I shouldn't subjugate my happiness/peace of mind for yours.

So there you have it. Just know I love you, and if I didn't it would be a lot easier to not care what you do.

I hope this makes sense to you.

==========

To: Lisa
From: Derek
Subject: what I've realised
Date: 08 June 2006 10:50 am

I guess I knew from Tuesday that you'd decide you didn't want me going to any friends' houses. So I am now looking at a year, 5 years, 10 years, forever, of never going beyond Seahorse.

I guess I've been hoping against hope that you'd eventually accept Meredith. Not necessarily embrace, but also not simply tolerate. And the prospect of losing that hope makes me very sad. And I have come to realise that it's not simply about Meredith being able to go out. There could be a million practical reasons why Meredith might be deterred, and they wouldn't matter as much. I think I have been pushing and badgering you because what matters to me are *your* reasons.

> I want you to know how much I appreciate you letting me go to
> Seahorse, when it is so hard for you to live with. I just can't
> help feeling rejected knowing that not only do you not want to
> have anything to do with Meredith, but also that you don't want
> anybody you know to have anything to do with her. It makes me
> feel like a leper that must be hidden away for the shame of it
> all.
>
> I can't make you accept this part of me. I don't think you can
> make yourself accept it. But I need acceptance, and validation,
> from people who know me, people who are more than acquaintances
> and strangers. So I turn to my friends. And now I can't do that
> anymore. And I feel as if I am alone.

It didn't take long for my sadness to turn into anger. I began to actively resent the fact that I was still being forced to hide myself, and I struggled not to push against my restraints. I tried to understand why Lisa wanted to keep Meredith a secret – I was prepared to deal with the consequences of coming out, but Lisa clearly was not, even if she couldn't articulate why. She told me that she wasn't ashamed of me. I was unconvinced. With a large, tight-knit circle of family and friends who might have differing, incompatible responses to Meredith's existence, it seemed to me that Lisa felt she had too much to lose.

And then, I wondered: was it that she was afraid of losing *me*? To Meredith?

None of Lisa's emails ever addressed the reasons behind her treatment of Meredith. Every time I tried to discuss her feelings about it, she made me feel like I was badgering her.

I was afraid of upsetting Lisa. So I stopped pushing, and tiptoed around her emotions. Seahorse was indeed just a monthly hobby, and my frustration became an ever-present binding around my heart.

Knowing what was at stake for Lisa didn't make it any easier for me to accept her limits. To me, her fears were unreasonable – rational or not. I understood that conceding Seahorse was difficult for her, and I was grateful for the extra space it granted me. But a walk-in wardrobe with enough room to breathe and move is fundamentally still a closet.

Chapter Twenty-Eight

Clandestine

Ironically, being forced to arrive at Seahorse as a man and changing at the venue has implications for privacy that Lisa might not have considered. As a closeted trans person, it feels risky to reveal too much about myself; the world of 2006 still hasn't evolved enough to feel safe having an open discussion about gender identity. Even in a transgender setting like Seahorse, people who haven't fully transitioned seem to be wary of other members they don't know. Revealing one's public identity in person feels a bit indecent, like the sort of thing you'd see on a tabloid TV show.

In the Seahorse meeting room, all we know about each other is our femme names and what we can observe. Outside lives are rarely mentioned – there are two separate worlds for most of us here, and there is an implicit, unspoken boundary between them. Every conversation seems to contain moments of hesitation, as if the speaker is choosing her words carefully and deliberately. Over time, this vigilance takes its toll: it's exhausting, always having to be alert and constantly scrutinising your interactions with others.

However, for me right now, as I become familiar with this landscape, it just feels like a normal part of the cost of living.

I don't know how much these privacy concerns play a part, but very few Seahorse members actually change at the venue. Those that do so hurry through the door, hunched over their bags of clothes and make-up, visible for all of five seconds before they disappear down the hall to the restrooms. Half an hour later they emerge fully formed as women, their secret identity safely hidden away.

I don't want to do that. But I can't change at John's place, and I don't want to use the shopping centre toilet every time.

There's a secluded carpark in the backstreets of an industrial estate, full of workshops and warehouses thrumming with activity during the week, but deserted and eerily peaceful on a late Saturday afternoon. There are no visible security cameras, and no windows on the corrugated steel sides of the adjacent buildings. The entire carpark is obscured from the quiet road used to access the entrance to the business site, and there is no other way in or out.[17] It feels relatively safe – there is absolutely no reason to expect anyone to be here right now. Someone with unsavoury motives looking for a target would be wasting their time here.

Dusk is falling on this unseasonably warm winter's day, and although the windows are open, the light reaching inside the car is fading quickly and I have to rush to do my make-up. I drop my eyeliner pencil down the side of my seat and swear out loud. I dream of having a luxury boudoir, with well-lit mirrors and air conditioning, full of comfortable, perfumed silken softness. Instead I have a deserted parking lot, my rearview mirror, and the smell of diesel and machine oil.

---

[17] There are security cameras at the entrance, and I know they will have recorded my car driving in and out. I reason that unless there is an incident reported, nobody will ever review the footage before it is overwritten.

This is how I change genders. Stripping down in the car where nobody can see, and reconstructing myself using grit and determination. And lace, frills and make-up.

I know that people would be surprised and concerned for my safety if they knew about this, so I keep it to myself. I don't even tell Lisa. She would be worried, of course, and probably angry at me for changing outside the Seahorse meeting venue. I don't want to risk her feeling like I am trying to manipulate her into letting me change elsewhere.

Late at night, on my way home, I find a quiet spot where I can change back. With no need for light, any street will do as long as there is no passing traffic. Still, even behind the tinted car windows, I feel exposed as I hunker down in my seat, once again stripping down and re-dressing, wiping away my make-up, wishing that there wasn't the need for this secrecy. Wishing that Lisa would feel comfortable with my friends seeing me. Wishing that there wasn't the expectation that I should be ashamed of this.

After several months of this, I muster up the will to push for a little bit of respite. I've gotten to know a few of the Seahorse members well enough to feel comfortable asking to change at their houses before the meetings. It feels like an imposition, but after months of using my car as a changing room I really want something better.

I don't want to hide it from Lisa, even if she doesn't know the people I'd be asking. It's so much easier if I don't have to plan my movements in secret.

But asking her permission is risky. If she says no, will I honour her wishes?

I can't answer that.

It's much easier for me to rationalise doing things behind her back if my actions never cross her mind in the first place. Ignorance is bliss, right?

On the other hand, changing at another member's house on the way to a meeting isn't *really* going outside Seahorse. It seems like a reasonable request. Maybe Lisa will say yes.

Would I even consider asking if I think she might say no?

I know the answer to that.

"I want to change at one of the other Seahorse girls' places before a meeting. Would you be okay with that?"

I can't interpret Lisa's expression. Is she simply processing my unexpected question, or is she annoyed that I've asked?

"You're pushing for more. I thought we had an agreement." I guess she's annoyed.

I consider trying to explain why I am dissatisfied with changing at the meeting venue. But while the privacy concern is justifiable, it's counter-intuitive and I don't think I can explain it without sounding like I'm arguing.

I decide to try a reassuring approach.

"I'll be going straight to the meeting, and it's a Seahorse person who already knows about me anyway."

"Who?"

"There's a few people I might ask. Emma. Rachael. Obviously nobody you've met."

Pause.

"Why? If you're just going to the meeting anyway, what difference does it make?"

"It… it just feels better walking into the meeting already changed. And my friends' places will be a lot more comfortable than the toilets at the meeting room."

"I guess." Lisa sighs.

This is so difficult and exhausting for both of us.

I am thankful for their kindness, but I hardly ever see my Seahorse friends at other times. In addition to the usual inertia of adult life and parenthood, which leaves me little time for socialising, there is the continued importance of keeping my transgender experience contained within the context of Seahorse. It feels a bit like breaking the rules when I do see one of my transgender friends outside of a meeting, even when I am presenting as Derek.

I should also acknowledge that whilst I yearn to be seen as Meredith by the world, I am still struggling with the fear that being visible in public alongside another trans woman, regardless of how I am presenting, will make me subject to ridicule or abuse. Internalised transphobia is hard to overcome, and I am still unlearning a lot of society's teachings.

It is many months before I realise how my situation, with its restrictions both real and imagined, has been impacting other people. One day I am changing at Emma's house, when she somewhat pointedly says:

"You know, it would be nice to see you when you aren't just coming over to change before a meeting."

I have no reply to that. It's true that I have been using Emma, and it's uncomfortable to acknowledge that, even if I think she should understand the limited options I have as a closeted trans person. But we're not close enough friends to have an open conversation about this. Instead, I just feel embarrassed and ashamed.

The next month, I return to using the carpark. It's depressing, having to choose between hiding and begging for the (not endless) generosity of other people. Even if my friends aren't necessarily put out by my requests, they have their own lives and are starting to move on from Seahorse anyway.

I long for the freedom to be Meredith on my own terms, living a life like Rachael and Emma do, where I don't need Seahorse at all. But they have both transitioned and are living full time as women. It's a familiar path amongst Seahorse members, using the club as an entry point, a safe space to explore and evolve until eventually transitioning and emerging into society. Leaving the secretive world of Seahorse behind as they proclaim their existence as authentic women.

But I am unwilling to give up my life as Derek. I don't suffer or struggle to be Derek. My pain is in the impossibility of freely being Meredith. If only Lisa wasn't afraid, or threatened, or whatever it is that makes her so uncomfortable with my female existence. I love my wife, and hate the fact that I am betraying her trust every time Meredith ventures beyond the edge of the shadows. But I can't see a way to reconcile Lisa's needs with my own. So everything about Meredith has to be carefully guarded, concealed not just from the wider world, but often from Lisa herself.

Part Seven

Chapter Twenty-Nine
Mover

I have a complicated relationship with gender stereotypes. As Meredith, I have embraced many things that align with society's prescription of femininity, particularly regarding appearance (even if it could be argued that some elements of this are counterproductive, on both personal and societal levels[18]). As Derek, however, I want to clearly distance myself from all of the problematic aspects of socialised masculinity. I am hesitant to allow myself to move through the world in ways that, if observed casually, might be assumed to be (or conflated with) "typical male behaviour".

    I suppose this could be considered hypocritical and a bit cringeworthy: am I really so earnest in my attempts to establish that Derek is "not like other men"? Am I doing a disservice to women when Meredith gets excited about being pretty and "girly"? But gender doesn't exist in a vacuum; as idealistic as it might be to claim that everything I am is internally driven, I

---

18 For all my attempts at progress, am I problematically setting the cause two feet back by wearing high heels? And am I causing my own two feet and back to suffer future problems in the process?

don't know how to define and present myself without at least acknowledging these references.

I also try to keep an open mind about others, but I don't always succeed in avoiding the shortcuts in thought provided by the convenience of such prepackaged definitions. Yet even as I slip up, I don't want other people applying those shortcuts to their interpretation of *me* – in spite of the fact that I *do* sometimes align with the stereotypes.

One notable area where this uneasiness makes me self-conscious is my longstanding interest in cars. Even though car culture can be quite diverse, people who don't share the interest might only think of the stereotype portrayed by tabloid news stories: crude, coarse men revving loud engines and behaving in antisocial and often misogynistic ways. I worry that people may connect me with this stereotype and that the association will somehow diminish the validity of my female existence. Nevermind that car clubs include plenty of women, and that applying the aforementioned male stereotype is quite unfair to many of the men.

Thankfully, as I become more comfortable in openly expressing and disclosing my dual-gender nature, I find myself growing less concerned about how these imagined stereotypes might inform the way others regard me. Years ago, however, when Meredith was still mostly a secret, I was very careful about navigating the car enthusiast world. Even if the people in that world might have been receptive and welcoming to a transgender woman, I didn't want to risk running afoul of somebody who did match the "unenlightened male" stereotype.

* * *

I've always been interested in cars that, rather than being flashy and expensive, are quietly unusual, significant only to car spotters who pay attention to details. In 2008 I purchased a car that would become a ten-year hobby: a 1998 Mitsubishi Legnum VR-4, a JDM (Japanese Domestic

Market) station wagon never officially sold in Australia, imported privately into the country as a used car.[19]

The Internet is full of car nerds if you know where to look. I became aware of my car's existence through a few JDM enthusiast websites after an unfamiliar and cool-looking station wagon caught my eye one day and I went online to figure out exactly what a "Legnum" was. Twin turbos and torque-vectoring all wheel drive in a body like the family Magna, except wearing a sharply tailored suit after hitting the gym for a year? It looked and sounded amazing – why had I never known about this car?

One of the sites I found was OzVR4 – an Australian forum dedicated to these cars, where members had already compiled pages of information and advice for new owners. Including how much a good example should cost – surprisingly, I could afford one. And even though the prospect of buying a complicated and high-tech foreign-market car made me nervous, the existence of OzVR4 was reassuring: all of the information I needed was available on the forum. Members had found online parts suppliers in Japan, and importantly, there were mechanics in Melbourne who knew how to service the complicated bits. Owning a Legnum would be more money and effort than owning my old Mazda Astina, but after visiting a JDM import yard and taking a test drive, I knew I had to have one.

Soon I was hooning around in my own dark purple beast that looked vaguely like a Magna but moved like an oversized rally car (such power and performance is what Mitsubishi's "VR-4" suffix signifies). I loved getting second glances and occasional questions from onlookers about what I was driving, and the astonished reactions when they realised it wasn't just a Magna with a fancy bodykit. I was also thankful that the Legnum's road presence was subtle enough that it usually went unnoticed, and I could

---

[19] I didn't have to import it myself – the interest in JDM vehicles is strong enough in Australia that there are niche businesses which exist for this very purpose, and once a private import has been registered, it can be re-sold like any other used car.

pretend to ignore any attention it garnered if I didn't want to engage with strangers.

I became very active on the forum, allowing my interest in the car to outweigh my aversion to the blokey culture that often pervades car enthusiast communities (OzVR4 being no exception). I made friends with a few forum members who taught me how to do my own maintenance. I went to local meetups and learned about modifying and tuning my car to make it more powerful. I even had car parts regularly delivered to the office!

One day, after about a year of ownership, I was idly musing about custom licence plates to Lisa, and I suggested the combination "MOO VR-4" as an option. I do like puns, and the car could certainly move, but it was intended as a joke – I have two personal rules about custom plates, both of which are broken here: first, I'm not a fan of putting one's own name on a licence plate (it just seems a bit gauche to me), and second, putting the car model or trim level on there is pointlessly redundant – it's already on the badges stuck to the car at the factory!

Even though I was proud of the pun I'd made, I didn't think there was anything else notable about my suggestion. Inventing licence plate wordplay for various cars is just an amusing pastime; that particular conversation with Lisa wasn't significant to me.

There was also another, more important reason why I wasn't serious about getting a custom licence plate. But since I'd considered my suggestion to be a throwaway joke, I didn't think to mention it at the time.

The Legnum was my only car, and Meredith drove it too. Putting "MOO VR-4" plates on it would immediately identify it as mine.

* * *

August 2010

It's my birthday and the extended family is gathered for a Sunday dinner to celebrate. I'm turning forty, which makes it a notable milestone. Lisa is excited about giving me my birthday present and asks me to open it as soon as I've blown out the candles on the cake.

It's a long, wide, flat package which doesn't weigh very much.

I tear the wrapping off, open the end of the box, and pull out two rectangular stamped pieces of metal. They both have the same dark blue letters on a white background.

MOOVR-4.

Oh, shit.

Lisa notices as I try to feign delight to cover my surprised horror. I'd completely forgotten about mentioning this licence plate idea. I certainly never expected her to take my suggestion seriously! The end result of my attempted facial discipline is a look of bewildered disappointment, which doesn't land well.

"Do you like them?" Lisa asks carefully.

I feel awful for not being able to be excited about this present. Poor Lisa was so eager to see my face light up and I've completely buggered up the moment. In front of the entire extended family. Who all know how much I love my car, and who *don't* know about Meredith, and are therefore puzzled about my strange reaction.

"Yes, thanks!" I say weakly.

"I thought you'd love them." Lisa doesn't really hide her own disappointment.

"I do. Really. I... they're cool. I'd forgotten I mentioned this to you."

Lisa nearly pouts. "*I* remembered. I thought you'd be so excited with them! I can't believe it."

The rest of the family wonder what's going on.

I can't reveal the real reason why I don't want custom plates. So I bumble through an explanation about my two rules.

"...but it makes a good pun, so in this case I'm okay with it," I conclude. I wonder if I sound convincing.

"Worst birthday present ever," says Lisa.

Later, when it's just the two of us, I try to explain.

"I never really wanted custom licence plates because I don't want to get spotted if I'm driving around as Merri."

"Spotted?" Lisa asks.

"It's a unique car. They're rare enough that other owners take notice and try to identify who it is when they see one. There's even a 'Spotted' thread on the forum to post about sightings."

"People *look* for each other's cars??" Lisa looks at me like I'm speaking out the side of my head.

"Yeah. People post things like 'whose purple Leggie was driving past Chadstone last night?' and stuff like that. It's fun." I thought about the MOOVR-4 plates in the back seat of my car, waiting to be installed. "Unless you're trying to remain anonymous."

"Car people are weird." She shakes her head.

"You don't ever notice your friends' cars?" I ask. For me, this level of awareness is almost compulsive in nature. "I always know what people drive. Don't you remember things? Like the Hello Kitty sticker on your own rear window. I even recognise some of my friends' licence plate numbers, even if they aren't custom."

"Nope. That's like... something a stalker would do. Maybe I'd notice a sticker. But who memorises peoples' licence plate numbers??"

Well, I don't *memorise* them as such. But I would recognise many if I saw them. Nonetheless, being spotted (and outed) by someone on the forum, or by anyone who knew my licence plate for that matter, was a scenario that simply never crossed Lisa's mind – if it had, she wouldn't have given me the custom plates. After all, keeping Meredith secret from people she knew was more of a concern for her than it was for me.

Luckily, I never got outed, even though I put the plates on my car. I know I got spotted at least once when driving as Merri, but the spotter wasn't certain of his sighting, or perhaps he had the courtesy to be discreet when he posted about it: *I thought I saw the mookermobile on the Monash Freeway the other morning, but it didn't look like Derek driving so I didn't wave.*

My first reaction was slight panic, even though the spotter mentioned not recognising me. Would I have to explain? Car enthusiasts can be very protective of their rides and it's unusual to see someone besides the owner driving a rare vehicle, particularly if it has been modified to the point where some road conditions might warrant extra care.[20]

I could have ignored the post, but I worried someone might comment wondering why I hadn't replied. So I answered with a simple *Yeah, I let my cousin borrow my car for the day,* prepared to spin a story that my car was the only one available to her at short notice. But there were no further replies, and the sighting gradually got buried beneath subsequent "spotted" posts about other cars.

I do have a cousin who looks a bit like Meredith. She lives in England though!

If it wasn't for the fact that Lisa didn't want Meredith to be recognised, I don't know that I would have taken pains to be so careful. The forum atmosphere was mostly focused on the cars and people didn't get overly involved in discussing their personal lives. There were a couple of prominent female members, and at least one gay man, and to my knowledge they never got any troublesome comments or attention.[21]

---

[20] Like many car enthusiasts do, I had lowered my car, causing the front bumper to scrape on steep driveways and excessively large speed bumps.

Eventually I decided that the Legnum took too much effort to keep running reliably (high-tech often means high-maintenance and high-cost as a vehicle ages), and in 2018 I replaced it with an Australian-market Honda Accord Euro which proved to be much easier to maintain. I had recently come out publicly as transgender, but since I was selling the Legnum and moving on, I didn't bother making an announcement about Meredith on OzVR4.

I briefly thought about tuning the Accord and getting "MOOGEN" licence plates,[22] but after lowering it and putting aftermarket wheels on it, I lost interest in further modifications. I'm still a total car nerd, but after spending ten years with my own car as a hobby, I decided I'd rather spend my time and money elsewhere.

---

[21] Over the years, my impression of the global car scene has been that it is quite inclusive and open-minded. It's considered uncool to disparage someone else's carefully chosen styling and performance modifications based on personal taste alone. Much like individual bodily autonomy, individual car-related decisions are treated with respect (as long as they are not reckless or unsafe for other road users). This extends beyond the cars themselves, and the same attitudes are exhibited regarding demographic diversity, at least at a grassroots level (broadcast media-driven professional motorsport is another story). In early 2022, two prominent online car-culture nerds founded an automotive blog called The Autopian, with the aim of creating *"fun, engaging content that fosters an inclusive, close-knit automotive community."* The site has become highly successful and features frequent contributions from Mercedes Streeter, an established writer in the online car scene for many years, who posted about being a transgender woman in late 2016. In the comments on Mercedes' articles at The Autopian and elsewhere, I have never read anything that suggests her gender is an issue for anyone.

[22] Honda has a longstanding motorsports partner called Mugen. I would break rule number one for this plate because I think it's hilarious, even if most people (except Honda fans who know my name) wouldn't get the pun.

Chapter Thirty
Navigating

In 2008 I started seeing a psychiatrist who specialised in gender issues. Lisa and I were still struggling to come to terms with Meredith's increasing presence, and our couples therapist Julie was at a loss to help us further. She thought it might be a good idea for me to see a specialist on my own – someone who could help me figure out Meredith's place within myself. Understanding this was essential to determining her place in the rest of my life.

    Julie did some research and found Fintan Harte, a well-regarded, genial man with a long history of helping transgender patients in Melbourne. Lisa came along for my first appointment, and left feeling somewhat reassured. Dr. Harte had a respectful and holistic approach. He was there to help me navigate the challenges of my life – gender related or otherwise – with full consideration for Lisa and my family, and he wasn't just going to send me down the path of transitioning.

The clinic was located just outside the Melbourne city centre, a short tram ride from my office. It turned out to be very convenient for me; I could commute to the city in the morning as usual, have my appointment, and then head off to work afterwards. Dr. Harte – Fintan, who wasn't into stuffy formalities – didn't care if I always presented as Derek; having treated many patients like myself, he understood the reality of living a closeted, double life.

However, after a few sessions, I found myself really wishing Fintan could meet Meredith.

I had female friends here in Melbourne who knew about my situation – cisgender women whom I'd known since well before I started attending Seahorse. My urge to share Meredith's existence was ever-present, and as Meredith emerged and evolved I kept these friends constantly updated. I wanted to cultivate and experience, face to face, the kind of sisterhood I had found online with the melons.

A few of these friends lived conveniently near to Fintan's clinic, and I nervously asked to use their houses to change early in the morning before my appointments. I worried a little bit about repeating what happened with Emma, but I was already close with these women and they were supportive and encouraging. They said yes, even though it meant they had to get up earlier than usual to accommodate me.

Fintan was quite happy to receive Meredith and did not discourage me. Indeed, he offered the use of the staff restroom at the clinic so that I had somewhere comfortable to change back into Derek before heading to work.

I was even lucky enough to have the use of a car park at the office, so I didn't have to carry Meredith's clothes, shoes and handbag around on public transport or hide them under my desk.

This became my routine for a while, and the only people to know about it were Fintan and my generous friends.

I felt guilty about hiding it from Lisa but not enough to risk the consequences of telling her. It was so much easier not to – even on days when I went straight to work I would leave the house while she was still asleep, so I don't think she took much notice of when my appointments with Fintan were scheduled. It was difficult enough to discuss Meredith's movements in the context of night-time Seahorse meetings and I wasn't keen to introduce the idea of mornings with non-Seahorse friends. Lisa also didn't know these friends like she knew the melons, so I rationalised the secrecy by telling myself it wasn't as bad because the betrayal was only personal on my own part.

I kept my actions concealed not because I thought they were wrong – on the contrary, I thought Lisa was wrong in her refusal to let me express myself and give Meredith freedom. No, I was simply afraid to have the difficult conversations with Lisa – and I suspect she felt the same. The emails that formed so much of our early discussions about Meredith are evidence of how painful it could be. With my visits to Fintan, I had found a routine that worked, and it was so easy to remain silent and leave the peace undisturbed.

Writing these words so many years later, I realise that this hasn't changed. I do intend to give Lisa editorial input around her part in this memoir, even at the risk of her wanting so many changes that I decide it's not worth publishing. But I haven't yet shown her any of the passages explicitly examining our relationship. I can justify this by arguing that doing so will change the thing I am writing about even as I write it, and it will make me question the viability of this project. This may be true, but there is a greater truth: I am more afraid of the consequences for me and Lisa.

I'm not rocking the boat. Yet. But I know there are some scary looking waters ahead.

"So how do you think things are going?" Fintan eventually asked, his warm Irish lilt adding to the comfortable feeling of his office. He usually waited for me to open the session and update him on my life, presenting whatever problems were affecting me. But I hadn't brought anything today – there was nothing specific I could think of that needed working through. I had sat down quietly, waiting a bit awkwardly in silence before Fintan spoke.

I relished my monthly opportunities to be Meredith when I came to see him. It was nice to just *be feminine*, with no anxiety, no second guessing of other people's reactions, no comparison with other women. Shifting in my chair slightly, I closed my eyes and breathed in, feeling the stretch of the bra holding the breast forms against my chest, feeling the soft silkiness of my pantyhose against the drape of my skirt.

"Things are pretty good. It's great being able to be Merri twice a month instead of just once." I paused, thinking about all the things that made up my life. "I don't know if I'd try to fit in more Merri time even if I was allowed to."

I was constantly trying to convince myself of that. In truth, I knew inside that I wanted to be Meredith more often than I was getting to be. My contentment was probably due to the fact that because there was no more space, I knew I wouldn't be making extra effort trying to squeeze her in. It would be many years before I had the freedom to realise that even back then, I was subconsciously balancing my desire to be Merri against the energy I was willing to spend on her. Looking back, I don't think I would have been content had I known what possibilities would eventually become real. But that reality hadn't happened yet.

Fintan smiled. "Well, it sounds like you're managing successfully around all the practical matters in your life." He was always careful with his words. "I get some people in here who are very... who have such unrealistic expectations, that it's difficult to come up with viable long-term strategies for them. There's no magic bullet solution to anyone's problems.

It's one step at a time. The question to keep asking is, are you happy with how things are going?"

Was I happy? Compared to not having the opportunity to be Meredith at all? Absolutely. At twice a month, I no longer felt frustrated and trapped when the urge to be female arose. I would only have to wait a couple of weeks for release, often less since I usually felt fulfilled for a few days after my stints at being Meredith. Then I could spend ten days or so looking forward with anticipation rather than dreading a nearly month-long dry spell.

Besides, the idea of being *completely* free felt like such an impossibility that it wasn't even a consideration on my scale of happiness. Yet – it was still an idea I couldn't shake, and it pulled with a tiny, inescapable weight at every feeling I had about Meredith's existence.

"I guess so. I don't see how things could be much better unless Lisa has a change of heart. And she's said that won't happen."

Fintan looked at me but said nothing.

I could never tell what he was thinking. Was he aware I was trying to convince myself that this was sustainable? That I could just keep steering my life through the dark corners of these mornings, without ever rocking the boat that carried my relationship with Lisa? For however long it took?

Until what? Where would Meredith be – or want to be – in a year? Five years? Twenty years?

Chapter Thirty-One

Daybreak

It sounds like a lot of effort to go through, making sure all the pieces line up to allow Meredith her time out in the world, but I often wonder what I would have done if I hadn't been able to make it work. Compared to someone with zero prospects of ever realising their transgender existence, I was very fortunate. The fact that I had the freedom to find these little corners of life to move around in was not lost on me, even as I dealt with the frustration of having to search for them.

It was a lot like having an affair – all the planning and sneaking around and careful disclosure of limited information. It was exhausting. I wondered what would drive someone to do this, if it were not for the feeling of freedom and release I had when I could be Meredith.

The secrecy added an element of thrill of the experience. But this was tempered by the knowledge that I was betraying Lisa's trust, even if there was no actual unfaithfulness. I knew that it would feel so much better –

maybe not as immediately exciting, but instead somehow deeper and more fulfilling – if I didn't have to hide it from her.

One morning, my friend Jane suggested that we start extra early so that we had time to get breakfast before my appointment. She had a cute café in mind, a cosy little place not far from Dr. Harte's clinic, decorated with retro memorabilia and run by a charismatic Italian man called Michael who called everyone "bella" and "bello". Thus began a treasured habit that I would continue for years. Once a month, it was lovely and affirming to walk into Michael's café to be greeted with a cheery "Good morning bella!" before sitting down for a coffee by the fireplace on a chilly morning.

Jane wasn't always available, and I didn't want to repeatedly impose on the same friend every month anyway, so I ended up bringing a few different people into Meredith's life with this routine. Curious friends willing to take time out of their morning to meet my female self for the first time; sometimes they joined me at Michael's café, and sometimes they only got to see Meredith briefly before I left their houses for the café on my own.

For many months I relished spending these mornings as Meredith, until one time when none of my friends were around and I was left with nowhere to change. I could have started the day feeling disappointed, but something made me want to push the boundaries a little.

Michael was behind the coffee machine, in mid-conversation with a customer as I came through the door.

"Yeah, as if that's what you'll be doing! I know you. You'll end up breaking someone's heart." His cheeky sarcasm peppered the atmosphere in the café, rising slowly with the wisps of steam glinting in the morning sun.

The woman laughed and shrugged as she received her takeaway coffee. She was attractive and wore a long green skirt that furled softly as she moved. "And what's wrong with a little holiday fling? Anyway I'll see you when I get back."

"Ciao!" Michael called as she departed. He turned towards me and a brief look of uncertainty crossed his face. Then bemusement, as he broke into a broad smile.

"Good morning... bello! Can I say that? Look at *you!*"

"Hello Michael." Grinning, I held my arms out from my sides, presenting the polo shirt and tan chinos combo that I always wore to the office. "This is my other self. I'm Derek. I dress way more boring than Merri does."

Michael looked at me in wonderment. "Hello Derek! You're so different. My mind is blown."

I gestured out the door. "I liked that woman's skirt. Merri hasn't got anything green though. Do you think green would look good on me?"

He laughed. "Stop, you're confusing me. I can't picture you in a skirt right now. So what's... why Derek today and not Merri?"

"I didn't have anywhere to change, actually." I shrugged. "And I thought why not surprise you?"

It felt a bit dangerous, revealing my male self to someone who only knew me as a woman. However, this interaction made me realise something. Maybe I wanted to share little glimpses of my fuller existence to people. Especially if they seemed like they'd appreciate it.

"You can change here if you want. Anytime." Michael nodded towards the back of the café.

"Aw, that's very kind. Thank you. But it takes me like an hour – I'm sure you don't want me monopolising the bathroom all morning."

He furrowed his brow slightly. "No, probably not. Why can't you change at home?"

"My wife doesn't want to see Merri." I didn't mention that Lisa wasn't even aware that Merri went out on most of these mornings.

"Oh. That sounds… complicated." Michael reached for the espresso portafilter. "I won't pry." He knocked the old coffee puck into the used grounds box and started the grinder. "The usual long black?"

"Yes, thanks." I headed past the coffee counter into the dining area. As I sat down I reflected on the separation of my two lives and how it felt to breach the border between them. It was always a little bit exciting introducing Meredith to friends who had only known Derek. But outside the context of a transgender environment like Seahorse, I had never really considered the inverse, where my male self was the hidden, intriguing one.

No matter how much the world tries to keep you in darkness, it's impossible to keep hiding when your heart and soul need to be seen. Little by little, the light was expanding over my complicated, strange existence. One morning at a time, slowly pushing aside the shadows that covered an undiscovered life.

Chapter Thirty-Two

Midnight

Sneaking Meredith out to Michael's café and Fintan's office once a month wasn't the only way I scraped out extra space for her. Even before I established those morning habits, I had known it wouldn't be enough just to stay within the comfortable closet of Seahorse and a few of its members' houses. Over a year of monthly meetings, I had slowly become envious of how some of the other girls[23] would continue their night out after the meetings ended.

A few of them would go to a late night café and I wanted to join them. I didn't expect Lisa to say yes. But in a moment of uncharacteristic bravery, I asked her.

"Do you know anyone who lives in St. Kilda?"

"No, why?" She turned the page of her book without looking up.

---

[23] I acknowledge the fact that it can be patronising to use the term *girls* when referring to adult women, but this is what many trans (and cis) women affectionately call each other.

"Some of the Seahorse girls like to go to a café after the meetings. I want to go with them."

Now I had her full attention.

"What?"

"I want to go out after Seahorse. There's a trans friendly café called Monroe's[24] on Fitzroy St. Do you know anyone who might be out late on a Saturday night around there?"

"How late?"

"I don't know. Maybe eleven? I think Monroe's closes at midnight."

She didn't stop to think for very long. "None of my friends would be out that late. Not in St. Kilda."

"So you're okay with me going out as Merri?"

"You won't be alone?"

I was so focused on thinking Lisa was afraid of me being recognised that I'd forgotten she also worried about my safety. St. Kilda was safer than its reputation suggested, but it still felt seedy at night.

Imagining myself as Merri alone on Fitzroy St. made me nervous. I quickly added my friends to the picture in my head. "No. There's about three or four girls who usually go there."

"Okay."

"Really?" I'd heard her clearly, but I didn't believe it.

"Yes."

"Thank you."

I wondered how Lisa really felt. But I didn't want to continue the conversation after such an unexpected gift.

It was liberating and surreal, being out in public knowing that I wasn't going behind Lisa's back. She'd said yes, but having permission only

---

[24] For decades, Monroe's was well known as a safe place for transgender people and the LGBTQIA+ community in general. It closed in 2012, and the site is now home to the Victorian Pride Centre.

changed the potential consequences of being found out: instead of worrying that Lisa would feel hurt and betrayed, I worried that she would be angry and say "I knew I shouldn't have let you go out" when someone we knew asked her what the hell I was doing.

Of course, this didn't happen. Everyone we knew was either too young or too old to be found hanging out in St. Kilda late at night. Including myself – nobody would expect to see Derek there either, so if someone did encounter Meredith they would have to really pay attention to recognise me.

After a few uneventful café visits, Tracy, one of the more experienced Seahorse members, suggested something a bit more adventurous.

"Have you been to Domicile?"

"No, but I've heard a few people mention it. What is it?"

"It's a nightclub. Very alternative. And very welcoming. It looks scary but it's really not." Tracy noticed as my eyes widened slightly. I'd never been to an ordinary nightclub, let alone an alternative one, whatever that meant. If it was anything like what I'd seen on TV and in the movies, then the idea of going as Merri was slightly terrifying. People went to these places to be seen and get drunk and find sexual partners, didn't they?

"You'll be fine. It's really trans friendly. Everyone just accepts people as they are. There's usually at least a few trans people there."

In the year 2007, if you walked into a random venue and presented as an identifiably transgender person, you would not necessarily expect a seamless, polite reception. You might not have any trouble, but there could be a definite awkwardness about your presence. Hearing that there was a place where trans people were *normal* was a revelation.

Terrified or not, I found myself interested, and somewhat intrigued. "Alternative? Like how?"

Tracy smiled mischievously. "It's… kinky."

Hmm. What would Lisa think?

When I mentioned it the following month, I just told Lisa it was a safe, trans-friendly nightclub, which it was. I just wanted to have a drink and hang out with my friends and see what it was like.

"You're pushing again." She sighed.

I didn't have a response.

She continued. "If I say no, you'll get all depressed and then I'll feel like the bad guy. I feel like I have to say yes."

I didn't want to argue. Lisa was correct in her assessment – I wasn't actually trying to be manipulative, but if she said no I would indeed get depressed. And resentful that she was keeping Meredith restricted. I just wanted Lisa to realise that she didn't need to worry. But it didn't matter how many of these discussions we had; she could never tell me what exactly she was afraid of.

I shrugged. "If you say yes, then the only thing different for you is that I'll come home well after midnight. But you know you're always asleep already anyway. And I'll still get up first in the morning." I knew how much Lisa treasured her weekend mornings, when she could sleep in without being disturbed by our two children. I wouldn't ask her to give that up so that I could be Meredith.

She frowned. "Are you going to be tired and grumpy?" She knew what happened when I didn't get enough sleep.

"I'll try not to be."

"You better not be." Lisa had very little patience for complaining, especially if the cause was self-inflicted.

We were establishing a pattern. Meredith could exist only in ways that didn't require Lisa to make any changes or deal with any consequences. As long as I minimised the risk of discovery and made sure there was no physical or practical impact on Lisa's life, then we never really had to work out any problems as long as we never talked about them.

For the most part, it worked. Meredith wasn't ever going away, but Lisa could essentially ignore her. Of course I wondered what Lisa thought about the situation, but not enough to risk asking her, not when things were peaceful on the surface.

Chapter Thirty-Three
Still Life

August 2008

There is a stray hair tickling my nose. The circulation in my right arm is being slowly restricted by the awkward position of my hand on my hip. The toes on my right foot are going numb, but I can't do anything to ease the pressure being channelled into the crowded tips of my stilettos. My perineum is also starting to get sore; the harness cradling my nether regions carries much of my weight down through the support pole positioned suggestively between my legs. I focus on these sensations until they blur into each other and begin to recede from my attention, becoming one persistent, slightly muted background presence against the distinct sounds and sights happening around me. The house DJ is spinning a deep trance beat that pulses hypnotically, leaving sonic after-trails that blanket the dark space and my drifting consciousness.

People wander past – a man in a silver latex bodysuit, a woman in a black tutu and long rainbow stockings. A dapper, immaculately presented being of indeterminate gender in long formal coattails and a top hat. A woman wearing an intricate web of chains around her torso and nothing from her waist down to the spiked ankle straps on her platform heels. Bodies in leather, in lace, in masks meant for mischief, in search of a good time. They pass in and out of my field of vision, most not stopping to take any notice of me.

This is Domicile – an "alternative" nightclub where people can seek adventures usually discussed only behind closed doors. The kind of place where adult humans come to be who they want to be without fear of judgement. Where people come to interact, with whom – and however many – they choose, regardless of what reactions this would elicit elsewhere. The kind of place where sex and gender, in all their forms, are considered part of the fabulous nature of our existence. The kind of place where it seems there are no rules, but where in truth there is a very strict rule – just one: "Be respectful".

In a TV show, this space would be portrayed as sleazy, depraved, and full of predatory characters. In reality, it is probably the safest nightclub in the entire country – every activity is 100% voluntary and consent is paramount. It's the perfect setting to explore my peculiar fetish, full of observers but not quite public, an environment that provides a receptive and appreciative audience.

I have dressed the part, aiming for that fine line between innocent cuteness and the suggestiveness that indicates I am aware that this is only the *appearance* of innocence. Satin bow in my hair. Corset top laced-up tightly, sweetly demure. Flouncy miniskirt and heels, legs out to play. Elaborate name tag hanging from a red ribbon tied to my wrist. I look like a cliché, but that is entirely the point. I want to be noticed, but only by those who take the time to observe their surroundings and who are interested enough to take a closer look. I ache to be somebody's delightful discovery: posed like a living picture, perfectly still on my stand, enduring my physical discomfort for the sake of the joy this fantasy brings me. It is an exquisitely romantic notion to me – I am my most feminine self, yearning, longing, helpless. Waiting.

I am a beautiful doll on a pedestal, frozen on display, blissfully enchanted.

* * *

September 1998

Ten years before finding myself at Domicile, I was cautiously, privately, exploring the idea of my femininity. I had purchased some nightgowns and high heels over the Internet, but in 1998 there wasn't much else to be found online in terms of women's fashion that would ship to Australia. And shopping for women's clothes in person, as a man, was not something I would feel comfortable doing until many years later.

So I had a few outfits that only ever saw the inside of my flat, where I lived alone with plenty of privacy and few visitors. My quiet evenings were often spent wearing lingerie and heels, practising my walk, my mannerisms, and generally fantasising about any and all things feminine. Lace and flowers and romantic prettiness, things I was too afraid to explore when I was younger. Dressed this way, I felt beautiful and sexy and desirable. An object needing the affection of an admirer.

Like a doll.

I wished I could be one of the girls in my drawings.

The aluminium pole appears to be the ideal length, going from the floor to my hip while I'm standing in the hardware store in my sneakers. I don't need to cut it down or remove any sharp bits off the ends. All it needs is a good wipe down so it doesn't get my clothes dirty.

Back home in my little one-bedroom flat, I quickly clean the shop grime off the pole and change into a lacy outfit, eager to start experimenting. Standing in my high heels opposite the full-length mirror on my bedroom door, I position one end of the pole between my feet and lift the skirt of my gown to check how it fits. It looks promising, but I'm going to need something to cushion the tip of the pole.

I fold up a small face towel and carefully place it over the end of the pole. It's an awkward sight in the mirror as I straddle the vertical arrangement, nestling the towel pad in my crotch directly under my perineum. Gingerly settling onto the pole I discover that this feels a bit like tilting forward on a bicycle seat. It's not uncomfortable.

It's not quite right, though. I have to bend my knees slightly and squeeze my thighs together to hold the pole in place. It needs to be a little bit longer. I dismount and look around my flat for something suitable, picking a random paperback novel from my bookshelf.

Repositioning myself in front of the mirror with the bottom end of the pole lifted by the book between my feet, I repeat my awkward straddle. It's immediately clear that even with fully straightened legs in four inch heels, the pole now exerts some pressure on my crotch.

It feels instantly compelling.

It's strong but not forceful. Solid, gentle, reassuring, Supportive. I let my hair down around my shoulders and breathe in deeply, summoning and channelling all of my femininity. Starting from the spot where the pole engages the core of my body, I imagine a soft radiance throughout my whole being, beauty and serenity emanating from deep inside, flowing out through my arms and legs and filling the room around me. Delicate, vulnerable, tender. I position my arms out slightly with my elbows and wrists flexed, like Barbie, and freeze with a smile on my face. My reflection in the mirror smiles back, perfectly still. Captured. Treasured.

I am a doll.

This feels so good. My smile is real.

The harness looks like some kind of medieval device used for punishment, if not outright torture. But it's not unpleasant to wear. I pull the laces firmly behind me and tie them together, feeling the harness pull tight around my hips and snugly up underneath me. It feels nice. The rigid lower section is held in place securely and I can still move and walk freely.

It's amazing what you can make out of a wire coat hanger, a washcloth, and some shoelaces.

There is a small tab bent into the wire, protruding downward from the bottom of the harness. I place the top of the pole under the tab and hold it there with one hand. Bracing the other end of the pole on the floor just in front of me, I step forward and let my body weight push the harness and the pole together. The tab is just wide enough to gently press into the top end of the pole and remain wedged there by itself, fixing the pole directly under my perineum.

Now the pole is attached to me and hanging down between my legs, reaching to the ground with the lower end just skimming the floor. I have to move around stiff-legged; the unyielding length of the pole means I can barely bend my knees. I awkwardly step onto the large wooden board I've placed on the floor in front of the mirror.

There is a small plug protruding up from the board, near the end farthest from the mirror. It's an attachment for the pole, made from a bolt and half a dozen washers stacked in a cylinder. Facing the mirror with the attachment plug just behind my feet, I hold the middle of the pole with one hand and manoeuvre the lower end towards the plug. I have to raise myself higher onto my tiptoes than my four-inch heels already do; when the tip of the plug is clear under the open end of the pole, I settle back down and let my weight press them together. I feel the pole slide firmly over the plug, ending with a solid click that transmits an impulse up the pole and through my entire body.

The impulse dissipates and leaves behind a quiet sense of fullness. I've set the height of the plug to match my heels so that the pole takes a significant part of my weight, and its constant, reassuring pressure bestows solidity and security onto the intimate core of my body. I am being held from my very centre, fixed firmly in place, unable to step off the base plate I'm standing on. Rendered helpless, literally attached to my delightful predicament.

I have created the perfect display for a living doll.

I spend many hours mounted on my doll stand, practising my poses, imagining myself as a beautiful woman captured in delicate, intimate stillness. It's an intensely private pastime and I keep it well hidden, like I do with my doll drawings. The lessons I learned as a child still resonate: protect the things that are dear to me, lest I be mocked for my weirdness or be asked to explain things I cannot convey.

Such complete and persistent secrecy can be wearying, though. And I yearn to be understood – by someone else, even if self-insight evades me. Perhaps it might not be such a bad thing to reveal myself.

* * *

November 1998

"Oh yum!" John whispers from the corner of his mouth. He discreetly raises his eyebrows in the direction of the doorway.

I glance up. A customer has just entered the café. Male, probably mid-twenties, dressed in a well-fitting T-shirt and jeans. Short dark hair, well groomed, trim but not skinny. A rather nice looking man.

I shrug.

"You know, I find you fascinating." John's eyebrows change from appreciative to thoughtful. "You're not gay, but you have no interest in women either. And you seem happy being single. Don't you want to find someone?" He drops a sugar into his coffee. Fancy brown demerara cubes presented in a little white bowl. "Or maybe you have a secret life nobody knows about?" He laughs as he stirs.

"I do like women. I just never talk about it." I sip my cappuccino, the cocoa powder on the milk foam leaving a trail towards my mouth. "But I'm not secretly dating anyone or going out looking for women."

Another customer walks in. A woman this time, also wearing jeans, paired with a loose and slouchy multicoloured sweater that hangs past her hips. Brown hair hanging in slightly messy curls on her shoulders. The broad hourglass shape of her body is vaguely apparent under the folds of her clothing.

"What about her? Does she do anything for you?" John asks quietly.

I roll my eyes. "How would I know? I can't tell anything about her."

I study the woman as she finds a table near the opposite wall. Her face is quite pretty, with large glasses framing her eyes to match the curls framing her cheeks. I imagine her job to be a quirky bookstore owner or children's librarian. This makes me smile because as I am thinking this she takes out a large book from her bag and opens it to read.

John notices my smile. "You do like her?"

I start to roll my eyes again and something stops me. I was going to repeat my previous retort but I find myself suddenly thinking: *if I was her, how would I dress? With a face that cute...*

"I think you do," John prods.

"Maybe..." This emerges hesitantly, but not because I'm unsure about finding the woman attractive.

John somehow senses I'm trying to make a decision that isn't about the woman in the café. He raises his eyebrows again. "Hmmm?"

I take another sip of my coffee. "So. You wanna know a secret?"

John's hug is very warm – he tends to run a bit hot when he gets nervous. And I think my own nervousness set him off; he's very empathetic. And, thankfully, non-judgemental.

"You keep so much hidden from everyone. I knew you were interesting before, but you might be the most interesting person I know." He releases his embrace and looks me up and down. "You're definitely the most confusing."

"I like to keep people on their toes, I guess. Do you want something to drink? A fan?" I laugh as I notice the damp spots under his shirt sleeves. "Hang on a sec." I put my hand on his shoulder, to steady myself as I dismount from my doll stand.

John winces as I remove the pole from between my legs and place it back on the base plate. "Amazing." He turns to the drawings I've spread out on the coffee table. "There's so much here. Thank you for trusting me."

I place my desk fan on floor in front of him, tilt it upwards, and switch it on. "Here."

John floofs his shirt to let the air flow past the fabric. "So... do you actually want to be a woman? Or just a doll?"

I start gathering up my drawings, gingerly stepping around the coffee table in my heels. "I don't know," I answer truthfully. "I wouldn't even know where to start." The idea of transitioning scares me. It also seems impossible. "How do people even know what to do? Just go to the doctor and say 'I want a sex change'?"

"I can ask people I know, if you want." John knows a lot of people.

"Um. No thanks. I'm not even sure what this is. A sex change is kind of extreme. And you're the only person I've told." I imagine calling my parents back in California: *Hey guess what?*

"Okay... well, I won't tell anyone else." He turns around to let the fan cool his back. "You know, I never actually thought you had a secret life. I was joking when I said that!"

"I know. I try to be quiet and boring." A survival strategy that became a habit.

"Well for what it's worth, I think you'd make a great girl." John looks over at – or through – the sheer folds of my nightgown skirt. "You have the best legs, too!"

Double Exposure

* * *

Ten years later, I am showing off those legs, indulging my fantasy in a not-quite-secret way. As I will do for years beyond, until Domicile closes down. Standing on display in this underground space every month, I slowly discover that my dollhood is much more than just the manifestation of an unusual fetish. It is a fundamental, essential part of my being.

The benefits of remaining still for a while are well known – ask anyone who regularly practises meditation. Left alone in my frozen reverie, I can allow my mind to drift free from the mundane concerns of daily life – chores, obligations, deadlines, these things all fade away and I am left in a pure state of being: I simply *am*. It is enough. Existence contains and provides its own worth. Freedom to be, on my own terms. Terms which include feeling feminine and beautiful.

It's ironic that I have set myself free by rendering myself completely immobile. Becoming a literal object that simply exists to be appreciated. I've mentioned the struggle to reconcile my fantasies with my feminism, yet I cannot deny how being a doll makes me feel inside: alive, visible, recognised. Helpless and secure at the same time. There is a strange power in this vulnerability; I can sense it with some of the people who observe and admire me. Almost as if it compels them to pay attention, to be more present, to be mindful of their actions: I am more than just part of the scenery, decoration to be taken for granted. Observers stop, and think, and question. Who has captured whom here?

This kind of passivity was not in the script given to me as a boy and as a young man. I did not consider that these kinds of desires and experiences could be rightfully mine to hold. Here in this nightclub there is no judgement, and I am finally claiming the things I have longed for all my life. I am proud and unashamed of my femininity. Being Meredith, embracing my inner doll, is giving me the freedom to appreciate all of my existence.

Part Eight

Chapter Thirty-Four
Bellie

When people ask me how I met my best friend, I delight in replying that we met in an online wedding forum – especially if I'm presenting as Derek while I answer. People get surprised at the idea of a man and a woman becoming friends in the context of planning their weddings to other people. And that's on top of the unexpected twist of me – the man – being the socially active planner of my own wedding, instead of my future wife Lisa filling that role.

Bellie is one of the original group of friends from the forum who became the denizens of melonworld, and has been a constant and supportive presence in my life throughout my evolution as both Meredith and Derek. I'm not sure when we realised we were best friends, but I'm almost certain we originally bonded over chocolate. Myself, because I'm a snob and usually prefer expensive dark chocolate, and Bellie because she can devour a 64-piece box of Koko Black truffles in approximately an hour. Followed by a two-kilogram block of Cadbury Dairy Milk.

Okay, maybe it took her a couple of days. I can't remember exactly.

Bellie

Bellie isn't her actual name but it's what everyone she met on the forum still calls her, even more than twenty years later. Her username was Annabel (also not her actual name) and when she was pregnant with her second child she shared a photo of herself which looked like the stereotypical cartoon rendition of pregnancy: a slender woman with a giant beach ball in her belly. So naturally we started calling her Annabellie, which then got shortened to Bellie because that's what Australians do to people's names.

After a few years of online friendship, Bellie and I met in person for the first time in 2006 when she came to Melbourne to visit relatives. Her family was somewhat apprehensive that she was meeting a man she knew from the Internet, but neither Bellie nor I felt nervous about it. We arranged to go get some chocolate for dessert at Koko Black, which hadn't yet expanded to Adelaide (I was intent on convincing Bellie that Koko Black was better than Haigh's). When I arrived at her uncle's house to pick her up after dinner it felt like we were simply hanging out again, as if we'd seen each other only that morning and weren't actually meeting face to face for the first time.

As I pulled away from the drive, Bellie remarked on this.

"Why doesn't this feel more weird? It doesn't feel like this is the first time we've actually met in person."

"I know! I was just thinking the same thing," I said. "But I probably chat with you online more than I talk to anybody in person. Even Lisa."

"I can't imagine talking to Richard as much as I chat with you." I was pretty sure Bellie grimaced a little; from what I'd gathered through our chats, her husband was an odd person to interact with. "I might talk to my sister as much though. And of course Dante never shuts up, does that count?"

"Depends if you have to answer him," I laughed. Dante was Bellie's five-year-old son.

Double Exposure

We drove in silence for a little while as I concentrated on navigating the unfamiliar inner-northeast Melbourne suburbs. There is a lovely vintage charm to the narrow streets and old terrace houses, but you need to have your wits about you when dealing with parked cars, daredevil urban cyclists, and twenty-tonne trams that can't swerve and don't stop unless they absolutely have to.

A fashion advertisement on the side of a tram caught my eye. The model was wearing a lovely flowing dress and an expression of carefree satisfaction. I sighed. It would be so nice to be Meredith and go out for dessert with my best friend. But that was out of the question. Meredith could only exist at Seahorse meetings, or online in the company of a select few melons.

Sometime around the beginning of 2007, Bellie and I were in melonworld chatting privately and I offhandedly mentioned how awesome it would be if I could visit her in Adelaide. As I thought about how I would plan the trip, I had a ridiculous pipe dream of an idea.

```
[mookers] I could probably get time off work around your birthday
[annabel] Ooh
[mookers] It's at the end of May, right? I think that's far enough
away that flights will be cheap if I buy a ticket soon
[annabel] Yeah
[mookers] I just had a crazy thought
[annabel] Tell me
[mookers] What if I brought Meredith
[annabel] DO IT
[mookers] I would love it so much
[annabel] Would Lisa be okay with that?
[mookers] I don't know
[annabel] Hmmm
```

[mookers] I don't think she knows anyone in Adelaide, so that might help

[annabel] Is she only worried about someone recognising you?

[mookers] I don't know. It seems like that's her main concern

[annabel] There are a couple of melons in Adelaide who don't know about Meredith, right?

[mookers] Yeah but I don't think Lisa would worry about them. It's more her family and work friends she doesn't want to find out

[annabel] What are the chances of that?

[mookers] Almost zero. I'll try and ask her tonight

[annabel] Yay! Good luck

"I want to go visit Bellie for her birthday in the last week of May. Will you be okay if I'm gone for three days?"

Lisa looks up from her TV show. She's in bed, or as she calls it, her Diamond Class theatre. Better than a Gold Class movie recliner. We only have a 30-inch screen but having a private lounge (and me as a dedicated personal server of drinks and snacks) makes up for it.

"Sure. As long as you're home on the weekend," she says. Fair enough. Because I leave the house early for work every weekday, Lisa has to wrangle both kids by herself in the mornings, making sure they're out of bed, dealing with breakfast and getting dressed and delivering them to school and daycare. Her disability adds a layer of difficulty – she can't move very quickly or carry a child very far on her own. Weekends are Lisa's opportunity to sleep in and rest while I take the kids grocery shopping and to the park or the play centre. Lisa really treasures her late mornings, and if I'm away on a weekend she won't get the chance.

"Okay," I say. That wasn't the hard part of my request. I peer through the darkness of the bedroom but the shifting light from the TV isn't enough to let me see Lisa's face clearly. "Do you know anyone who lives in Adelaide?"

She pauses the TV playback. "No, why?"

I steel myself slightly, leaning against the doorway as if it will somehow help. "I want to be Meredith when I'm there."

"Right." Then silence. Then, "You want to dress up during the day."

It's more than dressing up, but I let that one pass. As I always do.

"Yes," I say. How can I convey to Lisa what it means to me? I am tired of being only a creature of the night. I want to go shopping, have coffee at a nice café, be part of the everyday, normal world around me. I don't want to have to stay hidden, even if it means going to another city to feel free. But I don't say this to Lisa. Her reaction, I imagine, would make me feel greedy and ungrateful. Selfish. Why do I need to be Meredith to do these things?

I don't, but the freedom, the idea that I *can* be Meredith, makes it different. All these things are still enjoyable as Derek. Yet there's something… I'm not sure I even understand, but it pulls at me. I simply want to experience life as Meredith. But I'm certain that Lisa won't accept my inadequate explanation, and I'm too afraid of upsetting her to give her the chance to prove me wrong.

More silence. Then, "What about Bellie's kids?"

I was wondering if she'd bring them up. "What about them?"

"What if they come and visit us, and say something to our kids?"

"That's a pretty unlikely scenario. They don't come to Melbourne very often. Besides, Bellie can tell them not to mention it."

Lisa sighs. "It just feels… I just don't want someone else's kids knowing about Merri when our own kids don't know."

A thought immediately stabs through my mind. *Well, there's an easy solution to that problem, isn't there?*

Pause. Breathe. I resist letting my resentment take control. "I'm going to stay at a hotel since Bellie hasn't really got room for houseguests anyway. I'll make sure that her kids only see me as Derek."

"Okay."

Does Lisa have any idea just how much mental effort goes into planning every movement of every day of Meredith's existence, just so that she can remain secret?

Lisa returns to the TV. She's watching *Survivor*, where contestants endure hardship whilst carefully plotting and scheming with each other, spending all their effort to steer the world in a direction that will reward them with the grand prize – a million dollars.

My prize is being Meredith. For any other activity, the effort required would be enough of a deterrent to make me not bother pursuing it. I don't think Lisa is intentionally making things difficult for me – it's simply a product of the things I have to do to manage her fears about Meredith's existence.

I couldn't put a value on the stakes if I tried. I'm certainly not going to give up.

I check my reflection in the mirrored back wall of the lift. I think I look okay; mostly passable at a casual glance and dressed in an understated, modestly attractive outfit – a black fitted top with some lace detail at the collar, an A-line denim skirt, and black ballet flats with little bows on the front. Simple gold-coloured dangly earrings and a butterfly pendant necklace. My hair is down past my shoulders, parted at the side, and my make-up hides most of my beard shadow. Lipstick really makes a difference to how feminine my face looks – the one I'm wearing isn't bright or bold, but simply adding a bit of colour and definition works wonders.

I'm nervous and excited about Meredith facing the world during daylight. The only time I've done this before was in Sydney – behind Lisa's back. Today, in Adelaide, I don't feel the burden of my conscience and the anxiety of future confession. I feel free and light on my feet, my nervousness lifting my spirits instead of weighing me down.

And my companion today doesn't have to be my co-conspirator. Bellie is waiting for me in the hotel lobby as I step out of the lift alcove and her face lights up when she sees me. As we greet each other with a hug, I'm aware that the reception staff at the front desk may notice us; I wonder if they'll pick up on my female presentation. I dismiss my worries by reminding myself that they can't keep track of every single guest's appearance, and anyway, they wouldn't really care that I was a man last night and I'm a woman this morning. This might be a new experience for me, but hospitality workers have seen everything.

We head out of the hotel into the bright morning sun to find a café somewhere in nearby Rundle Mall. After breakfast we're going to visit the Haigh's chocolate factory; Bellie isn't yet convinced that Koko Black is better, and while I don't think she's trying to argue about it, a factory tour is a great excuse to have chocolate under the guise of gathering evidence. Bellie doesn't have a car, so getting there will involve a bit of walking and a short bus ride. It's going to be a good test of how the everyday world receives Meredith.

The purposeful bustle of the city morning means that there are a lot of people about. I feel self-conscious in a way that reminds me of when I was much younger – are people noticing me because I look weird? I get the occasional second glance but nobody says anything or gives me an uncomfortable stare. The people on the street don't seem to care who else is around as long as nobody is actively being a nuisance. Bellie and I are just another two humans going about our business in a crowd of thousands who are minding their own and not scrutinising everyone they walk past.

Even sitting in the café and on the bus, where there is more opportunity to observe someone at length, the other customers and passengers keep any inappropriate curiosity to themselves. It's heartening to learn firsthand that my existence is not a problem for society – at least not for the parts of it I've encountered this morning.

We arrive at the Haigh's factory slightly ahead of our tour start time. There are a couple other people here waiting already but not a lot of visitors in the factory shop. It's still before lunchtime and it's a quiet Wednesday outside of any usual holiday period.

When the tour guide arrives there are only six of us in the group – all women. The guide is a chirpy, engaging woman who introduces herself as Kathy and asks where we're all from. I'm a little nervous at having to answer in front of strangers with my not-very-feminine voice, but nobody remarks on it or gives any indication that they think I'm unusual. Kathy starts into a narration of the company's history as she leads us through some doors into a small waiting room outside the main factory floor.

There are a few props displayed on a table at the front of the room and a long couch along the opposite wall. Kathy motions for us to sit and begins giving us a description of the chocolate making process, starting with the actual harvest of the cacao pods. One of the props is an actual pod, which looks like a giant leathery almond about the size of a child's toy football.

Kathy picks up the pod as she describes how the farmers harvest and cut it open to obtain the beans inside. "This one's been dried to preserve it, but it was split first – you can open it and see the beans for yourself," she says, before suddenly tossing the pod gently through the air towards me.

I'm completely taken by surprise and instinctively reach out to catch it. I succeed; the throw was perfect and the pod would have landed square in my lap anyway.

"Good girl!" says Kathy.

WHOAAA.

Good girl.

She called me a girl!

In front of everybody!

I've been fixated on the possibility that someone might explicitly question my presentation, making me feel like I'll have to justify my transgender nature. I never considered the opposite. The affirmation is so completely unexpected and delightful and there's a warm glow of joy and satisfaction inside me that I never knew could be there.

Good girl!

I don't know if anyone else can sense the magnitude of what just happened. Did Bellie notice my eyes go wide? I look at her and she smiles at me.

I finish the rest of the tour feeling like I'm floating through a chocolate cloud.

Chapter Thirty-Five

Flying

May 2009

I've waited all year for this trip. For the third year in a row, I'll have four days of shopping, coffee and chocolate with my best friend, and I can be Meredith the whole time. Glorious, girly freedom. Day or night, anywhere we want to go.

In Melbourne, I can be a woman only in private, at night-time, in secluded and familiar spaces. In Adelaide I can be *out*, in the truest sense of the word. Openly female and sharing the experience with my wonderful friend who accepts and embraces every part of me. Two years ago, when I first convinced my wife Lisa to let me do this, it turned out to be a revelation. Now it has become tradition.

I've booked a seven A.M. flight so I can arrive with enough time to change and still have a full day to be Meredith. I want to savour every precious hour I can squeeze in.

You'd think I would know better than to risk being late.

"I'm sorry sir, check-in is already closed."

WHAT. No!!!

I'm already flustered from dealing with a self-check-in machine that stopped working halfway through my seat selection. I look at my watch. Six thirty-five A.M, still so early in the morning. Suddenly I'm aware of an assumption I've made without realising it: I pictured myself breezing through the airport without delays, anticipating an idealised scenario with hope so strong that it became my expectation. The vision in my head skipped over the time between check-in and boarding, so I haven't been considering the reality of airport procedures.

"You've got to be kidding me." This isn't part of the plan.

The service desk attendant shakes her head.

I've never missed a flight before. It was that god-damned kiosk. I fought with it for at least five minutes before giving up. I try to explain. "I was using one of those self-check-in machines and it was slow, and then it wouldn't respond, and then it wouldn't let me cancel and clear my details. I would have been on time otherwise!"

The attendant is so polite. "I'm sorry. It's a strict half-hour window."

I don't know how to handle this. My mind spins in a panic, trying to comprehend the implications of missing my plane.

Is my whole trip finished now? Ripped away at the last minute by an uncooperative, thoughtless machine? I rage at that damned kiosk.

Truthfully, though, this is my own fault. I know better than to assume there won't be complications. Why the hell didn't I get up earlier?

"Fuck!" It slips out, not quite under my breath. I want to yell at the top of my lungs. How the fuck did I let myself screw this up?

The attendant looks slightly resigned, prepared to suffer a torrent of belligerence and abuse. I take a deep breath and close my eyes for a few seconds.

"I'm sorry," I say, feeling embarrassed. "You must deal with this a lot."

Flying

She is unperturbed. "It happens."

"So what do I do now?" I ask. Thinking how much a new ticket is going to cost. "Can I get another flight?" When I booked this trip three months ago, there were lots of flights to choose from.

The slightest hint of caution darts across her face. "There's a fifty dollar re-booking fee. Are you okay with that?"

It stings a little, but it's less than I'd feared. "Yeah, okay."

She clicks a few times on her workstation. "There's one seat available on the ten thirty flight."

"Ten thirty?!" I repeat the time in disbelief. That's four hours from now.

"There's nothing sooner than that?" In four hours I'm supposed to be Meredith, relaxing with my best friend at the café down the street from her house.

"The eight thirty flight is full, I'm sorry."

Damn it! I try to think of a way around this. If only I could make someone give up their seat. Or make them late and take their place. Maybe if I went to another airline... but even if I found a flight, it would cost way more than fifty dollars. And I'd still lose time. Maybe even more than four hours, if that ten thirty seat disappears.

I sigh. "Okay, yeah. I'll take that. The ten thirty." That sounds so far in the future.

I hand over my driver's licence and credit card. Fifty bucks, burned like so much jet fuel as I'm stuck here waiting for take-off clearance, while fingers type, computers process, and airplanes come and go without me.

A few more minutes and it's done; my itinerary neatly reconfigured, unlike my emotions and expectations. The attendant hands back my cards and my new tickets. "Check-in opens at eight... and closes at ten o'clock sharp." She meets my gaze and smiles.

"I hope I didn't wake you up. I wanted to catch you before you got on the bus." The departures board says seven fifteen here in Melbourne, which means it's six forty-five in Adelaide. My original flight will be landing in just under an hour. Bellie doesn't drive, so she is going to catch the bus to the airport to meet me.

She sounds sleepy. "I was just about to get up. Why? What's going on?"

"I missed my flight. I'm so pissed off."

"Oh no! Are you still coming?"

"Yes, but I couldn't get another flight until ten thirty. So I won't be there until nearly midday. I won't be able to change for ages."

Bellie knows how much I want to maximise my time as Meredith, but she tries to reassure me. "You know I'm happy to spend time with you either way."

"Yeah I know. It's just so annoying that I've wasted the morning." I look at my new ticket. The 11:40 arrival time is depressing. After baggage collection and rental car pickup and travel back to Bellie's place to change, it will be three o'clock before I'm ready to go out as Merri. So much for a full day of girly shopping. "Anyway, I'm on flight VA221 now." I look around the terminal. "I need a coffee."

"Okay, well let me know if anything else happens. Otherwise I'll see you when you get here."

Five minutes later, I get a text message.

I had an idea. Why don't you change now, while you're waiting?

What??!

Because that would be...

Risky?

Maybe. What if one of Lisa's friends is here at the airport and notices me? I negotiated being Meredith in Adelaide only by pointing out how unlikely it is that I'll be recognised: if someone we know happens to see me there, they won't immediately wonder if the long-haired Asian woman is

Lisa's husband in drag, all the way over from Melbourne. But the airport is much closer to home.

Suspicious?

Will the airline think I'm trying to hide my identity? What will happen if I get stopped and questioned and they don't believe me?

Terrifying?

Yes. It will be all of those things. But it will be something else too.

Liberating.

It's a *brilliant* idea.

An opportunity out of my wildest dreams.

I sit across from the hallway leading to the toilets, fidgeting with the handle on my suitcase. Contemplating my decision – changing in a public facility is always a bit stressful, even without a gender swap. What if there isn't enough room to put my stuff down? Or worse, what if the floor is dirty and wet? Hooks on the back of toilet doors are often missing or broken, if they were ever installed in the first place. And then, since I'll be turning into a girl, I have extra considerations – more stuff than usual, for starters. Shoes, handbag, make-up… how am I going to do my make-up? There's no way I can manage that without both hands free, especially if I have to use my compact mirror.

I'm well practised at changing in my car, which is a tight space for wriggling in and out of clothing – but it's also clean inside, there's a built-in mirror, and there are empty seats and a dashboard to put things on. And nobody waiting outside the car for me to finish so they can use it next, which is a worry in a public facility when it takes me an hour to transform myself. I would love to be able to roll out of bed already looking feminine, but there are things that take extra time and effort before I feel like Meredith has fully emerged. Hiding bits, adding bits, making sure that my beard shadow is as faint as possible, using extra concealer and heavy make-up; all of this means that a full transformation, especially in an unfamiliar space, can take ages.

There's another thing, too – the toilets are gendered, which means both the men's and the women's would be wrong – I'm going to look inappropriate either going in or coming out, regardless of which one I choose. So that leaves the disabled toilet and the parents' room as my safe options. This makes me even more anxious about occupying the facilities for such a long time, but I've already scoped out the rest of the terminal and I couldn't find anything else.

If I'm going to commit, I need to know what I'll be dealing with. I wait until there is nobody around and I head over to the hallway. A quick glance inside the disabled toilet shows it to be reasonably spacious and clean. No door hook, though, but the floor looks dry. It'll do. I poke my head into the parents' room and find it much the same.

A twinge of anxiety makes me pull back and look around. I don't want to be questioned for entering these spaces without apparently needing a reason – people can get quite aggressive when challenging someone over the appropriation of resources.[25] Having an altercation while I'm trying to change gender would be an absolute nightmare.

I return to the bench across from the hallway and look at the time: almost eight. I need to get moving before the airport starts getting busier. Even if I don't get questioned or yelled at, I don't want to be monopolising the facilities when someone really needs them.

---

[25] I've been accosted more than once for using a disabled parking space to pick Lisa up. Even though we display a valid permit, people see me looking able-bodied when I leave the car and just assume I'm being an entitled jerk. One wheelchair-using guy even followed me for a bit, and when I turned around, he stood up and shoved me!*

* Wheelchair users are often capable of standing and walking. The media usually portrays disabilities as clearly defined and visibly obvious, when in truth many conditions are dynamic and symptoms can vary over time and circumstance, or even randomly. Disability can also lead to a healthy appreciation of dark humour: Lisa thinks it's hilarious that I was assaulted by a guy in a wheelchair.

I've decided to check in to my flight before changing so I won't have to explain myself when showing my I.D. This means transferring everything I need – make-up, boobs, outfit, shoes – into my carry-on backpack first. Then, after dropping my suitcase off, I'll come back here to change and hope that all of my male clothes and shoes fit into my backpack just like my girly things did.

I consider what might happen when I go through the security screening. I'm going to be a woman carrying a bag full of men's clothes. Should I wait until I'm on the other side before I change?

Actually, if I wait, then I'm going to be a man carrying a bag full of women's clothes through security, which isn't any less awkward. And what if I can't find a suitable place to change? There's no way to check beforehand. I decide it's better to change here, where I know what I'm dealing with.

Deep breaths. I'm sweating. Flushed and slightly panicky; my nerves don't agree with my decision. Kneeling in front of my bags, I dig through my carefully-packed suitcase, grabbing things and shoving them into my backpack, trying not to expose the items I am handling. Surely I look suspicious. I half expect airport security to descend upon me at any moment.

Nobody bothers me. Someone rearranging their luggage at the airport is not a remarkable sight. After I make a mess of my previously organised suitcase and stuff my backpack full of everything I need to become Meredith – including, somehow, my handbag – I head back to the check-in desk to put this terrifying, exhilarating plan in motion.

Check-in is routine and uneventful. Feeling determined afterward, and with some butterflies in my stomach, I stride back to the hallway. And stop abruptly.

There's a cleaner's trolley outside the disabled toilet.

Damn it! Should I wait? How long will they be? The airport is already getting busier. The longer I wait, the more chance that someone will come to use the facilities and make me wait even longer, increasing those chances with every delay.

I notice that I'm starting to sweat again.

I have to do this now or I might have to abandon this whole idea. I quickly slip inside the parents' room before anyone else approaches.

I lean against the inside of the door, feeling the cool surface against my cheek, waiting for my nerves to settle down. It feels like I'm in the middle of a real-life suspense thriller.

I don't like suspense thrillers. They stress me out way too much.

It's all strictly in my head, though – I have to remind myself that nobody's actually trying to stop me, expose me, or capture me for some nefarious plot. I'm just another traveller passing through, and from the outside, my baggage looks pretty much like anyone else's.

There is one worry that I can't rationalise away, though: as anonymous as I think I'll be to strangers, I don't have a plan for what happens if, after I've changed, I get spotted and recognised by someone I happen to know. I've decided to take the risk, and I'm trying not to think about the potential consequences. Would I ask a family friend – or even a relative – to keep this secret from Lisa? I don't know. All I know is I want to do this badly enough to accept whatever the results may be.

Thankfully, the parents' room is refreshingly pleasant inside, which helps to quell my sweaty nervousness. It's much easier to change into Meredith when I can relax and the surrounding air doesn't feel stuffy and hot. I hear the sounds of the cleaner through the wall: the faint hiss of running water and occasional clunks of equipment being moved around. I close my eyes, focusing on the noises, letting them distract me as my breathing slows. Soft piano music coming over the P.A. system helps to change the scene I'm enacting, from suspense thriller to slow, slightly offbeat independent cinema piece.

I hear the disabled toilet door close and the trolley wheel away. I listen for another minute, holding my breath. Nobody knocks on the door. I relax again – the cleaner's gone. I look around. They must have done this room already, because everything looks spotless. I won't have to worry about where I step or where I set my things down. I can even lay out my stuff on the baby change shelf. Perfect.

I unzip my backpack and set about my transformation. I find myself in an odd state of anxious calm – this is as nice a place to change as I could ask for, but I'm constantly aware of the possibility that someone might be waiting outside. I have to be careful not to rush. I don't want my undergarments and the extra bits I wear ending up misaligned and uncomfortably annoying. Also, there's no way I can apply my make-up cleanly if I'm in a hurry. Luckily, although I occasionally hear people and voices go past, nobody knocks on the door.

Just over an hour later, I'm finished. After checking the mirror one last time – seeing my reflection as Meredith always sparks joy – I exit the room to an empty hallway. Relief. And then, as I head towards the open terminal floor, I nearly collide with a woman coming around the corner on her way to the toilets.

"Oh! Excuse me, sorry." We don't make eye contact. Just a quick swerve and dodge and she is past me. People really are preoccupied with their own lives and mostly ignore what's going on around them. It may help that I am dressed unremarkably – a plain shirtdress, knit cardigan, ballet flats. I'm still finding my style, and I'm not yet daring enough to get on the plane wearing something overtly frilly or loudly, colourfully floral.

I'm not going to be able to avoid scrutiny for long, though.

If the other people in line read me as a man dressed in women's clothes, they don't give any indication of curiosity or unease that I notice. I try not to imagine what might happen if the security personnel decide I pose a potential threat.

I imagine it anyway. I remind myself that I'm not trying to fool anybody or fake my identity. I can simply answer questions with the truth: I'm dressed as a woman, but if you look at the photo of the man on my driver's licence you can tell I'm the same person under the make-up. My appearance should be irrelevant to the safety of the flight. I wonder how I might be able to prove this.

My hands shake as I put my things down on the rollers of the X-ray station. Is it obvious how nervous I am? I'm trying to blend in, but I feel like my movements are attracting attention. I'm also conscious that my backpack is stuffed full of men's clothes, which isn't what you'd expect to go alongside a woman's handbag. Will that be enough to trigger suspicion? Do they look for unusual evidence like this, or do they just scan for dangerous items?

A loud beeping startles me. The man ahead of me has just set off the metal detector gate. He backs up, removes his belt, and passes on the second try. Routine stuff. Now it's my turn. I look at the attendant on the other side. Can he tell I have a reason to be nervous? He waves me through. The gate is silent and I move past him to collect my things.

They haven't come out of the X-ray scanner yet. I wait.

After what feels like a minute, but is probably just a few seconds, the scanner operator calls out.

"Whose bag is this?"

I look over. My stomach drops.

She is holding up my handbag.

My mind panics, trying to prepare an explanation for the woman's handbag and carry-on full of men's clothing, before I realise that my backpack is heading down the rollers unquestioned, away from the X-ray scanner.

Why is my handbag a problem?

"Hi. That's mine." My voice sounds a little forced. I nervously raise my hand.

"There's a dangerous item in your bag. You'll have to surrender it if you want to go through." She gives me the handbag.

Dangerous item? Huh?

Oh shit! I forgot that I keep my old pocketknife in this bag!

I always like to have little tools at hand – I use them often enough to make it worth carrying them around. The pocketknife is small and hides away in my handbag quite easily. I usually carry its replacement – a bigger, more expensive Leatherman multi-tool – in my backpack, and in anticipation of this security check I had removed the Leatherman the night before. But I hadn't counted on having my handbag with me. It was supposed to be in my checked luggage – being Meredith right now wasn't part of the original plan.

I fish out the knife and look at it. It's a classic red-sided Victorinox model, one I've had for nearly thirty years. My first pocketknife, a birthday present when I was twelve. There's an old Dymo label stuck to the side, green plastic with "DEREK MOO" stamped out in slightly wonky raised white letters.

The X-ray operator looks at me expectantly. There are people waiting for their bags to be scanned.

How much do I value this object? It's more sentimental than utilitarian. I carry it just in case, and I've needed it only once that I can remember; if my Leatherman tool isn't available, I guess I never bother looking for a backup.

Goodbye, old forgotten friend. I used it a lot before I got the Leatherman, but if I've neglected it in my handbag I guess I don't really need it. I hand it to the operator. She barely glances at it before tossing it into a bin behind her chair. I catch a glimpse of the bin's contents as she tilts it forward for better access – dozens of pairs of scissors, knives, tools of various kinds. I wonder what happens to them at the end of the day. I hope they don't just throw them out.

Double Exposure

The operator nods at me without much expression. "Have a nice flight."

Airport coffee is rarely outstanding, even in Melbourne. My long black is predictably, generically adequate. The bitterness gives me something steady to focus on after the turbulence of the morning. I don't really need the caffeine though, since my nerves are still settling after my encounter with the X-ray operator.

My mind wanders to the upcoming flight. I have a window seat, which is good, because I'm going to be keenly aware of the person sitting next to me, and whether they appear to be uneasy about my presence. As Merri, I've never been confined to a small space with a stranger for any significant length of time before. A window seat means that if things get uncomfortable I can angle myself towards the wall. And thankfully it's going to be a short flight.

Does being transgender mean that I will always be anxious about how the world receives me? What an exhausting way to live. Yet I persist – the desire to be seen is so much stronger than the fear of consequences. And truthfully, the reality of being seen has not borne out my concerns. Instead, it has been quietly exhilarating: in my safe Melbourne spaces; out in the public centre of Adelaide; even with the incident at the security X-ray, nobody has questioned my gender. It's ironic to be elated about nothing, but it seems this is what acceptance feels like.

Recognition without spectacle. Implicit affirmation of my validity. Before Meredith, I took these things for granted. I'm starting to realise what life is like when things aren't so straightforward. And I'm thankful that I've been fortunate.

I finish my coffee and head to the departure gate.

I can't tell if people are paying any more attention to me than they would if I was dressed as Derek. Maybe my nondescript outfit is helping me go unnoticed. I'm trying not to look around too much – if you don't want everyone to stare at you, it helps if you don't act like you don't want everyone to stare at you.

The departure gate lounge is quiet. There are plenty of empty seats, and it's about ten minutes until we start boarding, so the flight is not going to be very full. I find a seat at the end of a row and park myself.

The usual smattering of announcements come over the P.A. system, which I automatically tune out as I concentrate on texting Bellie that I'm about to board the plane. But then I hear it.

Passenger Derek Moo, please come to the service desk at gate twelve.

Oh no.

Passenger Derek Moo, please come to the service desk at gate twelve.

Shit!

What now?

I look over and see two women behind the service desk. They don't seem particularly concerned with the whereabouts of Derek Moo – they're chatting to each other and paying little attention to the people scattered about the waiting area.

I put my phone away, pick up my handbag and backpack, and make my way across the room. Is anybody making the connection between my movement and the P.A. announcement? My fear of becoming a spectacle has reasserted itself; I'm trying not to panic on the inside, trying not to let the nervous dread show on the outside. How will I explain myself without making up some outlandish story?

Will they believe the truth?

One of the attendants turns to greet me as I approach. "Hi, can I help you?"

I brace myself for a reaction. "My name was just called. I'm Derek Moo..." I feel so self-conscious, and quickly continue before I have to contend with her reaction. "I look a little different than normal today. Is there a problem?"

The attendant smiles. "No problem at all. We paged you because we need to change your seat allocation. The flight isn't very full and we need to move some passengers to balance the weight in the plane."

I'm glad I hadn't actually panicked. I would be very cross if I'd had a heart attack and there turned out to be no reason for it. I'm still shaking a bit though – my head is relieved, but my body hasn't quite yet received the memo.

"Can I please see your boarding pass?"

I hand it over and the attendant starts typing into her workstation. There's nothing in her demeanour that suggests anything about me is unusual. I'm amazed at how benign my rather eventful morning continues to be.

I'm just another passenger to be served. I take my new boarding pass and sit back down. The attendants return to their conversation.

We move single file down the jetway, so the only person who can be staring at me is the woman just behind me. I don't feel any sense of scrutiny from her – not any more than I would be giving the man in front of me, whose carry-on makes a clunking noise when it rolls over the joins in the jetway floor segments.

I show my boarding pass to the attendant at the door of the plane. She briefly inspects it and doesn't look up as she speaks. "Welcome aboard, Mr. Moo."

Do I look like a Mr. Moo?

She's already reaching for the next passenger's boarding pass.

I can't decide how I feel about being called out and overlooked at the same time. Is it possible to be simultaneously thankful and slightly offended?

I move down the aisle and find my row. It's still empty. I stow my backpack, settle into my seat, and close my eyes.

Flying

After a couple of minutes, a voice speaks nearby, slightly louder than the background movements and conversations of passengers filling the cabin.

"Here we go. Do you want the aisle? I don't mind the middle."

I open my eyes. A woman and her school-age son are taking their seats. I check to make sure I'm not sitting on the adjacent seatbelt and move my elbow off the armrest.

"Thanks," she says, sitting down after helping the boy with his carry-on.

I smile briefly and close my eyes again.

The flight's departure is uneventful, and I'm relaxed enough to offer the magazine from my seat pocket to my neighbour when she discovers hers is missing. She shows no indication of surprise or unease when I speak.

When the in-flight trolley comes past, the flight attendant asks me "would you like something to drink, Ma'am?"

"Just some water please." I take the cup and she moves on.

By the time we get to Adelaide, I'm feeling pretty confident about my ability to navigate the world as Meredith.

Bellie's delight at seeing me come off the plane makes the gate lounge feel like a celebration at the end of a grand adventure. I return her enthusiastic embrace and soak up the affirmation of her presence. Two women, best friends, greeting each other after a long time apart. I suddenly understand that this is the kind of scene I've been yearning for all my life and never knew it. Recognition and connection entwined together, wholehearted acceptance and gratitude for our relationship and this shared moment of joy.

We head into the terminal. I'm not the slightest bit self-conscious in Bellie's presence, and I'm loudly animated as I recount my little diversions at security and at the departure gate. I feel so free, so feminine, so validated in my existence right now. We reach the baggage claim area, and as we stand waiting at the carousel, I pause to consider the significance of what I've done this morning. It's thrilling, but also a little bit scary to imagine the path I might take from here. If it's so easily fulfilling for me to be a woman, is it a sign that I'm *meant* to be one?

It's way too confronting a question to think about now, and I push it away. Besides, there's one more potential hazard to clear before I get properly – and belatedly – started on this visit. I've booked a rental car to use while I'm here because Bellie doesn't drive. And I've booked it as Derek, because that's the name on my licence.

We find the rental car counter and I present myself with a smile. After my previous interactions today, and with my best friend next to me, I'm not nervous anymore.

"Hi, I have a booking for today. It's under the name Derek Moo. That's me. I just look different today than I normally do." I hold out my drivers licence.

The man behind the counter raises his eyebrows briefly as he takes in what I'm saying. He reaches for my licence. "Thank you… I'll need a credit card also, for the security deposit. Just a moment please." He takes my cards and taps away at the keys in front of him. If he thinks I'm weird, I can't tell.

He hands my cards back, and places a clipboard and car key on the counter. "Head out the door to your left, and see the attendant in Lot B." He smiles. "I think you look great. Have a lovely time here in Adelaide."

Part Nine

Chapter Thirty-Six

Impasse

November 2009

For three years Meredith survived in the time and space outside of my conventional life. She usually emerged twice a month, once at night with Lisa's blessing, and once in the early morning without anyone knowing apart from a few of my friends and my psychiatrist. I really tried to believe I was satisfied with this. Practically speaking, I didn't have much opportunity to squeeze in more time for her anyway. But I was slowly coming to realise that it wasn't actually the restricted frequency that was bothering me.

The boundary of Meredith's existence was also determined by the risk of visibility – to the people in Lisa's life.

If I wanted to be Meredith during the day, in public, then I had to do it far from home. I'd managed to convince Lisa to let me visit Bellie in Adelaide, but I think that was only because Lisa didn't know anyone who lived there.

Merri had no trouble whatsoever being out in public during the day in Adelaide. I saw no reason why Melbourne should be any different. There were plenty of places in our own city that were unknown to Lisa and her friends.

My friend Nettie was turning fifty. She was a colleague at work who had become a good friend, and she knew about my double life. I wanted to go to the party as Meredith. Here in Melbourne – across town in an unfamiliar suburb, but at a mainstream establishment. During the afternoon.

"No." Lisa was firm.

I'd waited until the end of the day, when the kids were asleep and Lisa was reading in bed and there weren't any other distractions. I knew this wasn't going to be a simple conversation.

I cautiously nudged the discussion open. "You're annoyed I even asked, aren't you?"

She laid her book down on the bed. "Yes. I thought you were happy with our agreement. Why are you pushing again?"

I couldn't admit that I'd never been happy with the agreement. And given Lisa's reluctance to see or even talk about Meredith, I doubted that she was ever happy with our agreement either. It felt like a stalemate that we'd simply learned to live with.

Why now? Three years of frustration slowly building up and eating at me. "I don't know. I just… I can't explain, why it feels…" *Unfair.* I left the word unsaid. I just stood there next to the bed, awkwardly. "I don't know."

I suppose to Lisa it felt like I was the one being unfair – that I was disrespecting our agreement and being greedy, like an ungrateful child who was unsatisfied with what I'd been given. Unsatisfied being Meredith just once a month – as far as Lisa knew, of course – with a bonus trip to Adelaide once a year.

Well, yes. I was absolutely unsatisfied. I felt like a prisoner with an approved visitor list. Why did Lisa get to decide which of my friends were allowed to see me?

Yes, I could go to Nettie's party as Derek. Yes, I'd still enjoy it. But it wouldn't be the same. I knew I would spend the whole time wishing I was one of the women there, wearing a pretty dress, moving and walking and holding myself the way they did: so effortlessly *feminine*.[26] Wishing I could express myself completely, free of the invisible shackles I felt being male. This longing that filled my whole being, the female part of me making herself so clear in my heart and soul. I yearned to dance in the light, to be seen as Meredith by *everyone*. And I resented the fact that Lisa was stopping me.

Lisa was looking at me, expecting me to continue.

My fear of confrontation prevented me from speaking the whole truth. It was hard enough having the conversation as it was. If I voiced my resentment, I'd end up saying something hurtful.

I tried to address her fear that I'd be discovered. "It's in Eltham. That's on the other side of the city. We don't know anyone who lives over there. And even if somebody does see me – why would they have any reason to think I might be Derek dressed as a woman?"

"Nettie's from your work. What if your boss finds out about you?"

I'd already told quite a few friends at work, but Lisa didn't know this. Honestly, I half-wished that the whole thing would blow open, consequences be damned. I was sick of hiding. "What if? I'll deal with that if it happens. It's not like I can't still do my job."

Lisa sighed. "They can make your life difficult at work. I don't want you jeopardising your job." I knew that she meant "our livelihood" – even

---

[26] I realise that many women reject the notion that their femininity is tied to their appearance and clothing choices, but to me, and to many trans women (and more than a few cis women I know), it's extremely important to be able to choose these things.

though she also worked full time. Financial responsibility was very important to Lisa and she'd stress out if I lost my job.

I also knew that her perspective was coloured by her own work context: a Catholic secondary school, where more than a few staff happened to be gay and had to be extremely careful about their privacy. For more than twenty years, Lisa had never worked anywhere else. Of course she wouldn't understand.

"The corporate world isn't like a religious school. And there are laws about discrimination." Dammit, I was starting to get argumentative and I didn't like it.

She picked up on my tone. "I've said no, but you keep pushing me. I draw a line and every time you keep pushing. When is it going to stop?"

It would stop if she granted me my freedom.

"I don't know," I said uselessly.

"Well my answer is no. And I want you to stop asking me." She picked up her book, marked her spot as she closed it, and placed it on the bedside table. "Good night." She turned the light out and rolled onto her side, facing away from me. Leaving me standing beside the bed.

Darkness. Two feet away from my wife and unable to feel anything but empty. I knew that I loved Lisa. We had a happy, comfortable life in every other respect. Warmth and affection on our good days. Two small children and a large extended family where everyone enjoyed each other's company. I could gain Meredith's freedom if I left, but I'd lose everything else.

I wasn't about to leave, but stifling myself to save Lisa from hurting was going to kill me.

Chapter Thirty-Seven

Neverland

The world is dark. Outbound on the edge of the city there are scattered streetlights and the occasional passing car but I barely register them. I am feeling everything and nothing all at once and my body doesn't know how to respond. Overwhelmed by intensity and turmoil, my spirit has simply given up.

Anger, resentment, pain, disappointment, despair. They are all there, familiar companions. I *know* them, but they are not making themselves available to be confronted. I reach inside myself and find nothing. The road curves and dips slightly, and I mindlessly, instinctively follow it. I am driving aimlessly but deliberately, purposefully, searching for solace, or some kind of answer. To a question I can barely acknowledge. I am facing emptiness, and I am afraid.

Can I survive suppressing Meredith?

Can my marriage survive if I don't?

Either way, what will my life become?

What if it's a future not worth living for? Would I get to that point? I'm already close to tempting fate tonight. My car is powerful and fast. I could easily push my luck, accelerating headlong into the void, daring it to reveal an answer I won't see in time to swerve and reject.

The void is indifferent to my thoughts.

I want so desperately to escape this purgatory. To feel something besides empty, alone, lost.

Nothing.

I turn on the car stereo and start the CD that's already in the player. And I realise there is a song on this album that captures how I wish I could feel right now.

It starts slowly and quietly. Intimately. Like compassion gently approaching a soul in torment.

I drive on, letting the sound drift over me.

It's helping.

I turn the volume up as the music builds and deepens, and the realisation hits me.

Understanding. I imagine someone who *understands*.

The music hits a dramatic swell. And I break.

The tears come, suddenly and uncontrollably. In an instant, I am sobbing my eyes out. I should probably pull off the road for safety but I don't have the presence of mind to think about that. The song reaches full flight and I turn the stereo up as loud as it will safely go, the subwoofer distorting and rattling all of the panels in the back of my car. Out the windscreen my view is distorted to match; I am blinking and wiping the tears that don't stop and my whole world is rattling as I speed recklessly through the darkness.

The song is "Neverland", by my favourite band Marillion, and although I know it quite well, it feels like I'm hearing it for the first time. I never realised until now just how much it speaks to my existence.

When the darkness takes me over
Face down, emptier than zero
Invisible you come to me
...quietly
Stay beside me
Whisper to me "Here I am"
And the loneliness fades

You provide the soul, the spark that drives me on
Makes me something more than flesh and bone

- Marillion, from "Neverland"

The music is so passionate, so vital. Powerful. Moody and atmospheric, it envelops me completely. I am breathing in so deeply. Living, loving, crying. A tender, beautiful, heartbreaking catharsis, years in the making.

She is here, and *she understands.*

I haven't felt Jennifer's presence like this in a very long time. I always knew she was there but as my life settled down following my tumultuous twenties, she receded into my psyche, waiting until I needed her again. Perhaps guiding me gently. Perhaps I always knew the truth about her, even if I wasn't ready to understand. Even when Lauren told me that night in her hotel room in Kyoto.

I think she's just... you.

Did I really dismiss Lauren's words so readily? I didn't believe them, but I remembered them.

Now it was so clear. Jennifer, Meredith, whatever name she took, she was always me. The divine feminine within. She might still be more than I understand, but she *is* me.

And I have to be her.

And importantly, she has to be seen. She has to be more than a personal secret. I can't keep waiting for a Neverland that doesn't come true.

Chapter Thirty-Eight

Oxygen

The following night, after the kids had gone to bed, I steeled my resolve and approached Lisa again.

"Nettie's party." I started. Then paused. I'd rehearsed what I was going to say but it was gone.

Lisa looked at me impatiently over the top of her book.

"I'm going as Meredith." The air in the room suddenly felt close, yet inaccessible.

Lisa shook her head. "I can't believe you're doing this."

I breathed in but it didn't relieve the feeling of suffocation. I was so tired. Sick and tired of my cage. Of limits that had no basis in the reality I'd experienced. I could walk around as Meredith all day in Adelaide without any trouble. Did Lisa think people treated me like a freak?

It didn't matter. Lisa's desire to keep Meredith in the closet was driven by emotion, not reason. Anxiety, anger, fear. I could see those emotions now, as they surfaced in her eyes. There was exhaustion, too. But exhausted or not, the emotions weren't going to just give in.

Well, neither was I. I was exhausted too, living with an indefinite prison sentence. And my depression was only going to keep getting worse. I wanted Lisa to acknowledge this, but it felt like emotional blackmail to bring up how it made me feel. Even if it was true. I hated this. *If you don't give me my way, I'm going to be sad.* This wasn't an argument I wanted to use, but I couldn't stop it from coming out, even if I didn't explicitly say it.

Meredith had to be free, with or without Lisa's blessing. "I hate how it makes you feel, but I can't – it doesn't mean I'm going to end up transitioning, but I can't keep hiding. I'll just end up sneaking around again."

Anxiety, anger, fear. Both of us drowning in desperation and misery. Because of each other. Because of me. I was hurting the woman I loved.

I continued. "I'm not going to lie or hide it from you. I'm going as Merri. I need to prove to you that the sky's not going to fall in. I just wish you weren't so ashamed of me." I left the bedroom and closed the door behind me.

I collapsed on the couch, feeling like the biggest jerk I'd ever known. Loving husbands didn't blatantly disrespect the wishes and feelings of their partners.

There was an unfamiliar sound coming from inside the bedroom. A low drone broken up by occasional stutters.

In nearly ten years I had never known Lisa to cry openly, and hardly ever even in private. The ragged, wailing sobs now coming from the other side of the door tore through my heart. What the hell was I doing?

I was doing what I had to do.

In the morning my thoughts wouldn't give me peace until I wrote them out.

Oxygen

To: Lisa
From: Derek
Subject: Nettie's party and more
Date: Nov 04, 2009 9:49 am

It's not just about the party. The last couple of days I found myself unexpectedly depressed - more than I would be over just a night out. Each time we discuss Merri and you react negatively, it's a reminder of how ashamed you are of me. That's all I can think of. Every objection stems from shame. Without the shame there would be no need to fear the reactions of others. I know you are protecting our children but kids will find anything to tease someone if they want to. Our children are well liked and have good self-esteem. They are resilient - and if they are not, they need to learn to be. It's part of growing up and learning to make your way in the world.

I don't know what you think happens when I interact with people as Meredith. My guess is that you would not be able to see beyond Derek in a dress. The truth of the matter is that I have had nothing but positive experiences. Nobody stares and laughs. People take me as I am, and get on with their own business. More often than not, they are friendly and supportive.

How much ongoing stress is caused by the effort to keep this secret? How much stress do you suffer for fear of it being disclosed? I thought I could live with the burden but it's slowly taking its toll on me. And when the children find out, in their teens, 20s, or later (and they will find out, eventually, no matter what steps we take to keep it secret)... they are going to resent me for never telling them. And besides that, what kind of lesson will it teach them about being proud of who we are?

I am coming to realise that I keep pushing and pushing because any closet is still a closet, no matter what size it is. I resent the fact that there are still walls, regardless of whether I want to move past them. Allowing me freedom does not mean I will abuse it. You know that I am not going to transition

full time. I actually like the life we've built, you know.
Meredith will never draw me away from you and the children.

But it makes me so sad that you are ashamed of who and what I
am.

==========

To: Derek
From: Lisa
Subject: RE: Nettie's party and more
Date: Nov 04, 2009 10:22 am

It makes me sad too...... so very sad you have no idea. And you
get 'unexpectedly depressed' every time I say no. How often do I
say no???? Not very often at all. For this very reason. I read
an email from 3 years ago which covered exactly the same ground.
You want out of the closet... but I am stopping you. I love you
more than I can say, but this emotional blackmail is killing me
too. You are not respecting my views at all... because you think
they are wrong. I think I've been more accepting than a lot of
wives would be, but you are not respecting me. You are playing
the 'poor me' card... again. Yes... poor you... your life is so
fucking bad isn't it. And I am angry... angry that you keep
putting me through this. Angry that you keep pushing me. I am
sad that I am not cool and accepting enough of you... and for
you. Clearly you think you would be able to find someone else
who would embrace that side of you. Well... I can't. I thought
we had reached an understanding but apparently not. So there you
have it. You have backed me into a wall... and I either submit
or not.

So I say this finally... either accept the limitations without
the resentment or not. The ball's in your court. Next move is
yours.

Was she actually challenging me to take the obvious way out? To choose Meredith over her? Was she really so unwilling to try and understand my side of things?

I didn't care that some other woman out there might accept Meredith. I cared how *Lisa* felt about Meredith.

I realise now that I didn't consider how Lisa was feeling about *Derek*. And it wasn't fair to make Lisa the only one responsible for solving this problem, but I wasn't mature enough at the time to accept my own agency. All I felt was the suffocation. Desperately wanting to be free without facing the reality of sacrifice.

And I did love Lisa and truly believed that Meredith wasn't a reason to leave.

No matter how many times I mentioned shame, Lisa neither acknowledged it nor denied it. Would she rather have me leave her than face the idea of shame? Or had I got it completely wrong? Fifteen years later, I still don't know.

I also don't know if Lisa ever considered leaving. Given that I was the one who created the problem, was she just waiting for me do the leaving? I'd be the bad guy and Lisa could come away blameless. It's unlikely – I really can't imagine her thinking like that.

I wasn't ready to give up. But it felt like Lisa was rationing my oxygen, intentionally or not. Allowing me just enough to exist, but not giving me enough to truly *live*. As if my desire to breathe freely was unreasonable – as long as I wanted us to stay together.

How could we stay together?

Chapter Thirty-Nine
Answers

I knew plenty of transgender women whose marriages hadn't survived. Some of the separations were amicable, but others were traumatic with continuing fallout – even to the point where, in one example, the trans woman no longer had contact with her own children.

I also knew that Lisa and I didn't have to end up that way. There were couples who made it work, who embraced the challenge with love and courage. A few Seahorse members regularly attended meetings with their wives. There were even public figures, like politician Janet Rice and her wife Penny Whetton, who were well-known in environmental activism circles since before Penny transitioned. They demonstrated to the world that happiness was possible for trans women and their partners. And they had, in the early days of Meredith's emergence, given me a glimmer of hope.

But my hope was useless, because Lisa had never been interested in learning about any of it. There was a period where partners of Seahorse members had their own support group, but Lisa had immediately dismissed the idea when I told her about it. And we never continued relationship counselling beyond our handful of sessions with Julie. If I suggested anything to Lisa around exploring how Meredith affected her, she reacted as if I was just pushing her to get what I wanted – which was true, as much as I hated being manipulative. I just desperately wanted Lisa to figure out why she couldn't accept Meredith, but she wasn't willing to try.

What point was there in hoping when the goal was unattainable? Knowing that there would never be a chance, I tried to stop wishing that things would change. My hope turned into depression.

We had an otherwise strong relationship – which is why I was trying so hard to find a way to make this work. Meredith wasn't replacing Derek. Lisa really had nothing to lose, and possibly a lot to gain by accepting Meredith. A truly happy partner in Derek, for starters. Why couldn't she see that?

```
So I say this finally... either accept the limitations without
the resentment or not. The ball's in your court. Next move is
yours.
```

It was an ultimatum. But it was a Hobson's choice where we would both lose either way. There was no Neverland waiting for us, no happy ending where dreams came true.

The questions I'd asked myself, driving through the darkness, were getting the answers I always knew they would.

Can I survive suppressing Meredith?

Can my marriage survive if I don't?

Lisa had angrily pointed out that we'd gone through this before, and somehow nothing had really changed. Repeating the cycle... would next time be any different? I couldn't face endless years of this. If Meredith couldn't be free, it *would* be the end of us. Lisa would certainly lose me. One way or another.

One way or another. The question of survival wasn't just figurative. Already in a dark place, I could only see more pain and suffering when I looked down the road, whichever path I faced.

I really needed to talk to someone. Like my psychiatrist – but my next appointment with Fintan was weeks away and it didn't occur to me to ring up and ask for an emergency consultation. And although I had close friends who knew about Meredith, they mostly heard about the fun times – I hadn't revealed to them just how much I was really struggling, and I didn't have the energy to explain it now.

I was alone and lost. Untethered, my mind ran itself down the paths in front of me, catastrophising from the inside out. Unable to establish any kind of perspective on the situation.

What would happen if Lisa and I separated? I might gain Meredith's freedom, but everything else I valued would be torn away. Everyone else. The reality of sacrifice would be losing the life we'd built.

And then, as far as I could imagine, Meredith still wouldn't be completely free. I would still have to keep all of her things hidden so that my children wouldn't see them. I would still have to be careful about when and where she appeared, and I would have the additional anxiety of fearing chance encounters – if I didn't live with my family, I wouldn't easily be able to plan around their movements. The risk of Meredith being seen and discovered might be extremely small, but any risk at all would spoil my freedom.

I couldn't see Lisa being okay with me telling our children about Meredith. Or even telling the adults in our extended family. The decision whether to inform them would be mine, of course – but so would the responsibility: I could either heed Lisa's wishes or face the anger and animosity that would result otherwise.

I didn't want to end up as separated parents fighting over something so important. It was hard enough negotiating this while we were still together. If we separated over Meredith, then Lisa would already be extremely resentful. Revealing Meredith to the kids and the family would just give her more reason to blame me for making our lives a mess – and I didn't know how far Lisa would go. People can behave in uncharacteristic and unexpected ways during moments of crisis and trauma. And the reality of what happened to a few of the Seahorse members weighed heavily in my fears.

The trauma I imagined happening in the aftermath scared me more than the darkness that I was actually going through already. Separating from Lisa would make it *more* difficult and complicated to disclose Meredith's existence, not less. And only slightly easier to manage.

Even in my hypothetical scenarios, I was tiptoeing around Lisa. Avoiding conflict. As bad as things already were, the idea of becoming bitter exes, fighting over decisions that affected our children, seemed worse. But separating without fighting wouldn't improve anything either. We'd just be throwing away the life we'd built.

Things were already bleak enough to make me question our future. My future. What was I supposed to do when the alternatives were even more painful?

One way or another.

It was an uncomfortable reality, actually considering the possibility of suicide. The ultimate escape. To become just another statistic, choosing to join the ranks of the many – often unacknowledged – transgender souls who come to the conclusion that the world offers them no future worth living for.[27]

I couldn't follow these thoughts without the pain being subsumed into an even worse feeling of horror and dread; the idea of suicide was too

---

[27] The statistics around suicide of transgender people are impossible to determine accurately, due to the stigma and taboo associated with being transgender in many parts of society, in the past and even today. Even if a person is known to be transgender, this fact may be omitted from the official record of their death and the surrounding circumstances – and therefore missing from the resulting statistics.

confronting to give more than this uneasy acknowledgement. Intellectually it was a solution, but emotionally, viscerally, I wasn't ready to think it was an option. I am thankful that I never actually reached the edge of that abyss.

So I imagined choosing to live.

Together. To forever repeat the cycle of pushing Lisa for my freedom, and Lisa resisting. Both of us always suffering and hurting.

Apart. To somehow survive while constantly missing the closeness of my wife and children. Missing the extended family I saw so frequently and had grown to love so much. And if Meredith still had to remain secret, how would we explain why we separated?

Leaving would solve nothing, and hurt everyone. We were a happy family, apart from this one issue. One huge, overwhelming, all-encompassing dilemma of how I could truly be myself within, or without, that happy family.

Chapter Forty

Daylight

That day and the next, I sat there numb and listless, getting very little work done. My colleagues noticed how subdued I was and I told them I was just tired. At home, the unspoken tension in the air tugged at me like a constant weight tied around my chest, following me around wherever I went.

When Lisa and I interacted, we limited ourselves to safe, mundane concerns like dinner options and things to put on the shopping list. What I really needed was a salve for the anxiety tying knots inside me.

I was so caught up in my own misery that I didn't think about what Lisa was going through. But it turned out to be profoundly consequential.

The following evening – two days before the party – Lisa told me that she would talk about Meredith with one of her sisters, to get another perspective on things.

I couldn't believe my ears.

This was an extraordinary development – Lisa and her siblings were all very close, but they had been raised to be stoic and to hide their feelings. I had rarely known them to acknowledge or discuss anything that was emotionally troubling.

Sometimes, perhaps, the closeness of a relationship can make it harder to risk a secret – the stakes are higher and even the tiniest chance of rejection is enough to make us question our trust. I had been aching to tell Lisa's family about Meredith for years, certain that their response would be welcoming. Lisa wasn't so sure.

If her sister Claire's reaction was reassuring, then Lisa would reconsider her fears about Merri being out in public during the day. I was sure that Claire would be fine with it. She was a compassionate soul who had no time for discrimination or injustice, and I couldn't imagine her being anything but supportive.

Maybe things would actually be okay.

The next day was much like the previous one, but with a faint glow tinging the edge of the darkness – I wandered through a haze, not really able to focus on anything besides how uncertain the future looked.

```
To: Lisa
From: Derek
Subject: RE: Nettie's party and more
Date: Nov 06, 2009 8:42 am

I'm really glad that you've decided to talk to Claire. I
honestly didn't see a way past this where we didn't end up
separated. I know it sounds like I'm saying "give me what I want
or I will leave" but that's not it at all. Continuing the way
things are will be unbearable for both of us. It already is.

===============
```

Daylight

```
To: Derek
From: Lisa
Subject: RE: Nettie's party and more
Date: Nov 06, 2009 9:13 am
```

I really hope our love for each other and the kids is enough. The thought of not being together makes me feel ill. :(

===============

```
To: Lisa
From: Derek
Subject: RE: Nettie's party and more
Date: Nov 06, 2009 9:20 am
```

All I can think is that you let Merri free for, say, six months... and see that it has no negative (and possibly has a positive) impact on our relationship.

I believe she eventually has to be free regardless.

If I'm wrong, well, we're not going to be any worse off than we would with the alternative. And I believe there's a chance we could be whole lot better.

===============

```
To: Derek
From: Lisa
Subject: RE: Nettie's party and more
Date: Nov 06, 2009 9:24 am
```

When you say let her free what does that mean exactly?

===============

```
To: Lisa
From: Derek
Subject: RE: Nettie's party and more
Date: Nov 06, 2009 9:30 am
```

```
I guess I mean to let me use my judgement as to when and where
she appears. I have a feeling the frequency won't actually be a
problem, but the events and locations might make you worry. I
would try not to do anything completely stupid.

===============

To: Derek
From: Lisa
Subject: RE: Nettie's party and more
Date: Nov 06, 2009 9:43 am

OK. I would still like to talk to Claire about it all, but that
sounds like I could work with that. Obviously, frequency is a
problem since we are already so busy, but we can discuss that.

I am not ashamed of you, I am scared for me.
```

Was it really just the fear of losing me to Meredith? All this time?

On my way to Nettie's house to change before the party, I received a text message from Claire:

Derek dear, Meredith, we love you no matter who you are!

I was relieved. And thankful that Claire was Claire.

The darkness was lifting. I could see daylight.

The party itself went without incident. It was so liberating being able to breathe freely, to move freely, to be seen in the truth of my feminine self by friends and strangers alike, free of any culturally prescribed notions of masculinity.

In truth, a lifetime of being Derek was never intrinsically unpleasant – it only felt restrictive when I was forced to hide Meredith. Being Derek was like always wearing a comfortable, familiar jacket: not distressing or painful in any way, but sometimes I really wanted to take the jacket off. I wanted to feel what the world was like without it. Just being female, without any fanfare, quietly existing, open to whatever the world would bring me.

    Being Meredith at Nettie's party was exhilarating.

    I knew there was no going back.

When I went online the next morning, I found an email that Lisa had written while I was at the party.

```
To: Derek
From: Lisa
Subject: random thoughts
Date: Nov 07, 2009 11:48 pm
```

Just a few random thoughts that I need to get out, because I am having trouble sleeping, and am having bad dreams when I am asleep. Clearly I have some issues... :)

Let me start by saying that I am not looking to get out of our 'deal' in anyway. I am really going to try to give you the freedom you need. After I spoke to Claire, her reaction was positive so I feel a weight lifted off. She was, what you might say, my litmus test.

However, that being said I am concerned about a few things.

When I read your email the other day, the message I got was either give you freedom or our marriage was over. Not put that bluntly of course, but the same message. My choice... give you freedom or end the marriage. I think I used the phrase 'emotional blackmail' to you and you rejected that, so I think you were unaware that was what you were saying. Well... I can only hope it was you were unaware of the ultimatum, otherwise it would be a whole different thing.

I felt like I was the pathetic wife clinging to someone who wanted out, and that distresses me. And somehow it ended up with your initial request getting met - and you still weren't happy.

```
Now how the hell did that happen. I feel like I have been well
and truly mind fucked, as Julie would put it. Again, I am not
saying I am not going to try it your way, because I am. Our life
together means more to me than for me to be petty.

But, it seems to me that you do manipulate me, knowingly or not
(and I hope not) to get what you want in the first place. I
don't mean that to sound all evil and nasty, but any time I say
'no' or 'I'm not happy about that' it does become a big hoo-ha,
with 'poor Derek, sackcloth and ashes' at the centre of it. I
always end up feeling manipulated. The last time this happened,
you had known you were going to upset me, because you asked what
I was doing the next day, knowing I would be emotionally
drained. You told me that.

It seems to be a pattern, and not one I like. I know we can move
forward from all of this and I do feel more positive about Merri
than I have ever felt, so that has to be a good thing. But I do
also feel more insecure than ever as you were ready to call it
quits. That scares the hell out of me.

As I have said, I don't think you do this to me on purpose. But
it is not my imagination. There are other examples I could give
also. So you don't have to respond, but just getting it out
there will have to make my mind a little easier.

Love you very much.
```

As difficult as it was to admit that I had been manipulative, Lisa was right. I wasn't proud of it. And at the time, I knew in the back of my mind what I was doing, but the suffocation of being caged in and the stress of always worrying about discovery was so traumatic that I honestly didn't care.

I don't think Lisa realised that calling it quits — one way or another — was the only answer I could see, unless she changed her mind. My manipulation was borne from desperation.

Now, I had a little bit of hope. Maybe there was a future for all of us — Meredith included.

Part Ten

Chapter Forty-One
Fragile

It's May 2014 – late autumn here in Melbourne. Lisa's sister has just had surgery, and serious complications have set in. Life-threatening ones. Marie has been put into an induced coma in intensive care, and there is a very real chance that she won't make it. It's a sobering reminder that life can be fleeting and fragile.

The preceding six months have been a difficult time for many people in my life. Something is in the air – more than just the oncoming winter. As if there's some kind of cosmic reckoning approaching, and Marie is the latest to fall into its path. Every week someone else has more bad news to share; I watch as my friends and family struggle with loss and grief, with serious illness, the anxiety of uncertainty, and with guilt over relationships and lives cut short – all the things left unsaid and all the questions left unanswered, never to be resolved.

I think about what I would leave behind if the universe decided it was my time to go.

Marie eventually pulled through and made a full recovery, but she spent four months in the hospital. Her ordeal, and everything else that was happening to people around me, made me seriously question why I was hiding Meredith from the family. Lisa still didn't want them to know, of course – Claire was the only one we had told, and in spite of the long-running joke that Lisa's siblings couldn't keep anything secret from each other, as far as I know Claire never slipped up.

But how would they deal with Meredith's existence if something happened to me? Would Lisa want to keep everything secret, to be forever undiscovered? And what would I do if something happened to Lisa – how long would I honour her wish to keep Meredith hidden?

I didn't think it would be fair to the family if they only found out after it was too late to acknowledge something so important. I imagined the positions reversed, and realised that I would actually be resentful about being kept in the dark, as if I wasn't considered safe enough to trust.

I sit with these thoughts over the long winter nights, wanting to discuss things with Lisa but struggling to overcome my fear and avoidance. As with all of our conversations about Meredith, I expect it to be difficult and uncomfortable. The anxious tension in my chest has become a familiar companion, and I know it's unhealthy, but it never gets any easier to find the courage to push through it.

Finally, after several months of enduring my own dread, I let it out. Hoping somehow to avoid any drama. I bring it up as we're settling into bed on an otherwise uneventful Friday night.

"How would you feel about telling the rest of your siblings about Merri?"

Lisa doesn't take long to reply. "I don't want to. Why are you asking now?"

I've been worried she'll be annoyed, but I can't tell from her voice. "I've been thinking about mortality. Life is short. I haven't talked about it, but Marie's not the only one who's had a scare; other people in my life have been dealing with big stuff. Losing people. Life-threatening illnesses. And having scary close calls and things. And you know how Seahorse lost a member to suicide a couple months ago. And nobody saw that coming."

"You're not thinking about suicide." Her words come sharply, urgently.

I was expecting annoyance, and her alarm takes me by surprise. "No, I'm not," I say quickly. "But I don't want something to happen and end up leaving people to wonder, or find out that I had this big secret they never knew about. If Marie died and I only found out afterwards that there was some huge thing she never told us, I'd actually be hurt."

Lisa is quiet for a bit.

I continue. "People deserve to know who I am. I want to tell the adults in our family. Imagine if my parents found out only after I was gone. They would have a million questions and they might... they might end up guessing the wrong answers."

"Mmmmmm." Lisa is thinking, which is a good sign that she's not trying to shut down the conversation. But I can still sense her unease. She picks up her book, and then puts it down. Then picks it up again. "Let me think about it. I don't want to decide right now."

"Okay." I turn out my light and wait for sleep.

The next night, Lisa is already in bed when I come into the room for my nightly routine. Thoughts of mundane domesticity occupy my mind: running low on clean underwear, gotta do some laundry tomorrow.

"I don't know why I'm making this so hard for you," Lisa says quietly.

"What?" I stop halfway to the dirty clothes hamper.

"I don't know why I'm making this so hard for you. I really don't. You can tell my siblings about Merri if you want."

"Really??"

"Yes."

Wow. This is unexpected. "Okay! Thank you." Suddenly the immediate future looks full of new possibilities.

Well, maybe not completely full. Kind of like the laundry – I notice some of Merri's delicate lace in the hamper. Certain things need to be handled carefully. "I assume you still don't want to tell the kids." One step at a time. I don't want to push things.

"Correct. Not yet."

"Okay." I hadn't really expected a different answer. But this is still a huge step. "Thank you. I love you."

"I love you too."

"How will you tell them?" Lisa asks as I climb into bed after my shower.

"I'll send everyone an email. I've actually been drafting something for a while. But I wasn't going to send it without talking to you first."

"So you've been planning this." Lisa sounds unsurprised when she says this. She knows me well.

"I guess. It's more that I just wanted to write things down. Things I want to tell people. I started making notes so I wouldn't forget stuff, and it kind of turned into an essay."

"Okay. I want to read it before you send it."

"Yes, of course."

"I actually think everyone will be fine with it." Lisa slides closer for a cuddle. "But they're going to have lots of questions."

"I know. Your family is great. Thank you, I love you."

"I love you too."

Chapter Forty-Two
My Other Self

A letter to the adults in my family: my parents, Lisa's siblings, my mother's sister, my cousins.

November 2014

Apologies if this is a little bit disjointed and rambling. I originally started writing this back at the end of May 2014 and have set it aside to mull it over off and on since then.

The events of the past year have reinforced to me just how fleeting our time here is, and how we really need to make the most of it. Lisa's sister nearly died after surgery complications. Friends have lost friends, loved ones, beloved pets, and relationships. I lost a friend to suicide. Tragedy always leaves its mark and makes you stop to examine the things that are really important to you. And then you learn things about someone that you never expected and you wonder what would be different if you'd known.

I have an amazing life. A loving wife and kids and family, a good job, awesome friends, the luck to be situated in a first-world environment where comfort and opportunities are available to those with lucky circumstances like mine. And I get to do so many things that I want to do, that I end up complaining there isn't enough time!

So this isn't a whinge, or a cry for help, or a negative call out of any kind. I am writing this because I think you deserve a chance to know and understand more of me, and why I do what I do with the time I've got here.

Basically, I have two lives. And I'm tired of hiding one of them.

I am transgender.

The term *transgender* is extremely broad and includes many definitions. Maybe you are aware of this, maybe not.

Am I a drag queen? No. Drag queens are larger-than-life caricatures of femininity done mostly for stage shows. Drag is not the same thing as transgender, and although some drag shows are performed by transgender people, most drag performers identify as gay men.

Am I gay? No. Transgender and homosexuality are not the same thing.

Do I want to be a woman? Yes, sometimes.

Am I going to have a sex change? No. These days, it's more correctly referred to as gender reassignment surgery or gender confirmation surgery, and it isn't actually necessary to identify as the "other" gender. For various reasons, not every trans person has this surgery. As I will explain, I don't feel the need to have surgery. Unfortunately society and the media love to define people by their genitals - but just imagine if the most interesting thing about you to strangers was the shape of your private bits. Kind of rude and invasive isn't it?

Do I hate being a man? No, I don't hate it. I'm not a very manly man but I'm fine with that. I'm comfortable being me, as a guy. I don't have to be a woman permanently.

Am I a crossdresser? No. I think the term is too limiting. I will explain why later.

I am actually somewhere in the transgender territory overlooked by most treatments it gets in the media. They don't report on people like me because we don't fit into a neatly defined category. Gender expression can be quite fluid, in-between, mixed, alternating, or otherwise hard to define for the small percentage of people who don't settle conveniently into the usual male/female spaces.

This is important. You'll see a lot of talk in the trans community about moving beyond the binary – beyond the strict opposites of man and woman. We are brought up to recognise people as male or female but for a lot of us (more than you'd probably think) it's not just either/or; it's both, or neither, or somewhere in between.

I'm not ashamed of being trans. This is not a confession. I am not going to try and explain why I am this way, either - I don't see why I should have to make excuses, so I won't.

I know this is a lot to take in. You don't have to read this all at once. If you need to, have a break and process this at your own speed; there's no rush.

I'd like to introduce my other self. Her name is Meredith Lee, which I chose because I like the name Meredith but I wasn't going to be called Merri Moo, I wanted some other Asian-sounding surname, and you can make the anagram "red heel time" out of Meredith Lee. I like the wordplay and it makes an easy-to-remember email address.

Her clothes and personal effects take up 90% of my closet space.

She has a facebook account. In fact, facebook is so good at linking people by common friends and even network IP addresses, that you've probably seen her on a friend suggestion list. This is the reason why her profile picture has never been an actual photo.

There are lots of photos. :)

Lisa knows about Merri. Lisa isn't thrilled but understands that she is a part of me and needs to be accommodated. In return for Lisa's understanding, Merri stays out of the house even though all her stuff is kept here. There's no way it would all fit in my car!

I won't attempt to speak for Lisa regarding this. I hope it goes without saying that neither one of us expects to be judged on this - I don't think there are any moral considerations to being transgender.

There are certainly practical considerations though. And there are definitely things that need to be handled carefully.

More questions.

If transgender is such a loosely defined term, why not call myself a crossdresser? By the usual definition, a crossdresser is someone who "normally" identifies as, in my case, male, and sometimes wears womens clothing. However, there is really no "normal." To me, crossdressing implies that I am simply Derek in a dress. Meredith is much more to me than that. If you must put a label on me, then I choose transgender.

Am I going to rock up to your house, or to family gatherings, as Merri? No. I will not impose her upon anyone. I am not writing this so that I can be free to do whatever I want. I am writing this because I don't want to hide her anymore, which is not the same as actively flaunting her existence.

Do our kids know? As I write this, no. The question of when and whether to tell the kids is one of the biggest any trans parent faces. The common wisdom in the field of transgender mental health is that children handle it easiest when they are younger than teens, or already adults. My son is twelve and my daughter is nine.

Am I worried about my kids getting teased? Yes of course. But the act of hiding it tells them that it's something to be ashamed of, and that the teasing is justified. There is a tricky line to navigate between protecting the kids and showing them what is right and wrong. But there is also no reason to force anyone to be at the forefront of social change if it is going to hurt.

I won't hide the fact that I would prefer to tell them now, but Lisa has persuaded me to wait until they are adults. There is no way to tell whether it will weigh on them as a burden. They are well-adjusted but my son is very sensitive and it could cause problems. It pains me to know that I can tell strangers about my dual selves and I cannot tell my own children, but for now this seems to be the safest course of (in)action.

What if the kids find out anyway? This is a real possibility, and one that we will have to deal with if it happens. I honestly don't know because I can't predict how they will handle discovering it. In the meantime, Lisa and I would appreciate your discretion with respect to children that may interact with ours.

Do my friends know? Yes, most of them. They are almost all accepting and supportive of me. A few, as far as I can tell, are indifferent or simply keep their opinions to themselves. I have told somewhere around 100 people about Merri, and have lost exactly one friend because of her.

Do I have transgender friends? Yes, quite a few. You know how I go out a lot, and never really explain where I go? I am a member of Seahorse Victoria, a social and support group for transgender people, mostly trans women. In fact I have held the position of club secretary for the past year, which means I have obligations that take up a nontrivial amount of my time.

Why do I feel the need to be a girl? To be honest, I don't know and I don't particularly care why. Some of you may need a reason to help you understand this. I'm more concerned about acceptance. It is who I am. Fixating on "why" doesn't get us anywhere meaningful in my opinion. You may as well ask why I like coffee. Whatever the answer is, I'm still going to drink the coffee.

When did I first realise that I was transgender? It's hard to say exactly. I would definitely qualify as a late bloomer since Merri didn't really emerge until I was in my mid-thirties and many trans people identify as such in their teens or even earlier. However, looking back at my life I can definitely see that I have always identified more with women than I have with men. With few exceptions, my closest friends have always been female and I have always felt uncomfortable in groups of men. After Lisa and I got engaged I found myself quite at home on an Internet forum full of women who all joined up to socialise and talk about girly things like getting married! And now, when attending school functions and kids' birthday parties, I find myself gravitating towards the mothers instead of the fathers.

I didn't actually start trying on women's clothing until I found myself living on my own for the first time ever, when I moved to Melbourne. I think it never occurred to me as a possibility because I had always taken for granted there would be someone else in the dwelling to limit my privacy. For years I was too scared to tell anyone, so I made do with the very early days of online shopping - and the results were often questionable! Gradually though, my wardrobe improved to the point where the only thing stopping me from going out as Merri in public was fear and my lack of confidence. When I found Seahorse I realised this was Really A Thing, that others also understood and lived, and over the years I've grown confident and comfortable with it.

In fact, I believe that Merri has contributed a great deal to my self-confidence as Derek. She has certainly helped me to feel free of the social expectations normally placed upon men, and has given me the courage to push the boundaries.

How do I keep it secret? If you actually went snooping, you'd probably find evidence. I rely upon people minding their own business. I have garment bags, suitcases, and boxes. I hang the washing out so that Merri's clothes are obscured. I take precautions to ensure that things won't accidentally reveal themselves on my computer.

Where do I change? I rely upon the kindness of friends, the cover of darkness, tinted car windows, and isolated locations. I've learned to be resourceful.

I have been told that my trans journey, as far as it goes, is a selfish thing. I don't deny it. But there is a difference in being selfish for indulgence's sake and being selfish for identity's sake. I would have no problem giving up my time-and-money-consuming hobbies if I knew that the people I loved were directly suffering because of them. They are hobbies; they do not define who I am. My identity is another thing altogether. I may not be Merri full time, but being Merri is an essential part of who I am. The effects on my time and money may be similar to my hobbies, but the importance to my identity is much more profound.

So where do we go from here? What does this letter mean for you? Well that's really up to you. I'm still the same person regardless. Like I said before, I'm not using this as an excuse to bring Merri out whenever and wherever I like. She gets out enough anyway – it actually takes a fair amount of effort and I'm constantly tired as it is! You may have questions for me, or Lisa, or both. We will try to answer them as best we can. If we feel that a question is invasive or too personal we'll let you know.

Please remember that my children do not know about my trans nature, and therefore I ask that you be discreet when discussing it (not to mention that it is considered extremely bad form to 'out' someone to any third party without their express permission). If you have children of your own and wish to talk about trans issues with them, please consider how you frame the discussion and the possibility of details flowing on to other children including mine.

Otherwise, it's up to you how you respond to this. I'm happy to share this part of my life if you're interested. I'll still be around, busy doing all the things I do anyway. Sometimes wearing a dress.

Peace,
Derek / Merri

Seahorse's website can be found at http://www.seahorsevic.com.au/

* * *

My Other Self

My other self wants to be somebody else
Someone beautiful and mysterious
My other self leaves me messages on the phone
Telling me more than just words and pictures

My other self wants to hide out in the open
Behind a thousand expectations
My other self gets under my skin
Nursing the wounds that scratch that beautiful itch

My other self smiles that wicked smile
Enchanting all those other parts of me
My other self is a jealous child
Coveting all those beautiful untouchable things

Do I shout it out from the rooftops
Make wings and fly into the sun
I am falling off a mountainside
And my other self just laughs

My other self is the life of the party
And everyone wonders why and when and how
My other self is nothing but trouble
And always leaves me wanting more

My other self is full of questions
But never stops to look for answers
My other self is a victim of circumstance
Dancing spirals and sparks through the clockwork of my mind

Double Exposure

I will shout it out from the rooftops
I will grow wings and fly into the sun
I will fall up a mountainside
Falling
falling
laughing
crying
singing

My other self is a song in my head
My other self is anyone's muse
My other self might deny it but I sometimes think
My other self is me

Copyright Derek Moo and Meredith Lee, 2009/2025

Chapter Forty-Three
Plebiscite

In late 2017, Australians were asked about their views on marriage equality: should two people of the same sex be permitted to legally wed? To me, it felt like the country was struggling to grow up, shaking itself free of the restrictive ideals imposed by older generations and learning to advocate for itself. However, the question was being asked by a conservative federal government and I was cynical about their motives and methods.

The matter would be resolved by a plebiscite, in which the general population would advise the government of the majority's position. But the outcome of this vote would not be binding, and the government could ignore the result either way. The government could also simply introduce and pass legislation without the plebiscite. As far as I was concerned, marriage equality was a matter of human rights, and should have been encoded into law without having to justify the very idea in the first place. So to introduce this "debate" into the public sphere was like erecting a boxing ring, placing the LGBTQIA+ community in one corner, and giving permission for all manner of vocal opponents – regardless of their credibility – to jump in the ring and deliver a beat-up.

The resulting conversation was full of contested definitions, ambiguous terminology, and blatant misinformation and lies. The 'No' side was driven largely by the conservative Australian Christian Lobby – a political group who seemed to show up and make noise whenever the LGBTQIA+ community was in the news. Advocating for a definition of marriage as strictly between a heterosexual man and woman, and claiming to speak for Christians as a single demographic, the ACL were granted an inordinate amount of media coverage compared to the number of people who actually subscribed to their views (my Christian friends and acquaintances tend to resent being lumped in with this mob). Indeed, the ACL tacitly showed an awareness that they couldn't appeal to the public using their religious doctrine, which was centred around family and procreation. Despite their own convictions, they would have known that most Australians didn't think marriage was necessary at all – heterosexual or otherwise – to raise children or create a happy family.

So with no other compelling arguments to present, the 'No' campaign cynically turned to using the transgender community as a scapegoat. It didn't matter that the words "same-sex marriage" usually evoked images of two cisgender gay men or two cisgender lesbian women. Transgender people were cast as the primary villains – even though, from what I could tell, the general public didn't even realise how marriage equality would benefit the trans community (until same-sex marriage became legal, a heterosexual married couple would have to get divorced before one of them could legally transition). The public confusion between sex and gender was so prevalent that the 'No' campaign purposely conflated the two, and the resulting propaganda could have passed as satire if it wasn't so serious: somehow, *allowing gays and lesbians to get married would result in your children being molested in public toilets by men wearing dresses.*

Plebiscite

This argument, and others like it, were repeated often by right-wing politicians and ACL spokespeople, and loudly reported by the conservative-owned Australian media – under the guise of offering "balance" and presenting "both sides" of the debate. The effects on the transgender community cannot be understated. Already marginalised and vulnerable, we were exposed and repeatedly traumatised as fodder for the front-page news cycle. To be reminded, almost on a daily basis, that you were seen as a predator, a danger to children, a deviant, a freak, something that should be hidden away – or worse, eliminated – even the most resilient of us could be worn down and lose hope waiting for the rest of society to recognise the injustice and devastating consequences of these unwarranted attacks.

I thought I was resilient. Even though I wasn't fully out to everyone in my life, I was confident in my identity and unashamed to be Meredith. All of my close friends knew, as did my parents and many of the adult relatives on both Lisa's side and my own. Although I physically presented as Meredith only a few times a month, she was always present in my mind, inherently and instinctively colouring my interactions with others. Meredith was especially active online – using her own Facebook account – and I spent a lot of time there, following social justice and queer-centric pages, chatting with friends, engaged with my life as a transgender woman.

At the time, however, I was also dealing with some other, unrelated things in my life – changes at work that were disruptive and causing me a fair amount of anxiety. No doubt this hampered my ability to withstand the climate around the marriage equality debate, and even limited my own awareness of how it was affecting me. So while I thought I was comfortably settled into my dual-gender existence, traversing the boundary between Derek and Meredith with habitual ease, I wasn't prepared when everything finally caught up to me.

The fucking plebiscite broke me.

My children, aged twelve and fifteen, hadn't been told about Meredith yet because I'd agreed to wait until they were adults at Lisa's insistence. I had no idea if they suspected anything. They were certainly aware of the progressive attitudes held by Lisa and myself – both of us had made no secret that we supported marriage equality (and human rights for all, regardless of identity, background or circumstance).

I asked them one day if they understood what the plebiscite was about. Our family's circle of friends was pretty diverse, and my kids were well aware that romantic relationships came in many varieties.

"It's about whether gays and lesbians can get married, right?" my daughter asked.

I set my coffee down on the kitchen bench and looked at Alani to see if the injustice of the situation showed in their face.[28] It was hard to tell – they usually spoke their mind about things, but their older brother was always the one whose face reflected his feelings.

"Yes," I said. "What do you think?"

Alani was direct. "I think they should be able to get married. Why not?"

I looked at Alex, who said "Yeah. Doesn't make sense to stop people just because of who they are."

I retrieved a stack of leaflets from my backpack in the dining room. "I actually feel really strongly about this. These are for the 'Yes' campaign. I'm going to drop them in the letterboxes around the neighbourhood. Do either of you want to come with me?"

Alex shrugged. He doesn't really do outdoors, and I didn't expect him to say yes. He has a condition – the same as Lisa's, but less severe – which makes excessive walking a bit difficult for him.

Alani looked thoughtful. "Yeah, I'll come."

---

[28] My daughter began using the pronouns *they/them* at age sixteen. At their request I have used these pronouns when recounting events from their younger years, such as this one when they were twelve.

Over the next few evenings we wandered the neighbourhood, distributing leaflets to every mailbox that didn't have a "No Junk Mail" sticker. I briefly considered whether political material was classified as junk mail, but since there were still more than enough open mailboxes left to take all of our leaflets, it didn't really matter.

We didn't talk much about the plebiscite itself. Mostly we walked with a sense of quiet purpose, occasionally commenting on someone's yard if it had an interesting tree or unusual fence. It was clear to me, however, that my daughter felt strongly about the issue – each night they were eagerly ready to go and seemed as invested in the outcome as I was.

Of course, since I hadn't told them about Meredith, Alani didn't know *why* this was personally so important to me. And I had purposely refrained from mentioning the horrible things I'd seen in the media, because I didn't want to burden their twelve-year-old heart with the knowledge of just how awful other human beings can be. Life would let them discover this for themselves in their own time.

We were like spies, furtively tracing out the neighbourhood streets under the shadows of dusk, leaving our message – a simple one, stating the facts of the proposal without sensationalising or distraction – in unsuspecting letterboxes. I thought about the other side, doing the same thing in broad daylight, spreading their hateful rhetoric with impunity. I tried to imagine a mindset fearful enough to actually believe the things being presented by our opponents. In their fabricated dystopia, society would be held hostage by "gender ideology": children would be forced into genders decided by their parents, and would be sexually abused by men wearing dresses. The fact that these things were *already* happening in their conservative religious circles (do priestly robes not resemble dresses?) – for years, for decades, for generations – was completely lost on them. I wanted to shout into the void, to shake some sense into the closed minds floating in their sea of fear. But I worried that it would make people question why I cared so much, and my own fear was of the fallout if I broke my promise to Lisa that I keep Meredith hidden.

Transgender people posed a threat to no-one. I resented being dragged into this cynically manufactured conflict. A battle for the hearts and minds of the common people, where ideology and existence collided and the casualties regarded as acceptable collateral damage. We were on a noble mission indeed. Only for me, it felt like a fight for survival, one that I wasn't allowed to talk about, and it nearly destroyed me.

I sighed, slumping in my office chair. How many times had I tried to sit up straight? I'd spent the last thirty minutes staring at the grid on the screen without comprehending any of its contents. My job used to be enjoyable, or at least engaging. Now it was just misery. I couldn't muster up any motivation at all.

All these new terms and processes – software development concepts were so formalised that they'd become abstractions with arbitrary meanings. Why were *Bug* and *Defect* two separate things? What was the difference between *Test Plan* and *Test Suite*? It was an alien culture of made-up terms and made-up definitions of words I thought I already knew. There was something called an *Epic*. And we could assign *Story Points*. Was this computer programming, or some kind of classic literature competition? What was a *Burndown?* I imagined reading a medieval saga with flaming catapults and pitchforks.

I'm pretty sure my brain was having an epic burndown.

Somehow I managed to learn enough to realise an important detail: this system didn't actually fit our needs! It made assumptions that were incompatible with our team's processes and business model. But the decision to use it had already been made by corporate management, who didn't know or care about the details. My responsibility was simply to learn it and apply it to our operations – an impossible task. Every choice was ambiguous and led to dilemmas that could only be solved by someone way above my pay grade. But the people in my team who could make these decisions had delegated this to me because they already had too much to do.

To make matters worse, the damn thing was buggy! I spent ages going in circles before I realised that one of the pages was showing the wrong data. But only *sometimes*. So now I had to question the accuracy of all the other pages too – making it impossible to learn how the system was actually supposed to work. What a fucking waste of time! I couldn't help swearing out loud, repeatedly, even though it drew attention in an otherwise quiet office.

I didn't care. Not about disrupting my surroundings, nor about the seemingly impenetrable system in front of me. I resented this. I hadn't asked for it, but I was still expected to embrace this change, and all the new concepts it introduced, and to teach the rest of the team this new way of working. By last week, or at best, by yesterday – because we didn't have the time to actually stop working while we figured out how to work.

I was swimming in anxiety, feeling responsible for things I couldn't control. And I was angry. It felt unfair having this situation thrown at me. Yet at the same time, I understood that I was the only person in our team with the time and experience required to handle it. So I was trapped – angry and resentful, unable to solve the problems in front of me, and feeling unable to complain or even ask for help.

In hindsight, I think I also felt unjustified in complaining because all this work stuff didn't *matter* – it was just abstract concepts and technical details, unlike the marriage equality debate going on around me, which was directly affecting people's lives. So even though my job was causing me similar feelings of powerlessness, anxiety and resentment, I didn't allow myself to acknowledge their validity.

It felt like I'd been fighting the system for days. The online resources weren't much help, since they followed the same incorrect assumptions that were making this impossible in the first place. But I didn't know what else to do, so I clicked on a tutorial. In the ten seconds I waited for it to load, I got bored (frustration, ADHD, and slow computer systems are not a good mix). I flicked over to my other screen, where I always kept Facebook open (ADHD also means I can't resist keeping my distractions close at hand). At the top of my feed was a post from one of the social justice groups I followed, sharing a mainstream news report covering some right-wing talking head's recent press conference. She was insisting that marriage equality was akin to tyranny against heterosexual couples, calling LGBTQIA+ activists "gender Nazis" and claiming that transgender people were mentally ill. That we were paedophiles.

How could anyone take this woman seriously? Yet here we were, for the umpteenth time, giving some bigot a megaphone and free airtime, not just in the conservative-leaning media, but in re-sharing this bullshit in our own progressive circles! I knew that understanding one's enemy was important for effectively fighting them, but the weeks and months of endless exposure to this kind of hate was sorely testing my resilience.

I was exhausted, even without having to wrestle any inner demons of my own. I was proud to be transgender and I'd arrived at my current situation without ever having felt or suspected that anything was wrong with me. Any concerns I'd ever had were always about navigating *other* people's reactions to me. But I felt pain for those who were suffering through this debacle already burdened by their own internal conflicts and crises. How could someone still coming to terms with being transgender, in an emotionally fragile place, cope with this wall of hate, and the very real possibility of being harassed or assaulted by bigots who were emboldened by the public rhetoric? People were hurting. People were going to die because of this fucking plebiscite.[29] It was injustice on a nationwide, government-sponsored scale, and it felt like most people didn't give a shit.

And I was supposed to care about the minutiae of test procedures for Agile Software Development? Now here was something about which I didn't give a shit. But I had to learn the damn thing whether I cared or not. I turned back to my main screen, remembering the tutorial I'd loaded up, and started trying to read it.

I couldn't concentrate. The outrage in the comments on that Facebook post kept pulling me back. I was unable to reconcile a world where hate was given a voice with the world of my immediate surroundings, this peaceful office full of fabric-walled cubicles, my colleagues quietly toiling away behind their screens. Did this plebiscite affect them at all? I was pretty sure most of them would vote 'Yes', but for how many of them was it more than just an intellectual exercise? Our workplace culture was open to LGBTQIA+ employees, yet I had never seen a conspicuously visible rainbow flag in the office and none of my team had ever mentioned having a gay, lesbian or transgender friend or family member. Would any of them stick their necks out for me if they knew?

I was being held responsible for things I didn't care about, and I felt helpless to stop the attacks on people I *did* care about. Helpless to raise the alarm and find allies to share the burden and fight back, as the people around me remained silent, showing no indication that they were even aware of what was going on. There was a fanatical segment of the population who viciously slandered people like me, and their voices were being amplified by the media everywhere I looked. Voices of hateful people who opposed my very existence, and who were being given enough power to affect society as a whole. The bleakness of this reality made me despair for a future actually worth fighting for. And I wasn't able to turn to the

---

[29] The incidence of hate crimes rises when bigots are given airtime. The targets of this hate may also be struggling with their own self-acceptance. People die in these circumstances, whether by their own hand or by someone else's. This is what happens when society thinks it's okay to debate the validity of someone's existence.

people I saw in person every day, so I struggled to stay afloat by myself, trying to keep my head up, while the ocean around me kept getting darker and thicker and heavier.

Grace, the QA team leader, was going on maternity leave. I'd been hoping that the only extra responsibility I'd be given was to figure out this new computer system, but as her departure date drew closer and closer, the unspoken expectation became official: the only person in the team with the relevant experience and knowledge to take over her position was myself. So in addition to doing my normal product testing job, plus learning this new system, and teaching it to the team, I'd also have to track our development workflow data, manage two other people, send reports, and be held accountable for all of this.

I couldn't do it. Any of it.

I simply gave up.

I lay in bed, staring at the ceiling. It wasn't even eight o'clock yet, but I had no more use for the day. I wasn't sleepy, but I was weary – oh so weary, fatigued, worn down to nothing, unable to summon the will to contemplate anything but the ceiling fan above the bed. It was switched off and motionless, the cross of the four blades not quite lining up straight with the walls of the room. There was a thick layer of dust on the leading edges; nobody ever remembered to wipe them down. I didn't care.

"You're in bed early." Lisa came into the room, surprised to find me lying there.

I grunted.

She hovered for a second. "You ok?"

Did I want to try and explain? Did I even know? Too hard. "Tired."

I wanted her to ask more, but I also didn't. Too hard. It was highly unusual for me to be in bed this early, but it wasn't entirely unheard of. Except that the reason in the past would have ended with "tired" and not the unspoken "I want to disappear into oblivion." Oblivion would be sweet relief from the drudgery and pain of my job, of finding the energy to treat all of its bullshit as important because we needed the money to live, when the things that *really* mattered were already leaving me exhausted, when a whole community was hurting and having their rights debated, when so many people I cared about – not to mention myself – were being dragged through a public gauntlet of lies and twisted truths and hateful comments, facing the indignity of having the rest of society decide their basic humanity, all because of the fucking government and their god damn fucking plebiscite.

But I couldn't explain any of that. I couldn't even comprehend it anymore, lying there feeling nothing, wishing for nothing, feeling utterly overwhelmed by nothing.

Lisa picked up the iPad she'd come to retrieve, and left the room. A flash of irritation pricked my stupor, and I realised that I *did* care, that I wanted her to understand, even though I was too lost to communicate any of this.

I found the energy to start the conversation when Lisa came to bed.

"You didn't notice that I'm feeling like shit." Clumsy, but it was something.

Lisa put down her book, which she'd just picked up from the bedside table. "What? You said you were tired."

"I'm... I don't know..." I had no energy to express the persistent, hopeless wail I felt inside. "I feel like I want to die." Still clumsy. And maybe not exactly true, but the sentiment was the closest I could find in my current state.

She rolled over to face me. "Why? What's going on?"

"Everything."

Drawing herself close, Lisa reached around me and held me tight. And waited.

I took a deep breath. "I hate my job. It's so fucking pointless, the world is fucked anyway. I want to quit. I want to run away. I don't care anymore."

If only. I imagined being free from caring. What would it look like? Abandoning all my responsibilities. It felt like nobody was fighting for me, so why should I bother? "I want the government to go fuck itself. I want to be able to be happy without having to justify my existence. This fucking plebiscite... people are suffering and the fucking right-wing arseholes, fucking Rupert Murdoch, he's printing lies and making money from it. And people are going to die. And I'm supposed to put my energy into figuring out this god damned computer system that I didn't want to be responsible for, just because the god damned corporate management is forcing us to use it. As if it matters! I just... I want out. I don't want to deal with any of it anymore."

Lisa squeezed me. "Oh sweetie."

"It's killing me."

"Can you take some time off?"

I hadn't actually considered that. My mind had gone straight to quitting and running away forever.

Who would take over for me at work? I was already supposed to take over Grace's job for a year. There wasn't anyone else to do it. This fact wasn't important when I fantasised about quitting, but if I was just taking leave and coming back, it meant I still had responsibilities.

Our manager was already overburdened, but he was the most capable person I'd ever met. He was also compassionate and level-headed, and I'd never known him to be unreasonable. Would he let me take a break?

"I don't know." I pressed myself into Lisa's embrace. It was nice to be held. Usually I was the one on the outside of the embrace, doing most of the holding. "I might have to explain why. About how the plebiscite is causing me so much stress." My closest friends at work knew about Meredith, but so far I had avoided telling anyone in a position of authority over me.

"Do you really think so? You could get a doctor's note. If it's a medical thing you don't have to specify details."

Something inside me worked itself free. It was time to stop avoiding the obvious. Finally.

"I want them to know. I'm tired of hiding."

"But they don't need to know about Merri, it has nothing to do with work."

"I don't care. I just… I can't keep hiding. My friends aren't enough. It's too hard to go through this when I can't talk about it. It absolutely killed me to go deliver leaflets with Alani when I couldn't explain *why* this is so important to me."

Lisa was silent.

"I want to tell the kids. I can't wait another five years." There. I said it.

"Okay."

Chapter Forty-Four

Nevermore

Mornington Peninsula, October 2017

The morning sunshine permeates the cool air with quiet generosity. The road is free of traffic; I drive without urgency, noticing the trees, the sky, the hills touching the bay in the distance. It's a beautiful day, and the world seems large, the landscape around me gentle and sympathetic. Serene in a way that I am missing. I come in need of its comfort and its silent counsel. I hope that it is welcoming of my troubles.

I've been given leave to take shelter from the shitstorm I've been living through. My department manager Kevin was surprised to learn of Meredith's existence, but he was supportive and sympathetic, and dismayed at the amount of bigotry being shown in the current media climate. Even though my absence is going to mean more work for him – especially with Grace going on maternity leave – he said I could take as much time as I needed.

Nevermore

I pull into a lookout where I can see a hint of water through the bushes, down beyond the treetops poking up from the hillside below. I turn the engine off, but leave the CD playing in the stereo. Memories from twenty-five years ago appear when I close my eyes: sitting in my car at sunset next to the water, finding peace in the soothing waves of the Pacific Ocean. A sanctuary for my restless yearning, back when I was searching for things I didn't even know existed. But that was another time. Today I am seeking... what exactly, I'm not sure. Simple strength, perhaps. Some way to keep myself from falling apart.

Plus jamais... plus jamais...

Nevermore. The song unexpectedly pulls at me and the tears come flooding. I'm listening to Laurent Voulzy, a French singer I discovered years ago in Japan – it's not the music I would normally choose for a drive like this, but the album was in the CD player already. I didn't feel the urge to change it and now I understand why.

I know French just well enough to understand that he's singing about lost love, and while the song doesn't exactly address what I'm going through, it still hits me hard. I still feel the loss and the bittersweet mercy of its beauty. It's so tender and raw and I turn it up loud and play it again, twice. I'm a wailing, blubbering mess.

Nevermore. I imagine being free of my troubles. What that would actually mean.

Nevermore...

I am weeping for the love, the life, I *might* lose. The utter desolation I would face if I gave up.

At lunchtime, I stop at a small café in one of the little towns that line the peninsula. The woman behind the counter asks me how I'm going, and I answer truthfully.

"I've had... a difficult few months. I'm taking a couple of weeks off and I'm just making time for myself."

The woman leans forward with her arms on top of the pastry cabinet. I can't tell if she's noticed the smudged eyeliner and mascara from all my crying. Maybe she can tell that I'm transgender, and maybe she's aware of the shitty situation going on with the plebiscite.

She looks me in the eye and smiles. "Good on ya, darling. We have to remember to look after ourselves. And when it gets too hard, you can come to my café and I'll look after you. My name's Linda." She gestures at the array of treats in front of me. "Everything here is made with love. What can I get you to help you with your troubles?"

I don't doubt her sincerity. In a young adult fiction novel, she'd be the best friend's mother, providing shelter and wisdom and tasty treats missing from the protagonist's own troubled home. I wish that she could get me a new job and a government that cared about people, but I settle for coffee and the daily lunch special.

When it's time to pay before leaving, Linda compliments me on my earrings – large silver butterflies that I added sparkles and dangly chains to. She wishes me well and as I get back on the road I notice that I am feeling thankful.

I drive for a while in silence, thinking about small acts of kindness in the face of an oppressive world.

At the southern edge of the peninsula, I turn down a road heading to a nature reserve next to the ocean. I need to see and hear the waves, untamed and outside the shelter of the bays on either side of the land I've been driving over.

The road ends in a carpark on a hill overlooking the coastline. There's a path leading to a lighthouse at the highest point. The landscape isn't quite dramatic cliffs and wild spray, but the ocean is there, its vastness comforting me as I follow the waves rolling in to the rocky shore. It's peaceful right now, but I know the lighthouse would not be here without good reason.

My focus drifts out to the horizon. Ships and storms and dramatic possibilities arise in the distance. The lighthouse stands stoic, silent, protecting. How long has it been since its guiding light was needed? I imagine that I am out at sea in the swirling dark, losing hope. The lighthouse shines through the storm like a guardian angel.

My guardian angel. How long has it been since I've needed Jennifer? Or rather – have I somehow forgotten that I need her?

The road beckons as I crest the hill and see the sweeping curve heading down into the next valley. The music is charged – I've switched to Marillion now – and the timing is absolutely perfect. I turn the volume up two more clicks, ease the car from fifth back into fourth, and hold it there for two beats… one beat… blip the throttle, grab third gear and plant my right foot to the floor as the song jumps off the cliff of the chorus into the swirling, searing fire of the guitar solo. I'm pressed into my seat as the car surges forward down the hill, the trees in the valley rushing up towards me. The turbos whistle and the engine sings like it's part of the music. I haven't felt so alive in years.

I'm being reckless but I don't care. They say you should never drive when you're emotional but I need this, I need this in a way that fills my soul that has been so battered and torn and unable to hold anything so vibrant, so fantastic, for so long. So long that I didn't even know I needed this until this very moment.

I tear open my pain with a long, formless wail to echo the cry and sorrow pouring out from Steve Rothery's guitar. Mine is an ugly, tortured accompaniment – yet it is beautiful in its savage honesty. The car's power carries my voice with it as I let it all out. I'm driving a well-engineered, immensely capable machine, but I'm pushing it past the edge of reason, well beyond the safe limits of the road and of my own reserves. I am lost in the moment, letting my fate ride on the wings of my feelings. Of my guardian angel.

The road pulls me forward and challenges me to dig deeper, harder, feeling the tyres sing as they trace out the curves, telling me exactly how much more they can hold on. The car plays its part well, working with me and encouraging me to explore its dynamic talents, instead of refusing to follow my lead or biting back sharply when my guidance isn't perfect. I'm lucky to be driving a car like this, and not something that would punish me for attempting this flight through the twisting landscape of my feelings. Perhaps it wouldn't even occur to me to make this experience happen with a different ride, not that any of this was really planned or expected.

The tears start flowing again as the stormy angst of the song's outro fades into the bright, peaceful beginnings of the next piece. I don't know if I'm happy or sad anymore. I am running on raw emotion that has no recognisable form. After several corners finding my line through a watery haze I ease off the throttle, letting the car relax into a sensible cruising pace as I recover my composure.

I know that my little jaunt could have ended badly – it could have ended me completely. I don't know that I didn't entertain the possibility. Perhaps I drove to oblivion and back in that moment, and the sound of my own cries made me realise that I'm not ready to give up.

Nevermore.

I'll probably never do something so recklessly dangerous again, but… fucking hell, I needed that. I needed that like my life depended on it. It was perfect, and the tears are still coming, quietly, beautifully, comprising the very essence of my being. Proof that I am still here.

Chapter Forty-Five
Disclosure

A few days after my drive around the peninsula, Lisa and I sat down with the kids for a rare family talk.

"Daddy has something to tell you." Lisa's voice was steady. She was always so stoic and outwardly impassive, I couldn't tell if she was nervous.

Alex and Alani looked at me expectantly. Were they worried? This was the kind of moment that usually meant bad news.

"It's okay," I assured them. "I'm not dying or anything. There's nothing wrong."

Pause.

"I'm transgender." Was this how I imagined I'd tell them?

Silence.

"Do you know what that means?"

Nods.

"I'm weird though. I mean, you already knew I was weird. But I'm not going to transition permanently. And I'm not leaving Mummy. So I'm still going to be me. I mean, Derek. Like this." Gesturing at myself. This was awkward.

I took a deep breath. "I use the term 'dual-gender' since I'm not going to stop being Derek. But I am transgender, I have a female side. She's called Meredith. Or Merri, for short. And she's, like, really girly."

I looked closely for any signs that pennies were dropping, that sums were suddenly adding up. Nothing. My kids' faces were still blankly neutral, waiting.

"Have you ever wondered about the meetings I go to every month? On Saturday nights?"

They shook their heads. How often do young teenagers care where their parents go without them?

"You've never noticed anything about my laundry? When I hang it up to dry on the racks in the other room? Girly clothes that wouldn't fit Mummy. Things that aren't Mummy's style. I mean, you wouldn't see them unless you looked behind other things because I always make sure they're obscured. But I always worried that you might find them. No?"

Alani looked at me like I'd suggested they read the instructions for the microwave. "It's your laundry. Why would we go looking through your laundry?"

Kids! All that effort I'd been making to ensure I was never accidentally discovered. Was there ever any significant risk? And even if they'd found out, would they have cared?

I thought back to my own childhood. I never went snooping around my parents' stuff explicitly searching for things I wasn't supposed to see, but occasionally I did look in cupboards and closets – including the ones in the master bedroom – out of innocent curiosity or when trying to locate a specific item. I reckon I would have noticed clues about someone's secret second life. But that's because I was always hypervigilant about my own secrets.

Disclosure

I'd spent so much of my life hiding the most precious, treasured parts of myself that it had become second nature, shaping how I interacted with the world around me. As I've written elsewhere, I'd mostly avoided feeling shame about the things I kept secret, but I still worried about the consequences of people finding out. What was it like to live a life unencumbered by such anxiety?

Less exhausting, that's for sure.

Of course, that's why we hadn't told the kids before now. To save them the effort of having to keep a big secret. But the fact that we hadn't told them when they were younger just made the secret even bigger. Instead of being a fact of life that they'd grown up with, now it was a surprise revelation with unpredictable consequences.

Including, apparently, not much at all.

I tried to get something out of them besides blank looks. "So how do you feel about this? That your father is sometimes a woman?"

Shrugs.

Bloody kids!

"Do you have any problem with it?"

"Nope." Alani fidgeted with the pencil they were holding.

I looked at Alex, who just shrugged again.

"I want to be clear that I'm not ashamed of this. Not at all. We kept it secret because... because we decided it was easier that way. But... well, we think it's time to tell you."

Nods.

I looked at Lisa, and then allowed a little bit of resentment to slip out. "I wanted to tell you when you were much younger, but Mummy didn't want to. She didn't want you to have to worry about keeping a secret. She wanted to wait until you were adults, but... I couldn't wait any longer." The turmoil of the past few weeks was suddenly present, feeling heavy around me.

More nods, but still no clues to their thoughts.

Did they understand the nuances of navigating a society where it was potentially dangerous to show the things about yourself that you loved? My kids have always been pretty perceptive. I wanted to believe that this turned out to be as much of a non-issue as their reactions suggested. I suppressed the urge to say to Lisa, "See? It's not the end of the world. We could have told them years ago."

I looked at Lisa. Her face didn't give away anything either. If she was annoyed that I'd brought up her reluctance to disclose Meredith, she didn't show it.

Tough audience, my family.

Was Lisa worried about the fallout? Frustrated at the lack of reaction? Bewildered? Relieved?

And the kids – what were they feeling? And how would they feel later – tomorrow, next week – after they'd had more time to process what I'd told them?

Resentment? Why didn't we trust them to be able to keep a secret? Shouldn't they know such an important fact about their father?

Anxiety? Would they worry about what this meant for the future?

Curiosity? Outright acceptance?

Would they want to meet Meredith? In their own time, of course. It wasn't as if I was suddenly going to parade around the house in make-up and heels, especially not with Lisa's reluctance to interact with Merri.

"So you don't have to see Merri if you don't want to. Mummy doesn't want to see Merri, so I don't change here at home. But you don't have to keep it secret – although you can if you want. I'm not going to go around advertising it to everyone, but I'm going to be visible, I'm not going to hide anymore. So if there's anyone you *don't* want to know, tell me so I can be careful."

Alex spoke up at last. "Who else knows?"

"All of the adults in the family know. Your aunts and uncles. My parents. Most of my friends. Not many of Mummy's friends. I guess all your cousins will find out now."

Nods.

"So that's it. I'm transgender. Do you have any questions?"

Blank looks. Shrugs.

"I will always be your father and I will always love you. Can I have hugs?"

They both gave me a hug. They just felt like normal hugs. The whole conversation – if you can call it that – had been so uneventful.

"So, no questions? Nothing?"

Alani spoke, looking slightly embarrassed with their query: "Do you have boobs?"

I suppose I should have predicted that. "Yes. I have fake boobs. I keep them in a box with all my girly stuff."

Fake boobs. Real smiles.

Smirks, actually.

Bloody kids!

Chapter Forty-Six

Official

December 2017

I'm so nervous. I was hoping that I'd be able to arrive with Nettie or Joan but we couldn't make the logistics work. So I'm on my own. I wiggle my feet into my strappy heels, leaving my flats behind as I lock the car and click-clack my way to the parking garage exit.

It's only a block to the venue, and I've walked through the city many times as Meredith before, but my heart is racing. This feels dangerous, like the morning when I secretly dressed as a woman and walked from the train station to my office. So many years ago. Back then I was breaking the rules, full of nerves and excitement. Right now I feel the same electricity in my body, as if I'm doing it again.

Except that I'm not breaking the rules now: I no longer have to keep my secret. I no longer have to hide my things or carefully contort my movements through the world in order to evade discovery. Now that my children know, anyone can know, and I am free to be Meredith on my own terms. Well, mostly – as long as I take care not to cross paths with Lisa until I'm back to being Derek.

This feels dangerous, not because of any rules, not even because I'm worried about my physical safety – that kind of nervousness feels completely different, and this part of the city is not scary in that way.

No, this is somehow more vital, more primal, than plain, physical fear. More *meaningful* – I feel this anxiety deep in my soul.

This feels dangerous because there's no going back now. After tonight, everything will be different.

I channel my anxiety into my determination, into each step forward as I approach the bar. I know that even though I don't *have* to keep my secret, I could still *choose* to keep it. But I am choosing to leave that emotional safety behind. Breaking the rules has become irrelevant; I'm breaking up what's left of the closet.

And I'm doing it rather dramatically: coming out to my work colleagues by showing up to our Christmas party wearing a dress. Self-consciously choosing the scenario like I'm writing a scene in the movie of my life.

Dramatics aside, the Christmas party is the perfect opportunity to present myself: it's after hours on a Friday and it's at a venue outside the office. If anyone has a problem with me and goes as far as complaining to management, I can't be accused of interfering with actual work – regardless of whatever legal protection I may have, which I'm unsure about anyway. Not that I expect to encounter any trouble. I don't know all of the people in the office, but my immediate colleagues have always seemed accepting of diversity, and if I was worried about negative reactions I wouldn't have considered doing this at all.

Inside the venue, I carefully climb the stairs to the second level where our party is being held, making sure not to trip in my heels. I'm fifteen minutes early; the background music is playing quietly and I can hear a couple of workers talking about last-minute details of the event setup.

The second floor is a long space with a bar down one side and an open area at the end, a DJ booth in the corner and a small dance floor overlooking the street. I find myself a spot at the bar with a good view of the stairwell and wait for others to arrive. I'm looking forward to greeting people – those who know Meredith will be delightfully surprised to see her, and those who only know Derek could be in for quite a shock.

The first person to come up the stairs is Joan, who gives me a big smile when she sees me. "You look great!"

I give Joan a heartfelt, thankful hug. "I'm so happy you're here."

She squeezes me tightly. "I was hoping you'd go through with it."

Over the previous day or so I'd been hesitating and reconsidering my choice. I'm glad I didn't bail. Now that Joan is here, my nerves are subsiding and I'm excited to see how others react when they realise who I am.

As the party gets started we're given sticky labels for name tags so that we can introduce ourselves to colleagues we haven't met face to face. It's so affirming to be able to write "Meredith" on mine. I briefly wonder if I should add some kind of hint or explanation about my identity, but decide to simply write "(Merri)" underneath.

"What?! How...? You look great! Why...?" Sandor gestures up and down at me with wonderment.

"This is my other self," I say. "I thought it was time everybody met me." I shrug slightly and swivel back and forth playfully on my barstool. Sitting with my thighs crossed demurely in my short cocktail dress, my glimmery stocking-clad legs and sparkly heels on show, I feel beautiful and sexy.

"You are amazing!" He looks at my name tag. "Meredith. Merri. I am so happy to meet you!" Sandor, ever the gentleman, makes an exaggerated bow complete with the tip of an imaginary hat. "Would my lady like a drink?"

"Oh, no thank you, I already have one." I smile and reach for my glass, glad that my interactions have been so positive. Nobody has reacted quite as theatrically as Sandor but they have all been welcoming. Exactly as I hoped.

More than a few people want to know why I'm suddenly Meredith tonight. I skip over the complexities of my journey, simply stating that my gender changes according to how I feel, and that parties are way more fun as Meredith.

Not least because I can dance. Rather, I actually *want* to dance. Out on the dance floor, I feel free and feminine and expressive and so grateful that I get to do this. That I get to experience this evening so openly as my female self, something that for so many years I only ever dreamt about.

* * *

March 2018

It's Harmony Day (introduced in 1999 to acknowledge Australian multiculturalism) and the Melbourne office is celebrating with a potluck lunch. Everyone is invited to bring a dish to represent the culture they identify with. We're also encouraged to dress in traditional style if we want to.

As far as I know, there's never been any specifically transgender food, so I don't bring anything to contribute for lunch. However, I'm not going to pass up an opportunity to wear a dress to the office.

And not just any dress. I show up in a vibrant purple lace and velvet medieval-style peasant dress, floor length and flowing,[30] teamed with black suede stiletto calf boots and ornate filigree silver jewellery. I add a transgender flag badge with "Meredith" written on it and spend the

---

[30] This would be the first and last time I wore a floor length dress when spending the day sitting in an office chair with wheels on it. (How many women reading this right now are laughing? And how many men had to think for a second? It's amazing how half the population can be aware of things that the other half never even considers.)

morning gathering reactions from people who hadn't attended the Christmas party. Most of them don't know what to say or ask, which is understandable: not only am I dressed as a woman, I also look like I should be at the Renaissance Faire instead of a corporate office.

"Wow! Um..."

"What's this all about?"

"Well, this is different!"

I explain as best I can in these brief hallway encounters. "This is my other self, Meredith. Sometimes I am female."

I watch as they process this. Then I answer their puzzled looks regarding my outfit – for Harmony Day it's a more fun and interesting choice than a standard office skirt suit. I say that I come from a culture of magical trans women, and it's clear that some of my colleagues can't tell if I'm serious or not.

We gather for lunch in the break room, where I feel slightly out of place – not because I'm the only one wearing something unusual, but because my outfit is the only one not referencing a geographical or national identity (the medieval Anglo-Celtic style of my dress notwithstanding). A handful of colleagues have also dressed up for the day: I see a couple of colourful saris, a sleek cheongsam, a kilt (but no bagpipes, sadly – or thankfully, depending on who you ask). There's even a full Morris dancing outfit. Flags of many countries decorate the break room walls, and someone has cheekily added the United Federation of Planets from *Star Trek*. It's a fitting vision for Harmony Day, if a bit optimistic.

After lunch, when everyone else has gone back to their desk, I ask my manager Kevin if anyone has said anything to him about me.

"Vince asked if you were doing this as a joke. I told him 'No joke, this is how she is. At least I think so!'" Kevin looks at me for confirmation. "I don't want to speak on your behalf of course."

I chuckle. Vince is one of a few people who I thought might be visibly uncomfortable with Meredith, or even make inappropriate comments. "Thanks. What did he say then?"

"He said you were confusing. And that you looked great!"

"Good!" I don't mind being confusing. In fact, I have spent years becoming known as the resident eccentric in the office: I made a wide-angle periscope for my cubicle so I can see the rest of the office over the partition wall without having to stand up. I built an Evil Supervillain Death Ray control panel for my office chair (complete with flashing lights and variable kill-o-tron setting). I walk around with a little stuffed lion hanging off my ID badge lanyard – he even has his own tiny ID lanyard with matching photo on a tiny badge.

I didn't start out with an explicit motive, but somewhere along the line I realised that cultivating this reputation could make it less surprising if I ever came to work as Meredith. I had even joked about this with people who already knew about her, wondering if my colleagues would be so used to my weirdness that they'd simply take it in stride.

"I think everyone is fine here. People know you, you've been here for years, and you're still the same person." Kevin is reassuring. Matter-of-fact. He doesn't readily suffer fools, and that includes people who exhibit intolerance. I'm happy that he's my boss.

*　*　*

About a month after Harmony Day, I decide to be Meredith again at work, this time dressed in a pencil skirt and blazer, with classic high heeled pumps. My colleagues are curious again but not so surprised this time; I don't have to repeatedly explain myself and introduce the concept of being dual-gender. I do get a few comments, mostly complimenting my appearance and the apparent ease with which I present myself this way – including my ability to walk in four inch stilettos. But for the most part, it just feels like a normal day, rendered slightly surreal, like I'm inside an alternate reality.

At my desk in the middle of the afternoon, I pause between tasks, distracted. This isn't unusual; I often have trouble concentrating on things that don't fully engage my interest. Usually I just follow whatever grabs my attention – Facebook, incoming emails, the discussion happening over at a colleague's desk – but this time I focus inward.

Sitting quietly, I close my eyes and breathe in deeply. I feel my fitted shirt and blazer pull tight around my breast forms, the softness of the fabric against my skin, my long hair laying gently against my neck and shoulders. I shift back in my chair, bringing my knees together, my feet perched in their high heels in front of me. Delicate, feminine, pretty. It's a significant feeling, even though I know the catalyst is superficial; am I not the same person as always, under my clothing and cosmetics? Yet somehow, the effect transcends the materials that make up my presentation: creating, nurturing, manifesting my experience of being female. For all the artifice of my outer appearance, my femininity inside feels wholly natural.

This isn't an alternate reality – I am actually living it. It's happening. Right now, I am a woman, and I feel blessed.

"Hey Derek, can I talk to you for a sec?"

It's another couple of weeks later, an ordinary Monday morning in the office. I'm headed to the break room and Em is coming the other way down the hall. I don't mind being interrupted; conversations with Em usually involve discussion of something fun, like a party or a new dress, or else there is some kind of office intrigue that I am inevitably the last to find out about.

Curious, I say, "What's up?"

Em looks around. "Um, this is maybe kind of a delicate matter... should we find somewhere more private?"

I don't know if I should be worried. "Was anyone in the break room? I was gonna make a coffee."

"Nah. Someone might walk in though."

Now I'm really curious. What needs to be a secret? "I really need a coffee. Come on," I motion down the hallway. "Just talk quietly."

We enter the empty break room without further discussion.

"So," Em starts as I rinse out my mug, "it's about Merri."

"Oh?" I have a brief flash of anxiety.

"I was approached by HR because they know we're friends and asked if I already knew about Merri. I said yes and they asked if I could help them. Someone else approached them already, asking about you."

"Yeah?" I'm not surprised. I've tested the waters twice, three times if you count the Christmas party. I expected there would be some kind of acknowledgement eventually. Is this going to be bad news? Em doesn't seem concerned, so I'm not sure what to feel.

She continues. "This person didn't want to do or say the wrong thing. They asked HR if there is a company policy. And there isn't!"

"So it wasn't a complaint?"

"No, not at all. It sounded like this person wants to be supportive, but doesn't know how."

Ha! My instincts about my colleagues haven't let me down; I'm glad I haven't wildly underestimated the risk of coming to work as Meredith.

We stop talking for thirty seconds while the noisy coffee grinder does its thing. The aroma it creates adds a welcome softness to the somewhat clinical, utilitarian atmosphere of the office break room.

Reaching for the tamper, I ask, "Why didn't HR come to me directly?"

"I don't know. I think they also don't want to do the wrong thing. They know they need to come up with something, but maybe they figured it would be better if a friend approached you first."

"Ah. I guess that's good. I suppose." It seems a little neglectful of HR to be caught unprepared. But I've also never heard of a company planning for these situations ahead of time. And I've been neglectful too; I never actually looked at our company policies myself.

We stand in silence again as the espresso machine pulses and hums, the coffee dribbling slowly into my mug. The smell grows stronger as the liquid splashes and releases little wisps of steam.

"Well, I suppose I need to contact HR and help them write a policy!" I laugh. This is as good a situation as I could ever hope for. A far cry from the disciplinary action I would have imagined receiving a few years in the past.

So I return to my desk with my coffee and draft an email to HR. I send it along with some links to prominent transgender organisations' resources and guidelines pages, and it's not long before I receive an appreciative reply. It's timely; the updated policy that results from our exchange is perfect for highlighting in the company's newly formed Diversity and Inclusion initiative.

* * *

Official policy notwithstanding, I'm prepared for questions and comments regarding Meredith's presence in the women's restroom; I have no intention of using the men's room as a woman. Surprisingly, nobody at work ever raises the issue – either to question the situation or to explicitly support me. It feels like everyone simply expects – correctly – that I use the toilets befitting how I present at the time. When I encounter other women in the restroom, they acknowledge me with a nod or a smile as they would anyone else. The only people who ever ask me about the toilet situation are outsiders, astonished to learn that I am successfully existing in two genders at my workplace.

The HR staff even figure out how to shoehorn both of my names into my employee record – sort of. I have two different first *and* last names (Derek Moo and Meredith Lee), but the system only accommodates a single "Preferred Name", which replaces "First Name" when strict legality is not required. Entering my preferred name as "Meredith Lee / Derek" produces an output I find acceptable, either with or without "Moo" following it. At least the office systems never call me "Merri Moo"!

Regardless of what the computer thinks my name is, Merri begins showing up to work regularly – about once a week. Wearing skirt suits and pretty floral dresses with hemlines that don't get caught in my chair wheels.

Eventually, after getting used to seeing my double account name in the corner of various system screens, I decide that it would be nice to have a double profile photo to match. My current photo just shows Derek, and it feels like Merri should be visible online where her name is displayed. I don't know if there is an official company position regarding profile photos, but I'm going to find out.

It takes me a while, but after looking through hundreds of photos of Merri and a handful of photos of Derek – no surprises who likes being seen more here – I find a suitable example of each to use for my combined picture. It's not the first time I've looked at my face as Derek and Merri side by side, but seeing both of me together still has an impact that I don't take for granted: it's an affirmation, a celebration of this strange dual existence I embody.

Using an image editor I crop the sides of each photo so that they form a square when I put them together. It looks good, but the backgrounds blend awkwardly at the seam where they join. It needs a border. I try a thin white line, a few pixels wide. Nope. How about a dark line. Better. Then I have an idea.

Playing around with the fill pattern options, I manage to turn the thin line into a rainbow spectrum, like the ones you see in science demonstrations, turned vertically. It's perfect.

I attach the image to an email and send it to HR, requesting a change to my profile. The reply is positive; the next day the double photo pops up when I log in.

From now on, every online interaction with my colleagues will be accompanied by this visual declaration and reminder that I am Meredith as well as Derek.

I'm sitting in the office, but I feel like I'm standing outside in an open field. Surrounded by countryside full of colour and trees and open roads. The sky is dotted with clouds. There are some dark patches in the distance, and I know that storms will happen, but I feel no apprehension. I understand that they are simply a part of how this landscape lives. The wind breathes with freedom and possibility.

I have to stop and pinch myself and reflect on how I got here – somehow living a reality that I once considered unattainable.

Part Eleven

Chapter Forty-Seven

Body

September 1984

It's always uncomfortable, having to change for P.E. in the boys' locker room. For one thing, my family has never been all that free and easy about nudity and it feels scary undressing anywhere but in a private space. Additionally, though, I am uneasy about the teenaged body I have to expose to everyone in this awkward, smelly, anxiety-inducing place with its stark fluoro lighting and rows of cold metal cabinets and hard wooden benches. Even though the reality might actually be less unpleasant than my worst fears suggest, it has the air of someplace that *could* breed the kind of meat-headed bullies found in Hollywood movies about teenagers – depictions that I usually find unwatchable, so averse am I to the hostility, inflated ego, and aggression embodied by such characters. I try not to think about how it would feel to be shoved up against the lockers, or to have my head forced into a toilet bowl. There's no way I would be able to prevent it – I'm simply not physically big enough.

Body

My body. I don't think I'm ashamed of it, but I am well aware that it is lacking in the qualities I have been led to believe are desirable. I'm on the short side of average, and I'm extremely skinny. Thanks to my Chinese genes, I don't expect to ever have hair on my chest or anything approaching a full manly beard. This physique, along with a reputation for academic achievement, makes me the stereotypical Asian nerd: an easy target should any jocks decide to pick on me. It also makes me feel completely unattractive to any girls who catch my eye. But my fourteen-year-old self is too awkward around girls to attempt conversation, let alone ask someone out, so my primary concern is simply to avoid getting harassed or beat up. Thankfully, I must lack whatever the behavioural characteristics are that attract the attention of bullies, because I might as well be invisible, which suits me just fine.

It is swimming season in ninth grade P.E. and that means even more exposing of bodies than usual. Plus, it means wet swim trunks, which is the absolute worst if you are self-conscious about showing a bulge in your crotch. Yes, I have penis anxiety. Ever heard of it? Me neither. It's a term I just made up to describe something that might actually be commonly experienced, but I can't imagine any boys or men actually discussing it.

We're sitting against the wall at the end of the swimming pool, waiting after having taken our turns to swim the single lap we are required to complete for grading. I'm not exactly sure what the expectations are, since swimming ability varies widely, but I've managed to slowly finish my lap without incident and now I'm dripping and shivering as my body tries unsuccessfully to absorb the afternoon sun's warmth. There's no heater for the pool and even on a hot day the cold water feels like punishment, not relief.

I'm very conscious of the fact that the chill has caused my penis to contract into a little stub that isn't long enough to lay sideways or hang down, meaning it protrudes through my wet swim trunks as they stick to the skin around my groin. I adjust the way I'm sitting to fold my knees up; even though it exposes less of me to the sun, it allows me to pull at my shorts so that they're a bit loose in the front, causing multiple folds to form and hide the evidence.

I glance sideways at Tom sitting next to me. He's tall and lanky and has stretched his legs out in the sun. He looks bored watching the other kids swimming, and appears completely unconcerned about the bulge showing at the front of his own shorts. I wonder, would he ever nervously glance around at other boys' pants?

At least Tom isn't giving off any hostile or intimidating vibes. The other boys sitting around me are similarly benign; three of them are talking about a baseball game from the other night and a couple more look like they'd rather be somewhere else. We've been sorted alphabetically by our last names, and it's just luck that I'm not stuck here with meatheads and bullies.

Nevertheless, I hate P.E. and can't wait for next year when it's no longer mandatory. Being confronted with the reality of physical bodies is so uncomfortable. Even if I might find it enjoyable to think about the girls across the yard, their bodies still so mysterious to me, I don't dare let myself because I can't risk getting an erection when I'm already so nervous about how my crotch appears.

I doubt that the things I felt as a teenager would qualify as dysphoria, but it's interesting to think about it from a transgender perspective. Plenty of cisgender girls go through puberty feeling anxious and self-conscious about their budding breasts and other visible changes in their bodies, so it makes sense to me that cisgender boys might have similar experiences. I wonder if penis anxiety might be an actual phenomenon – what kind of feelings and reactions do cisgender boys and men have about drawing attention to their crotches? Penises can certainly be unpredictable but culturally we seem to let them hang however they please – as long as they're covered, there's no expectation to explicitly rein them in unless it's necessary for playing sports.

I've never personally asked anyone else if they get self-conscious about a bulge visible in their crotch, or whether they perhaps consider it desirable to show one. I suspect it's simply one of those things that remains unspoken until something notable comes along – the collective reaction to David Bowie wearing tight pants in the movie *Labyrinth* suggests that there are plenty of people who do appreciate a well-endowed individual showing the goods. But whatever the prevailing social norms, the appropriateness of a person's crotch presentation is not a trivial matter in the transgender world.

* * *

May 2006

I squirm in my seat for the fifth time in the two minutes since I've sat back down with my new drink. Tucking is bloody uncomfortable. I'm constantly aware of my penis trying to unfold itself from between my legs, where it feels like it's in the way. I haven't learned about taping, so I'm relying on my undies being tight enough to hold everything in place, which is not entirely successful. How do people do this? What happens when you get an involuntary erection?

I'm at my first Seahorse meeting and it's an odd experience. It's awkward sitting at a table with strangers where nobody is talking. I'm finding it difficult to relax and the discomfort of my inadequate tuck job isn't making it any easier. I wonder if the others here ever become comfortable enough with each other to discuss such intimate physical concerns (over the coming years I will learn that indeed they do, although I very rarely witness it). Luckily nothing embarrassing happens, but after this evening I decide that I need to find a better solution.

I'm not that familiar with the existing devices transgender people can use to assist with their presentation. At this point, I am vaguely aware of a thing called a *gaff* (for tucking and preventing crotch bulges) but I don't know how it differs from normal underpants and I wouldn't have a clue how to obtain one. In 2006, transgender content on the Internet is still largely underground and heavily skewed towards fetish porn sites. To search for a gaff I have to use the words "penis" or "cock" and I really don't want to wade through the results in the hopes of finding something useful.

Thankfully, it's easy for me to imagine something homemade. As Derek I am already well-known for making odd creations and fixing things using random objects and materials. Given my surname – Moo – it isn't surprising that I've earned the nickname "MooGyver", after the 1980s TV series *MacGyver* – the show's title character is famous for improvising solutions to technical problems using everyday items he finds lying around. In popular culture, the term "MacGyver" has become a shorthand verb for implementing such fixes, and I have been known to MooGyver things that last for years.

When I am faced with a problem like this, my initial thoughts usually go towards inventing my own solution rather than buying something. Besides, a gaff still requires tucking and that doesn't appeal to me. Making something myself is also likely to cost much less and will be easier to keep secret – I can work on it after the kids are in bed, and we rarely have unexpected visitors in the evening (extended family members frequently drop in unannounced during the daytime). I won't have to discuss it with anyone or worry about explaining or hiding an unexpected parcel delivery. It's also not unusual for me to be tinkering late at night, and it's never that clear exactly what I'm MooGyvering amongst all the bits and pieces scattered over the dining table I use as a desk.

I've used a plastic file folder and some long shoelaces. The contraption looks like a BDSM device, but it works. The laces make it obvious that it's a binder of some sort, but it's basically an elaborate, fiddly G-string. The plastic sheet is cut closely to match the shape of my groin, narrowing to a strip going between my legs with small tab at the tail to receive the web of laces strung over my hips from the sides of the front section. It's stiff enough to stay flat at the front but flexible enough to move with me. I can wear it over my undies and tie the ends of the laces at the back; nothing shows even when I wear a tight pencil skirt.

Over the years I will improve on this, making it more comfortable by using heavy cotton fabric for the central piece and turning the plastic part into an insert. Some versions will get straps and buttons instead of laces, for slightly less hassle in securing and releasing. I never quite manage to get it to a point where it conceals things enough that I'd feel comfortable wearing a swimsuit, but that's okay – I don't have any interest in going swimming as Meredith anyway.

I realise that I could probably publicise and share my designs and experience, but as I mentioned above, the concealment of one's penis is – perhaps surprisingly – not something I've heard much discussion about among the transgender women I know. Maybe after my story gets published, I'll end up regretting that I didn't patent my design, cornering the market and making a fortune!

* * *

There are other aspects of having a transgender body that I've learned to navigate on my own: primarily boobs and hair, both on my head and on my body (the hair I mean, not the boobs!). I actually let my hair grow long several years before I started exploring my gender (although it's quite possible that growing my hair out *was* exploring my gender, albeit subconsciously). Because a man with a ponytail is not that unusual, few people ever questioned my motives. For those that did, my answer of "because I like it" was enough to satisfy them. Once I started discovering

Meredith, I was able to present as female with my own hair – to this day I've never tried on a wig.

One thing that surprised me in the early years of my journey, when I was still keeping Meredith largely secret, was my reluctance to let my hair down as Derek. People would ask to see what I looked like without the ponytail and I always felt like I was revealing too much when I obliged. As soon as my long hair fell down around my face and over my shoulders, I felt my femininity wanting to surface. I'd leave it down only briefly before nervously tying it back up again.

It did feel a little odd, having long hair and being apparently unwilling to ever let it out. I wondered if anyone else ever thought my hair was pointless if I was always going to keep it tied up. But I was too scared to give away any hints about Meredith's existence, especially to my young children. Even an innocent remark from my daughter ("haha, you look like a girl!") would give me anxiety. Because I had agreed not to tell the kids about Merri until they were older, I was genuinely afraid that Lisa would blame me for being careless if they found out.

Interestingly, my son, who is now an adult, has much longer hair than I do, and it is gloriously full and effortlessly wavy and I am extremely envious. He has never shown any signs of gender questioning, and seems completely comfortable wearing his hair in whatever arrangement suits the circumstances – leaving it out, tied in a ponytail, up in a towering top knot, whatever. He even lets his younger sister put it in braids or pigtail plaits as he sits and plays video games. How times change.

Of course, since I've come out to everyone there is no longer any question of hiding Meredith's existence, so leaving my hair down as Derek feels neutral – and fairly natural – to me now. I still leave it in a ponytail mostly because it's easier to keep out of the way, and I'm a creature of habit – it feels like Derek has always had a ponytail as the default presentation. On the odd occasion that I leave it down, there's no anxiety. There's just a very slight feeling that my identities are blurring together. If anyone who doesn't know Meredith were to remark on how feminine I look as Derek with my hair out, I would probably tell them "Funny you say that – as a matter of fact, my alter ego is a girl!"

I lean my head back into the wash basin and settle my neck against the cold porcelain of the cutout. As the warm water hits my scalp I breathe deeply and try to relax. I feel somewhat exposed – having my hair wet and pulled back means there's nothing framing and softening my face, and even with make-up on I think I still look like a man without my hair to help feminise me. But I try not to dwell on this, and concentrate instead on letting myself absorb this experience.

The hairdresser slowly works her hands through my hair: shampooing, rinsing, conditioning, and then, after a brief pause, I feel her fingers press gently on my temples. I wonder what she's doing, and then as she begins to knead my scalp I realise that she's giving me a massage. She presses more firmly as she gets into it, and – oh my God, this is the best thing ever. Does this happen every time? Is this the reason women go to the hair salon?

It's blissful and I keep waiting for it to end too soon, leaving me unsatisfied, but the hairdresser is generous and indulges me without me asking. I reckon she takes a good five minutes and when it's over I wonder why I waited so long to try this.

Men have no idea what they're missing out on.

This takes place in the middle of 2008, on a visit to Adelaide to see my best friend Bellie. It's a rare chance for me to be Meredith freely, during the day, out in the open. I'm using the opportunity to experience things normally off-limits to me.

I haven't paid someone to cut my hair for over a decade. After I decided to grow it out, I just asked friends or relatives, or Lisa, to trim it straight across the back once every few months. For the last couple of years, however, even in the limited circumstances where I present as

Meredith, I've wondered what it would be like to have my hair properly cut and styled by a professional.

It's expensive, for starters. But the experience of being pampered and fussed over is so amazing that I can't wait to do it again. It's easy to dismiss the hairdresser (and the entire beauty industry) as being trivial and superficial and primarily about the capitalist drive to keep consumers spending – such criticism certainly has its place – but the way I feel, sitting in this chair, is a revelation: regardless of how I look, I feel *valid*. I feel *seen*, and I feel *worthy*. The fact that I am paying for the privilege does not diminish the sense of affirmation that I get, as a transgender woman, about the inherent beauty of my existence. And I suspect the transgender perspective here only magnifies the fundamental truth. Hairdressers aren't considered stand-in therapists for no reason: their clients *matter*.

"How do you want it cut?", Tham, the hairdresser, asks as she re-ties my apron and gathers the tools around her station.

I look in the mirror and squint a bit, since my glasses are sitting on the shelf in front of me and everything's blurry. "I don't know, really. I'm not always like this... a girl – so I need to still be able to tie it back in a ponytail when I'm a boy."

Tham takes this completely in stride, like she has dual-gender clients come in every other day. "Okay, so no fringe or anything. How about just a simple shoulder-length bob?"

"Sure." I have no idea what would look good. A bob would just be a shorter, neater version of my untrimmed look, so I figure it's a safe bet. I leave my fate in Tham's capable hands.

Bellie is having her hair straightened, which is quite an undertaking since she has thick, messy curls reaching halfway down her back. I hear Bellie mention to her hairdresser that this is pretty much the first ever salon visit for both of us. When we're finished, we have to mark this occasion, and Tham obliges us with a photo before we head off to find somewhere to feel fabulous while drinking coffee.

"I like how it looks, but my hair feels icky with all this product in it." Bellie is a no-nonsense, earthy soul who rarely bothers with dressing up or primping and preening her appearance. She sets her coffee down and gathers a handful of glossy locks hanging past her shoulder. As she examines them I can see the mixed feelings on her face. Of course, she still looks like a woman with zero effort, salon hairstyle notwithstanding – in contrast, I have to go through a ringamarole or I'll look like Derek in a dress instead of Meredith. When it comes to Bellie's hair, though, I can't blame her for rarely spending time on it. She had the ends trimmed, but that part took maybe ten minutes out of the two hours we were in the salon. The rest was spent taming the curls.

"It's so sleek. It's like you're Bellie but not really Bellie. I don't know what to think." I laugh.

"I'm Bellie's evil twin now. Muahahahaha."

"Hmmm... that's perfect, because I'm Meredith – Derek's evil twin!" I flounce and flutter my eyelashes menacingly, and primp my newly-coiffed hair.

Bellie smiles. "My hairdresser asked me if you were a man or a woman. I said... 'both?'"

"What did she say?"

"She was confused a bit. But I asked her if it really mattered, and she said 'I guess not'. She did say you looked beautiful with your hair done. I agree."

I find this affirming, and fulfilling.

It turns out I am a creature of habit. I've kept this hairstyle ever since that day, and currently have no plans to change it.

* * *

I've mentioned before that I've never had a lot of facial hair to remove – even before I started presenting as Meredith, a couple of minutes with an electric razor was always enough to deal with the daily stubble. I did have reasonably hairy legs at one point, but I discovered wax-at-home strips and even purchased an epilator in the years when I was still very private about being feminine. While I was a bit anxious about showing some unusually smooth legs for a man, I knew that I could explain them away with my Chinese ethnicity, at least to anyone who hadn't noticed my leg hair in the past. If they had, well then I would simply have to let them wonder.

Over time, as I became comfortable in my own (hairless) skin, I found the occasional awkward moments kind of amusing.

It's 2016, the middle of summer, and I'm wearing shorts to the office, because the air conditioning is never effective enough to stop me sweating in long pants when the weather's this hot. I'm sitting against the wall at the back of the board room; three different divisions of the company are assembled for a staff meeting and there are not enough chairs. It's not overly crowded but there are plenty of people I only know by face, through the occasional passing encounter in a hallway or in the lifts.

The man standing next to me glances down at my legs sticking out of my shorts. I hardly register this, because I'm used to being known as the weirdo who does things like fix the hot water tap with a piece of cutting board, turn paper clips into fidget toy spinning tops, and wear shorts to the office with my ID card and lanyard hanging from my hip together with a little stuffed animal mascot.

I look up. It's Tony, a manager from one of the other teams. I've noticed him often carrying a gym bag when he leaves the office. He always looks sharply masculine, and he's certainly fit; his well-defined frame is readily apparent under his tailored shirt. He's handsome, with subtly spiked short hair and a hint of beard shadow.

"Do you ride?" He nods ever so slightly towards my legs.

It takes me moment to understand what he's getting at. Oh! My legs are quite shapely and devoid of any hair. He's asking if I'm a cyclist.

I look at him a bit quizzically, and then give a short, bright answer. "Nope!"

This takes him by surprise. "Oh."

I don't say anything else.

Tony looks around the room for a few seconds, and then awkwardly wanders away.

* * *

It will probably come as no surprise to find out that I MooGyvered my first pair of boobs. I had acquired a self-adhesive "magic bra" – basically two small silicone cups, shaped like padded bra inserts, attached together at the middle and intended to enhance and somehow support a natural bust. The cups didn't really do much for me on their own, but when I inserted more padding in between my own chest and the silicone, they gave me a pretty decent shape when held in place by a conventional bra.

The first time I wore my boobs for more than an hour, though, I discovered that the adhesive on the silicone wasn't very nice to my skin. It's kind of embarrassing to be in the middle of a social situation and realise that your chest is itchy, but the area you want to scratch is *behind* your breasts. It's not a good look to be fingering your boobs like you're digging for treasure. Luckily this happened during a Seahorse meeting, which only lasted a couple of hours. I couldn't imagine trying to put up with it all day long. And it would have been much worse without the additional padding I used under the cups; instead of two red rings matching the borders of the silicone, there would have been a solid rash across my entire chest.

I solved this problem by fabricating a liner from an old towel, to match the outline of the breast forms. I didn't really need the forms stuck to me because my bra held everything in place anyway. Plus, a layer of terrycloth under the forms had the additional benefit of helping absorb sweat – silicone stuck to your skin means it gets hot and there's no airflow.

After a couple of months I cobbled together some thicker and slightly more realistic looking forms by cutting up a second "magic bra" to fit inside the first one, using silicone caulk from the hardware store to glue the pieces in place. A liner made this viable because it covered the resulting mess, which was still sticky in many places, and made it possible to wear it against my skin. I made a few liners since old towels are ubiquitous and it meant I'd always have a clean one available.

I relied upon my own ingenuity and crafting skills to provide my breast forms partly because of the expense in buying actual prosthetic forms, but mostly because of my concern for secrecy. Stick-on "magic bras" were available at any shop that sold women's underwear, and it was easier to endure an awkward moment making a quick purchase than it was to have to explain why I needed prosthetic breast forms to a specialised dealer. Ordering online was an option, but given the expense of good quality prosthetics, I wasn't going to risk it unless I knew they were exactly what I wanted. Plus, as I've mentioned, I only had any real privacy in the evenings, and I didn't want people curious about things arriving to the house during the day.

Eventually I made a contact in the local transgender community who was able to sell me a pair of very nice prosthetic forms, and I retired my MooGyvered set for good. I went up a cup size in the process, needed to make new liners, and had to purchase some new bras, but my friends say that my hugs feel much nicer now!

* * *

July 2006

I'm surprised by my phone ringing in my handbag. I rarely get phone calls, especially in the evening.

The background chatter in the Seahorse meeting room isn't too loud, so I answer the call without leaving my seat. "Hello?"

It's Lisa. "Hi, I had to restart my laptop and I forgot the Wi-Fi password."

Ugh. I hate dealing with technical issues like this, especially over the phone. "Hmmm okay. It's supposed to reconnect automatically. I hope it's not -"

Lisa interrupts me. "What's with your voice? It sounds fake."

I cringe a little. Is that how other people perceive the way Meredith talks? "Well... yeah... is it a problem?"

"I don't like it."

I close my eyes. "Hang on a sec."

Getting up from my seat, I quickly head out the door into the lobby next to the meeting room. There won't be anyone out here unless they're passing through to use the toilets.

"Okay. Is this better?" It feels uncomfortably revealing to speak in Derek's voice around Seahorse members who only know Meredith. It also feels wrong when I'm wearing a dress and make-up. Like I'm out of kilter somehow. Stuck halfway through a dimensional phase shift.

"Yes," Lisa says.

I want to get this sorted out quickly so I can get back to being internally consistent. "Right. So is your laptop trying to reconnect and failing?"

"No, it didn't do anything and I had to tell it to connect again."

"Okay. That's probably a good sign." I give her the password, spelling it out carefully.

I wait in silence for thirty seconds.

"Okay it's connected now. Thank you." Lisa sounds happier.

"Great. Did you tick the 'reconnect automatically' box?"

"I don't remember."

I roll my eyes. I hate tech support. "Nevermind. We can check that later. All good?"

"Yep. Thanks. Love you."

"Love you too. Bye."

Around the end of 2005, when I had realised that I wanted Meredith to become part of my life, I spent an evening searching the Internet for information about altering my voice. Most of what I found required interactions with other people that would be hard to keep secret: appointments with voice therapists, singing and acting coaches, even vocal cord surgery. Since I was very guarded about Meredith's existence, none of these options were viable.

But my searching eventually led me to a site which was perfect for my needs. It was a random transgender woman's personal account of her journey, and contained a page explicitly devoted to the technique she used to feminise her voice. The instructions could be summarised as follows: *Make as if you are going to speak falsetto, but lower the pitch of your voice without changing the tightness of the throat muscles.*[31] When I tried it out, it was easier than I expected, and to my surprise, I instantly felt like I should be carrying myself in a more effeminate manner.

I didn't have many opportunities to practise using my feminine voice, though. Occasionally I would try it out when I was alone, but I always felt ridiculous because I couldn't think of anything to actually say besides "Hello, I'm Meredith!" For some reason it never occurred to me that I could have picked up a book or loaded a page from the Internet to read out loud.

One day, going to lunch with a friend at work, I decided to experiment.

Nobody else was leaving with us, but I waited until the elevator doors closed. "I'm looking forward to this. I haven't had a good curry in months."

---

[31] It's commonly understood that women's voices are naturally higher pitched than men's voices, but in reality much of the difference comes from the harmonics – the frequency overtones – and not the fundamental pitch. A female and male voice both at the same fundamental frequency will still sound different, and the female voice will register higher to the ear. The harmonics can be affected by the way the voice is used; many singers and actors know this well and are trained to take advantage of it.

My voice cracked a bit as I concentrated, tightening the muscles in my throat while speaking.

Nadia smiled. "Oh hi Meredith!"

I had become close with a few people at work, and told them about Meredith, even though I hadn't introduced her in person yet – this was back before I'd even attended my first Seahorse meeting. I needed to share what I was going through, and since I was afraid to talk to Lisa about it, I turned to my friends. They were supportive and interested in my journey. I'd shown them photos of my clothes and shoes and explained my desire to sound more feminine when I talked.

I was a little concerned about being incongruous, using a girly voice while presenting as Derek. "Does this sound weird?"

"Hmmm. A bit. I think maybe because I know you already. To a stranger, you could be a gay man, or maybe someone who just talks camp."

I nodded. "That's what I was hoping. I'm going to try to use this voice until we get back from lunch."

"I wonder if it'll be affected by a spicy curry." Nadia laughed. "Maybe that will help!"

As we exited the lift, I looked around the lobby. "As long as nobody I know shows up and sits next to us."

Nadia shrugged. "I'm sure it will be fine."

Sure enough, the staff at the restaurant just accepted the way I sounded without batting an eyelid. If they thought it was strange, they didn't show any indication.

* * *

Early 2018

After I'd told my children about Meredith – twelve years after I'd first given her a voice – my son Alex waited a few months before meeting her in person. I don't know why he was more hesitant than my daughter was;

Alani had wanted to meet me right away. It may have been age – Alex was fifteen and Alani was twelve. Perhaps Alex was preoccupied with the concerns of teenage existence, and social expectations of masculinity, more at fifteen than he would have been a few years earlier. He didn't say much regarding his position other than "not yet", and I didn't pressure him. I tried not to place any expectations upon him.

When he finally did meet Meredith, he seemed mostly indifferent to how I looked. The thing that surprised him the most was my voice.

"Ewwww, you sound weird!" He made a face.

I rolled my eyes. "Gee, thanks for that."

"I can't help it… it's so weeeeiiirrrd!" Shrugs.

"Well this is how I talk as Merri. It's been this way for so long, I can't help it either!"

We were at my mother and stepfather's house.[32] I was preparing to go shopping with Alani, who was waiting for me on the couch.

They looked up from the book they were reading and said, "You get used to it."

My mother walked into the room and laughed. She'd first met Meredith a couple years earlier. "Kind of! Merri still sounds funny to me."

I sighed. I know everyone was accepting, but it still stung a little bit.

Later that day, Lisa asked the kids how it went.

Alex: "Her voice is annoying."

Alani: "Merri's or mine?"

Alex: "Hers. Your whole thing is annoying!"

I know that I could develop Meredith's voice further, to make it more convincingly feminine. My male and female voices feel very different to me when I use them, but as it is, if I answer the phone as Meredith, most

---

[32] My mother and stepfather obtained Australian residency and bought a house in order to spend six months of every year living near their only two grandchildren.

people assume that I'm male. Even if they already know about my dual-gender existence, Meredith's voice on its own isn't enough to immediately shift someone's perception: the caller usually addresses me as Derek if they aren't already aware of how I'm presenting.

I do find this situation mildly annoying, but in the grand scheme of things it's not a big deal. Regardless of whether I present as Meredith or as Derek, I am still inherently both inside. No matter how I conceal, reveal, augment, and adorn the various physical parts of my body, I will always feel like I am truly Derek as much as I am truly Meredith. For many trans people, being casually misgendered or misidentified can inflict serious harm, but when it happens to me it's much less harmful than it is philosophically intriguing: the person assessing me is not actually *wrong*: I don't cease to be one gender just because another one is more prominently in view at the moment. In this sense I am extremely lucky, but I also think it is reflective of the confidence I have gained in forging my path and surrounding myself with loving and supportive people. I know who I am, and the important people in my life know who I am.

Chapter Forty-Eight

Emergent

Being Meredith feels completely natural to me now, but in the early days it did feel a bit awkward – kind of like I was inhabiting an unfamiliar, alternate reality. I wanted to be feminine but I had to practise at it somewhat. However, even though I had to consciously think about how I moved and acted, it never felt forced – not even Meredith's voice, which initially required some concentration but still felt comfortably like *me*. I couldn't tell if I was adopting a new demeanour or simply loosening years of socialisation enough to allow my natural inclinations to show through.

I still don't really know. Being Meredith feels different than being Derek but it also feels every bit as genuine. I know that my mannerisms change, my voice changes, even my posture changes – but I can't explain why or how these things went from conscious to automatic. I think that it has simply become part of my natural expression. I find myself occasionally channelling Meredith when I am presenting as Derek, not realising it until after the moment has passed.

Apparently this started happening years ago, long before I came out publicly.

* * *

September 2010

"Oh man, this is heavy." I haul the garment bag out of the wardrobe, awkwardly banging it on the door, and set one end down on the bed. I lay it back and let go of the handle, and it falls flat with a loud *thwump*.

"How many clothes have you got IN there?" Bellie asks, laughing.

I pull the zip around the edge of the long rectangular bag and flip the cover open, revealing a jumbled mess of colours and fabrics. Black lace, red and pink and purple florals, cream and white lace, ribbons and ruffles. All compressed mostly into the end that was at the bottom when the bag was hanging vertically. I would love to be able to store everything nicely separated and easily accessible, but my two young children don't know about Meredith so I keep things hidden. I'm pretty sure the kids wouldn't notice the clothing, or make the connection to me (Lisa and I wear clearly different sizes), but I don't want to take the chance.

"I seem to be building a bit of a collection." Discovering Meredith inside me has led to the discovery of my love for pretty clothes. "I don't even know how, since I really only go out shopping on my trips to see you. I'm probably buying more things online than I realise."

Bellie is visiting from Adelaide for the weekend, and I'm showing her all the things in my wardrobe as I try to decide what to wear the following day. I'm Derek at the moment because I can't be Meredith with my family in the house, even after they've all gone to bed.

I hold up an ivory satin skirt with a print of delicate purple flowers on it. "Remember this? I should find a top to go with it. And maybe some purple shoes." I suddenly remember a shop window I walked past a week ago. "Oh, I saw the most beautiful purple satin heels last week! They had cute little bows on them. They were two hundred bucks though."

Bellie looks at me with a slightly puzzled, amused expression on her face.

"What?" I ask.

"Your voice. You just sounded like Merri."

"Really?"

"Yeah. I think talking about clothes and shoes is making you girly." She laughs.

I guess I shouldn't be surprised, but I think this is really cool. "That's hilarious. Are you sure?"

"Definitely."

I'm not sure what to do with this information. I decide to treat it as an affirmation.

* * *

April 2018

It's been four months since I came out publicly. I'm in the back room of my mother and stepfather's house, getting ready to go out for the day. I'm fortunate that my parents have made their place available; it's convenient and I'll never have to impose on my friends or change in the car again.

I'm in my underwear, and I've just finished donning my bra and inserting my breast forms. I have no make-up on yet and I'm still wearing Derek's glasses.

My mother calls out through the closed door. "Where are you going to meet your friend? Are you going to go past the Asian supermarket? I need some more dried mushrooms for dinner tomorrow."

I start to answer, and a strange sound comes out. I stop before the first word is finished. I don't know if I'm a boy or a girl right now.

I have to concentrate.

"Um. Hang on." I use Derek's voice, but it's awkward and feels wrong.

I relax into being Meredith. "Just a minute." My female voice is still a little bit forced, but it feels more appropriate if I've got my boobs on. I hurriedly pull my top and skirt on, and open the door. My mother isn't in the hallway anymore; she's gone to do something else instead of wait for me.

The clothes complete my internal transformation. It doesn't matter if my face still looks like Derek; it feels normal to use Meredith's voice now. I call out. "I didn't know which voice to use! Isn't that hilarious?"

My mother emerges from the laundry room, holding a basket of sheets and towels. She smiles. "It's fascinating. I have no idea how you manage all this."

"Neither do I, really. Anyway. We're going op shopping, so we're probably gonna drive all over the place. I can make a point of getting dried mushrooms if you want."

"Yes please. I need them tonight so I can soak them. It saves me having to go out this afternoon. Back up, let me see your outfit."

I step back and smooth out my skirt.

"That looks nice. Are you going to wear high heels with that short skirt?" She's trying not to purse her lips, I can tell.

I raise an eyebrow and try not to roll my eyes. "Maybe!"

Chapter Forty-Nine

Conspicuous

Sometime in 1998

"That guy just totally checked you out." John says offhandedly, as we weave around two more people coming the other way.

"What?" I chuckle nervously. I can't tell if he's joking or not. My attention is focused on watching where I step, and not at the faces of other people. It's an effort to keep up – John's pace is quite brisk and we're walking through a busy shopping strip. I don't want to be the person causing a traffic jam on the footpath.

"I just saw that guy look you up and down." John states this as if it's old news being repeated.

Well of course he did, I think. I'm awkward and funny looking. That's why I don't like to draw attention to myself. I'm nearly thirty years old, but I've never really felt at home in my body. At some point over the previous decade I went from 'boy' to 'man' without ever coming to terms with my scrawny Asian physique. This may have something to do with the fact that

I managed to get through seven years of University and living in four different countries without ever getting a girlfriend, or even going on any real dates.

I shrug. "He probably thought I looked weird," I say. Not as weird as the guy with purple hair sitting at the café we just passed. This is Fitzroy, an inner-Melbourne community filled with all manner of hipsters, self-identified queers, and arty-farty bohemian types. A world away from the upper-middle-class conformity of the Silicon Valley suburbs where I grew up. My own weirdness sticks out here as being self-consciously uninteresting. Dorky. Naïve. Inexperienced.

"Oh no darling." John's voice bears a conspiratorial edge, his pronouncement delivered with the authority of a gay man who's been around the block a few times. "I know when someone is perving. He was checking you out and he liked what he saw." John's eyes twinkle as he smiles.

I don't believe it. "Nobody ever looks at me like that," I say flatly.

"How do you know?"

You know when you have to stop and re-evaluate a whole bunch of things you once took for granted? If this was a movie, there would be a montage of flashbacks here. Moments in time marked by embarrassment, shame, awkwardness, or simply a keen sense of enduring unwanted scrutiny.

When I see photos of myself as a child, I see a dorky nerd who looks very uncomfortable having his appearance be the focus of attention. Skinny with big ears, big nostrils, thick glasses, and a decidedly home-grown haircut.

As I grew into my teens and twenties, the haircut got better, but the feeling of self-conscious dorkiness never really went away. My habitual non-effort regarding my appearance was really an attempt to blend in, to be boring, unremarkable, overlooked — so that nobody would notice, and remind me, just how awkward I really was. I did put some effort into my hair, but only because I kept it short and I didn't want it to stick out unevenly. The effort was purely so I wouldn't attract undue attention (I would later come to understand that I took my male privilege for granted here; this strategy of being inconspicuous is not nearly as effective for girls and women).

At nearly thirty years old, the idea that somebody would find me attractive and desirable was still a completely foreign concept to me, as unexpected and incomprehensible as actual snow at Christmastime in Australia – it's just not something that ever happens.

I wasn't filled with self-loathing or shame, at least not consciously. I had faith in my intelligence, my skills, and my ability to navigate life on my own. But when it came to my appearance, and my physicality, I had internalised the idea that it was easier to be invisible than risk being found inadequate – I wanted to avoid getting teased or ridiculed, regardless of what I actually believed about myself. I lamented the fact that I was awkward and geeky, but my negative thoughts were mostly aimed outward at the social pressure so ingrained in the culture around me.

That moment, walking down Brunswick Street with my friend John, was the first time I ever realised that my physical presence was not something to be treated as an afterthought, as a side-effect of knowing me and interacting with me. It was the first time I ever considered my physical body as something people might actually *want*.

It wasn't a dramatic epiphany that changed my entire world overnight; I didn't suddenly decide that I was no longer awkward and that strangers should covet my skinny body. But that moment planted the seed of an idea, the beginning of an awareness that would grow in time. Growth that was helped in no small part by Meredith's eventual emergence and the positive reception she got from the world. Realising that other people consistently found me attractive slowly built up my confidence in my presentation, not just as Meredith, but also as Derek.

There are other factors of course. Finding a girlfriend (and eventual wife) who liked the way I looked certainly contributed to my awakening. When our first child was born, I embraced fatherhood wholeheartedly, which to me includes the acceptance that anything I do to avoid attention will be easily (and automatically) defeated by my offspring. In return, I have countered that with the willingness to be ridiculous whenever I want to embarrass my offspring in public. There is a little bit of truth in the joke that once you become a parent you may as well forget about your dignity. To their credit, my children were quick to embrace me as Meredith and have never been ashamed to be seen with me in public – if I want to embarrass them, I have to do it using my behaviour, not my appearance.

There is also the element of age, and the accompanying insight and wisdom that comes if you're paying enough attention as you experience life. Over the years I have realised that energy spent worrying about whether others think I'm awkward is energy I could spend on something more useful and rewarding. Like embracing, and nurturing, the things that make me uniquely myself. Things that a lot of other people, incidentally, seem to find beautiful.

* * *

Today, Last Week, Ten Years Ago

I look in the mirror on my bedroom door and wish that I had hips. This never changes. I can wear prosthetic breasts that I am happy with, but the one time I tried wearing padding on my hips and my bum I found it impractical and not worth the discomfort of the restrictive, heavy extra layer.

I also see my wide shoulders and the muscles in my upper arms. I've never worked out or attempted to enhance my physique, but I can't help seeing the shape of my upper body as so very *male*. Without some width below my waist to balance it out, I have no hope of achieving the classic hourglass figure that I find feminine and desirable.

If things were reversed – if my body was curvy and I had narrow shoulders – would I feel dissatisfied at how I looked as Derek?

I don't know. I'd love to have the opportunity to find out. But I don't want to take hormones or have surgery. I don't think the effort and expense would be worth it, even if I could convince a doctor (and Lisa) that I needed those things.

When I started attending Seahorse meetings in 2006, I learned to take notice of what other trans women wore that I thought looked good – and not so good. There seemed to be an unusual penchant for stretchy, tight skirts, which served only to make wide shoulders and chests look excessively top-heavy. I realised that this was why I'd never been quite satisfied with the way I looked in some of the things I bought when I first started wearing women's clothes – those outfits were designed for people with hips wider than their waists.

I began wearing A-line skirts and tailored dresses that held their shape on my body. As much as it would be nice to swan around in a fluid, flowing, elegantly sensuous number, I just don't have the curves for it. I would simply look (and feel) like a lamppost wrapped in satin.

I also learned how to use Lisa's old sewing machine. The ability to alter garments to suit my body turned out to be one of the most useful skills I ever learned. Because of my wide shoulders, if something fits me on top it will usually be too loose and baggy below my chest; taking in the sides of a top is usually a simple task and does wonders for my figure, especially when paired with a full skirt.

With practice, I moved beyond shirts and tops, becoming more ambitious, tackling skirt waistbands and hemlines and even a fully lined blazer jacket. Being able to alter my garments meant I had many more options to choose from when searching for clothes – and this turned out to be perfectly suited for the new hobby I discovered: op shopping.

I would recommend to anybody experimenting with their personal style to start at the op shops ("op" is short for "opportunity", and "opping" is the Australian term for "thrifting"). Op shops, at least in Australia, are not just a last-resort dumping ground for old and tired items. You're just as likely to find a lightly-used $200 dress as you are to find someone's old scruffy T-shirt. And if you want to try a new style you can do so without risking half your paycheck on something you'll never wear again – if you donate it back after you decide it's not for you, you've basically rented it, probably for less than the cost of lunch.

Once I discovered the joy of op shopping, my wardrobe grew well beyond what I actually needed for Meredith going out only two or three times a month. I stored many of my new acquisitions next to the sewing machine, and the pile seemed to grow by three or four items for every one that I managed to finish altering.[33]

With a selection of stylish outfits, I earned a reputation at Seahorse for being one of the best dressed members. It was an unfamiliar feeling at first, because I'd grown up so accustomed to thinking of myself as awkward and funny looking. Lessons learned in childhood are hard to escape. I'd spent much of my life trying not to attract undue attention for fear of ridicule, and it was a significant mental shift to accept positive comments and sit with the resulting feelings.

* * *

May 2011

These are pretty fancy restrooms, even for a nice department store in the centre of Adelaide. Maybe it's a women's toilets thing; I've been in the men's room at David Jones in Melbourne and they weren't anywhere this

---

[33] To this day, I have never reached the bottom of the pile.

posh. It's comfortable here. The soft décor and warm, muted lighting are helping to soothe a few of my anxious thoughts.

I look in the mirror and wince slightly. I can't help but focus on my prominent Adam's apple. My face is androgynous enough that I can make it pretty using make-up, and I've learned to use my clothing to visually narrow my shoulders and widen my hips. My boobs look pretty damn great, too. But I can't do anything to hide the sharp lump sticking out at the front of my neck. To me, it's an obvious marker, betraying the nature of my male body. I've learned to live with it – minimising it would mean undergoing a medical procedure involving sharp instruments. The idea of being cut into for any reasons besides treating illness or repairing damage makes me squirm. I don't even have pierced ears.

Bellie and I have been out wandering the markets and the shops in the city. Throughout the morning, I haven't noticed many people looking at me closely, or if they have, they haven't stared long enough to make me uncomfortable. I've also been trying not to pay too much attention to others; this is my now-annual trip to Adelaide where I'm not restricted in my movements (it will be years yet before I am able to move freely about in Melbourne). I'm thankful that I have a best friend to share this experience with. Bellie understands how much it means to me to be Meredith out in public..

I'm not trying to fool anyone – I want people to treat me as a woman, but I'm not ashamed of the fact that I am transgender. I guess I just don't want my Adam's apple to make people second-guess my presentation and let it colour the way they interact with me. It's been heartening to find out that most people either don't even notice, or they are open-minded enough for it not to matter.

I finish washing my hands and step over to the hand dryer. There is a full-length mirror at the end of the row of sinks and in the reflection I see Bellie waiting in one of the armchairs at the other end of the room.

"Hey, let's take a selfie in the mirror." I pull out my phone.

Conspicuous

Bellie gets up and comes over, shaking out her skirt. Another woman enters, sees us posing in front of the mirror, and gives us the once over before she heads into a stall. I can't tell if she was looking at me specifically or not. Being a transgender woman in a public restroom is not an experience I take for granted.

But I have decided that I belong here, that I am entitled to this space, and that I will not let anxiety shape how I carry myself. We take our photo, then a few more, making funny faces and posing this way and that. I look around at the softly furnished waiting area, with its little table lamps and make-up nooks. I walk over to one of the little desks and sit down to touch up my lipstick. As I finish, I hear the hand dryer and look up to see the woman from earlier. She glances over at me as she leaves, and I give her a smile.

* * *

October 2018

Many years ago, I thought I was invisible. Over time, as a result of me proudly embracing who I am, I have learned to be comfortable being seen. Conspicuous to the point where my visibility and reputation actually precedes me.

"Excuse me, are you in an op shop group on Facebook?" The woman looks a little embarrassed as she approaches me.

I smile brightly as I take a skirt off the rack to have a closer look at it. This never gets old. "Yes I am," I say. I know what comes next.

My enquirer relaxes a little. "You're Meredith! I love your photos. Your outfits and your poses are so beautiful! I am your biggest fan!"

Based on the comments I get in the "I Love To Op Shop" group, I actually have more than a few biggest fans, which amuses me a lot. "Aw, thank you!" I nod appreciatively. This is the fourth or fifth time that I have been recognised in person from my posts online. My younger self would be shocked to know that I am putting myself out there in a group with a hundred thousand members.[34]

I hold the skirt up against my waist. It's my size. I look at the tag. Eighteen dollars is a bit pricey for an op shop – however, it's an expensive brand and it would have retailed for more than ten times as much when new. It's really well made and I like the colour. And it's in really good condition. "What do you think?", I ask.

The woman nods approvingly. "I love it. It's totally your style. I wish I could still wear things like that."

"Oh all right. If I must." I laugh, hooking the skirt hanger over the strap of my handbag. I think to myself: she *could* still wear things like this if she wanted to; it just comes down to what she's comfortable with. With fashion, the *way* you wear something – not just arranging and accessorising, but your confidence, your attitude and comportment – can be just as important as *what* you wear. However, that's a complicated conversation to have with a stranger you've only just met. "What's your name?"

"Penny."

"Nice to meet you Penny." I smile again. "Thanks for saying hello."

Penny grins and nods. "You too! I better leave you alone to find more treasures. Happy op shopping!"

* * *

March 2019

"Good morning! You look gorgeous!" Kate looks me up and down, clearly approving of my presentation. The other passengers waiting on the

---

[34] Social media has an often-justified reputation for harbouring toxic behaviour and discourse, particularly in groups with large memberships. But the ILTOS group is an oasis of positive and uplifting content. This is due not only to the attentiveness and principled stance of the admin, but also to the kind and caring nature of its members – thrift shops, after all, exist largely in the domain of charity, which implies some element of generosity about those who participate.

platform glance at us briefly, but they give no indication that they've noticed anything unusual about one woman greeting another.

Yesterday I was here in this same spot, greeting Kate in the morning chill with mostly the same bystanders around, and I was a man.

My usual commute involves catching an early train from a station near the end of the line, meaning that I normally encounter the same cohort of other early morning travellers. We're a small collection of regulars – maybe a couple dozen people at most – and I recognise many of the others by sight: there's the man with the dark green overcoat who walks with a limp, the woman who always wears long floral skirts, the couple who always arrive at the station together with matching takeaway coffees. It's not until later in the morning, or further along the line into the city, that there are enough passengers to make a crowd you can blend into.

The train pulls in and we board in our usual place. I scan the carriage and see a hand waving. Our friends have saved us some seats, as they do every day.

Judith looks delighted at my outfit as I slide past her to my spot by the window. I've set off the red and pink florals of my dress with a vibrant red cardigan, red heels, and a large red bow in my hair.

"Nice colour," says Judith, tilting her head to show me the flower in her own hair. It's the same shade of red. Judith is eccentric and crafty with a quirky style, and I enjoy seeing and hearing about the clothing and artwork she makes.

Phoebe is sitting across from me. Quiet and observant, she seems to be perpetually amused by Judith's presence. She smiles at me as she shifts her bag to make room for Kate, and I think how unremarkable this is: four people, connected only by circumstances of habit, the comfort of familiar faces and a passing interest in each other's lives. Each of us has a story that runs much deeper than what we reveal in the context of a shared morning commute. One of us just happens to live in a story where the cover picture changes dramatically every now and then.

Unremarkable and familiar. A morning routine similar to so many others, notable only because I once thought it would be impossible. Presenting publicly as a woman at all, let alone in an environment lacking the safety of anonymity? I hardly dared to imagine such a life. It still amazes me that I have made it reality. I once nervously ventured out on carefully planned missions under cover of darkness. Now I find myself inhabiting the everyday, my own unusual self being fully visible and identifiable through my difference.

A few weeks later I take a little bit too long in my morning routine – dressing as Meredith takes time and getting out of bed early is difficult – and I miss my usual train. This happens occasionally, and like today, I often find my friend Jeddy on the train that follows. A gentle and softly spoken woman, with a lovely, kind face, Jeddy has a tendency to befriend other travellers who look as if they would appreciate someone to talk to.

"I met a nice man last week who works in the building next to mine. I've seen him on the train a few times but we never really spoke to each other before." She leans toward me a little bit. "He asked about you."

"Oh really?" I know where this is going, and I'm intrigued. And thankful, because I've honestly been hoping for questions and none have been forthcoming. Questions from others will help me gauge the level of acceptance and understanding society has about gender nonconformity – at least, the specific slices of society I regularly encounter – but I've found most people are too afraid to ask.

Jeddy recalls the man's awkward phrasing. "He said, 'I was wondering about your friend I see you with sometimes. The... person who... changes?'"

I laugh. That's one way to put it. "What did you say?"

Jeddy shrugs. "I said that sometimes you are a man and sometimes you are a woman."

"And?"

"He said you were very brave, and that he admired you."

It says something about society when being yourself is considered an act of bravery. And I do wonder sometimes, how often admiration is rooted in envy. Before I felt free enough to be Meredith in public, I would absolutely have admired someone I saw doing the things I do now.

"Isn't it funny how people always use the word *brave?*" I furrow my brow. "It's like there's this expectation that my experience is going to be negative. I actually feel very lucky that I *don't* expect to have trouble. Society has actually made progress."

I look around the train carriage. The other passengers are reading, sleeping, sitting with their eyes closed and headphones on, or talking to each other like me and Jeddy. A young woman looks up from her phone and catches my eye as I turn around. She smiles at me.

I smile back. It's genuine. There is joy and freedom in being Meredith and I am glad that others can see it.

* * *

May 2019

After about a year of showing up to the office as Meredith roughly once a week, I get featured in the company newsletter as a representative of the kind of diversity our workplace strives to foster. It's part of the company's celebration of IDAHOBIT (International Day Against Homophobia, Biphobia, Intersex-phobia, and Transphobia).[35]

It's only a brief article but it's an important milestone, and not just for me. A few days after the newsletter comes out, I receive an email from a colleague I don't know, from one of our offices overseas.

---

[35] I think it's a silly acronym but that's what it is. It's also pronounced "I da hobbit" (not "Idaho bit") which seems even sillier to me. But I don't make the rules. And I am waiting for someone to announce "U da wizard" day.

I think I'm transgender, and you're the first person I've ever told. I've never acted on my feelings because I've always been too scared to try anything. But seeing your article has given me hope that one day it might be possible for me.

I feel incredibly honoured. This person trusts me enough to share their secret, even though they've never met me. I am evidence that they are not alone in their struggle. The power of visibility cannot be overstated.

I reply: *It means a lot to me that you have reached out. I hope that you can find a way to explore and express who you are, safely and with support. It can be a daunting journey but for some of us it is necessary and inevitable. Only you can decide for yourself what your journey should be, but please know that you are definitely not alone.*

I never receive anything further after this (sadly I neglect to follow it up myself), and I can only hope that things have gone well for them.

* * *

January 2020

I'm attending a musical tribute show at the Crown casino, in the fashionable Southbank riverside district of Melbourne. It's not something I would normally consider, but my friend Vicky has free tickets from a social media promotion. The show is called "Legends" and it includes tribute acts for Elvis, Neil Diamond, Diana Ross, and other stars, most of whom had their heydays in the decades before the beginning of the twenty-first century.

The majority of the audience is a fair bit older than middle-aged, and not as visibly diverse as the communities I usually travel in. There are some young people present, but only a smattering; it's far from a hip and trendy crowd. I joke with Vicky about the stereotypical demographic for a show like this – perhaps unfairly, because we aren't exactly hip and trendy ourselves, but we do feel rather out of place.

I've come to the show as Meredith, and it may be my imagination, but I feel like people are staring at me more than usual as we wait in line at the theatre doors. I'm used to the occasional double take or lingering glance, since I often dress in colourful florals or lace, and I do feel that a significant percentage of the general public can read me as transgender if they pay attention. But normally, people don't make a big deal of it and just treat me like any other random stranger.

After the show – which is surprisingly enjoyable – we slowly file out to the lobby, and I once again feel conspicuous. My outfit isn't particularly bright or eye-catching; in fact, apart from a pale denim jacket folded over my arm, I'm dressed in solid dark colours. I still notice a few people casting glances my way, with what seems like curiosity in their eyes. This interpretation is probably influenced by my preconceived expectations about the crowd at this show. But nobody is being rude or indiscreet so I just smile back.

It won't cross my mind until much later that this show featured celebrity impersonators, and I've attended it presenting in a way that, once upon a time, would have been labelled "female impersonator". Perhaps it's a stretch to imagine that this had anything to do with the attention I felt I was receiving. However, it does make me aware of how the idea of "passing", and its implications, has evolved over time.

It's a concept loaded with nuance and complexity: passing, for many transgender people, means being seen as their true gender – the one that matches how they feel – instead of being mistaken for something they are not. Passing can allow trans people to blend in to society, and can be a form of privilege – one which is definitely not distributed equitably by the combined forces of genetics, socio-economic position, and life opportunities.[36]

The archaic term "female impersonator" expresses how society once interpreted the existence of transgender women; the term implies that they were considered performative and possibly insincere. There are still people

---

[36] The standards for passing are inextricably tied to cultural standards of beauty and appearance in general, and increased diversity in these standards will benefit everyone.

today who reject trans identities, and who view passing as a form of deception. For a trans person presenting authentically in a hostile environment, the anxiety can be overwhelming and debilitating: failure to pass convincingly can bring unwanted attention and mark you as immediately worthy of suspicion, yet passing completely does not bring with it any guarantee of safety – it still requires constant vigilance, lest unanticipated circumstances render you suddenly exposed with unpleasant and severe consequences.

None of this is occupying my thoughts as Vicky and I thread our way through the groups of people milling about in the lobby after the show. I have been fortunate in my circumstances, able to explore my gender while living in a large, socially progressive city, and lucky enough to mostly fit into cultural standards of feminine appearance. I've been presenting as Meredith for years with only the occasional curious stare indicating that someone might notice something different about me. Over time, I have become comfortable in my own skin, and clothing, regardless of how I choose to dress or how I am received.

The performers are all gathered at the side of the room for photos with audience members, and we decide it will be fun to get one for ourselves. I'm heading towards the line of people waiting when someone stops me.

"Excuse me."

There's a nervously energetic person in front of me. They look young, about twenty, and female, although I'm not completely sure and I don't want to make assumptions.

This is not the first time I've been randomly approached in public. It seems to happen fairly regularly, as a consequence of my visibility in certain circles online. I fully expect this person to ask me, "Are you in an op shop group on Facebook?"

Instead they look at me earnestly and say, "I noticed you might be trans and if you are I wanted to say congratulations!"

I am speechless.

Before I can think of something to respond with, they continue.

"I'm LGBTI as well, and I have a friend who is just coming out and hasn't decided on a name or pronouns yet, and I wanted to say how nice it is to see someone like you!"

I remain speechless for a bit longer.

After years of being Meredith and having very little trouble with public interactions, I'm not unduly concerned about strangers discovering my transgender nature – indeed, I have become accustomed to openly disclosing it whenever it seems relevant. However, until this moment I've never been randomly approached by someone clearly indicating that I'm not passing successfully! Being *congratulated* for it feels very bizarre. Congratulations for what, in essence, is me being myself, following years of struggle and growth. The sentiment is particularly jarring when it's coming from someone less than half my age.

Pointing out that someone "might be trans" could go very badly depending on who is being addressed. Obviously I am unashamed to be transgender, but there are people, both trans and cis alike, who might not welcome the message. A transgender person attempting to pass might be disappointed to find out that they are failing at it. And a cis person with an unfavourable opinion of trans people would consider it an insult to be told they looked like one. Even someone cisgender who holds no conscious bias, but who is insecure about their appearance, might be inadvertently hurt by hearing that they don't meet conventional social standards of presentation – and, presumably, attractiveness.

Ultimately – regardless of the implications or the consequences – it is considered an egregious act to "out" someone in public without their consent.

I briefly consider trying to convey all of this information to my admirer. But a thirty-second interaction of random strangers in a theatre lobby isn't the appropriate situation for such a discussion. I figure that they probably haven't interacted with very many trans people in public – if any at all – so I try to be gracious. I hope that they might learn these lessons in due time, as they bear witness to their transgender friend's experiences. Perhaps, if society progresses enough, some of these lessons won't need learning at all.

"Yes I'm trans, and thank you." I say. "It's an exciting time when you're coming out and deciding all of those things. Tell your friend they're awesome."

They beam like I've just given them a holy blessing as they walk away.

* * *

I know that my worth is not, and should not be, tied to my appearance. But it's hard to ignore the confidence boost I get when someone tells me that I'm beautiful. I am extremely lucky that Meredith is considered attractive, and I try to remain humble while feeling empowered at the same time.

I get perved at a lot now. Far from wanting to disappear into the background, when I am Meredith I choose to dress in outfits that I find eye-catching. Reds and pinks and purples, bright floral patterns, bows and flowers in my hair, skirts and heels that show off my legs. I know this attracts attention; I love being pretty and I no longer want to hide myself like I used to. It sounds shallow but I don't pretend that it's anything but a bonus on top of everything else I am as a human being. And I am well aware of how much privilege I am afforded as a result of my appearance.

Society has always preferred those perceived as beautiful, even as the standards of beauty change over time. The advantages of being beautiful, however, do not come without strings attached – beauty standards are enforced by society in many ways that create and perpetuate overall gender inequality, regardless of attractiveness. And within the ranks of women, the hierarchy of privileged beauty has very real implications for physical and emotional well-being.[37]

For transgender women, this hierarchy is reinforced by the fact that our chances of passing are tied directly to how well we meet those beauty standards. This can lead to uncomfortable situations where identity rights get jealously guarded: someone who has spent an enormous amount of time, effort, and money to achieve a socially appealing presentation may resent sharing the label "transgender woman" with someone masculine-looking who constantly gets questioned and misgendered. This kind of lateral violence within the community is less common than it used to be, but it can still happen when individual insecurity wins out over solidarity.

Feeling pretty makes me happy. I know that I am not obliged to smile for anyone – indeed, I believe society should stop placing such expectations upon women. However, I do want to be seen for who I am, and when I am feeling good about myself, I smile. If my smile makes someone's day a little brighter, I'll happily take that as a bonus.

I am not dismissing the lived experiences of women who grew up with the patriarchal expectation to smile and be pretty for men. It was different for me. Growing up as a boy, I wasn't expected to follow the same standards of behaviour. I also wasn't consciously aware of my male privilege back then.

In many respects the social standards haven't progressed very far. Based on things I see online and conversations I have had recently, women who find themselves sharing space with men can still feel pressure to smile, even if only as a pre-emptive, defensive tactic to smooth their passage through that space. It may not always be expected, and many women

---

[37] Decades and bookshelves full of feminist discourse are available if you want to more fully explore the effects of cultural beauty standards and read other writers' thoughts about them. This is just my memoir so I am only writing about how they affect my own experiences.

choose refusal, but the absence of a smile can still be an unfavourable if not downright risky choice.

Having gained a bit of insight into these dynamics, I have discovered that things are different again for me now: as Meredith I am much more inclined to smile and engage with *women* than I am with men. Being a transgender woman, I am keenly aware that the biggest threat to my safety is transphobic men who think that I am somehow trying to trick them into desiring me. Because of this, as Meredith it feels more risky to smile at a man I don't know than it does to act indifferent towards him.

When I am Meredith I do find that women smile at me more than men do, regardless of whether I smile at them first. Perhaps this is simply because women have been taught to smile at everyone. If this is true, then I hope at least to make it genuinely worth their effort. I don't think there is anything wrong with spreading a little bit of happiness, however fleeting or insignificant. And I'm not expecting anyone, myself included, to smile if they're not feeling so inclined. Nobody hates being told to smile more than someone in a bad mood!

Simply being seen and accepted as Meredith makes me happy – even though I know that this social acceptance, and feeling of liberation, is a result of my adherence to the very same cultural beauty standards I find problematic. But when I'm feeling joyous and free, I'm not going to discourage myself from smiling just because I want to dismantle the patriarchy. My freedom lies in rejecting the idea that being born and raised male means I can't indulge in overtly feminine things. I don't care if I earn a place on some feminist-traitor list somewhere just because I express my happiness when I wear make-up and pretty dresses – not to mention the fact that I enjoy being a literal living doll.

I like pretty things. I have always liked pretty things, even when I only felt safe appreciating them in secret. Now, I am unashamed to openly celebrate pretty things – including myself. I don't pretend that there is any deeper significance here. I am a woman who likes to feel pretty, and ultimately, I will make myself pretty regardless of whether anyone is watching.

* * *

Back to the mirror in my room. I'm wearing a purple lace top and a black A-line miniskirt with a provocative split up one thigh. My legs – my best feature, the cause of many an admiring comment – catch the light in their sensuous, glimmery pantyhose. Standing confidently in my four-inch heels, I strike a suggestive pose. My carefully made-up face appears reasonably feminine when framed by my long hair. I throw myself a mischievous smile and covet my reflection. I feel no shame in believing: *I am fucking sexy*.

Before Meredith emerged I never would have imagined a moment like this. Being raised as a boy meant that the body standards I was judged against were about size and strength – attributes I did not possess in remarkable quantities. I tried to cope by deciding that these standards didn't really matter to my value as a person, but I still ended up feeling scrawny and awkward. The best I could do was view my body as an arbitrary vessel for my existence; I certainly never thought to treat it as something worth *celebrating*. Even after meeting Lisa, it was difficult to reconcile the knowledge that she found me attractive with the physically unflattering self perception I had held for so long.

Accepting my own physical desirability as a man has required me to unlearn my personal feelings of inadequate masculinity. It turns out that being accepted as a woman has been helpful here: somehow, the freedom to be female and beautiful has removed whatever hangups I previously had about being seen as acceptably male. I no longer care that I am skinny or physically weaker than someone who regularly works out; the pressure to prove such things about my masculinity has completely vanished. I'm not exactly sure why or how this happened. I'm much more confident as Derek than I used to be, and I believe my positive experiences as Meredith have been a big factor. My best guess is that the effects of the compliments I receive as Meredith have diffused across gender boundaries inside me, and have settled onto some internal core beneath Derek and Meredith alike.

It's possible that people call Derek "handsome" no more frequently today than in the past. But receiving such a compliment used to feel *weird*. It felt like people were being polite because it was expected of them. Being told I was handsome was like being handed a coat that clearly wasn't going to fit me, and being asked to wear it anyway to avoid offending anyone.

Nowadays, if someone tells me I'm handsome, I am able to believe they actually mean it. I still consider myself skinny (and occasionally awkward, sometimes on purpose), but I don't connect my masculinity to how big my muscles are. My body does its job pretty well; I no longer think I'm funny looking. I reckon Derek looks pretty good, and I know that Meredith can be a knockout when she tries.

I also know that if I moved through society and *never* heard that I was handsome or beautiful, but instead only heard negative things, then my insights, self-image, and approach to the world might be very, very different.

I didn't set out on this journey with any goal other than my own peace and happiness. Along the way, I have learned that being visibly transgender and unapologetic about my appearance makes me powerful. So I figure if I'm going to exist, I might as well be conspicuous.

Chapter Fifty
Trans Enough

I am living a life where I am free to be male or female whenever I want, yet I still struggle with self-doubt. Not often, but it's definitely there, and I may never be entirely free of it. Some people might argue that I am simply a man who is appropriating womanhood when I feel like it.

Nowhere do I feel this more keenly than when I am in explicitly feminist spaces, especially when there are no other transgender people present. When people see Derek, they see an ostensibly cisgender heterosexual male. Middle aged and middle class; the only missing piece of privilege is the fact that I am not white (although, if examined, my cultural biases would reveal themselves to be mostly white; I grew up Chinese-American in an environment where Asians collectively assimilated enough to be labelled a "model minority").

So when I present as Meredith, I can't be sure if people really accept me as a woman – particularly if they also know about Derek. Meredith appears very feminine, and this probably informs their behaviour towards me; we make assumptions all the time about people based on how they present to us. But in reality, nobody knows how anyone else actually feels inside. Who are they to tell me what I should feel as a woman – or for that matter, as a man?

I think that the argument is irrelevant: self-expression is not a zero-sum game. Gender is infinite in possibility and I am simply occupying two small points that I have become comfortable with. I don't entertain anybody's prescriptive definitions of "male" and "female". The rules of society regarding gender are constantly being negotiated, at both an individual and collective scale, in many cultural contexts.

Identity is personal. Calling myself transgender does not diminish or alter the lived experience of another transgender person, and their identity does not affect my own. Calling myself a woman does not diminish or alter the womanhood of other women. These things are true regardless of whether our identities are straightforward, or complex and nuanced: I cannot control another person's sense of self. I am not ignoring or disregarding the struggles and oppression faced by women today and throughout history, nor am I jumping on a bandwagon or attempting to displace anyone. I am adding my own contribution, standing beside other women in solidarity.

It's a strange place to be, facing potential flak both for being transgender as Meredith and also for being "not trans enough" due to not rejecting Derek. I could point this out to anyone who accuses me of appropriating womanhood without forfeiting male privilege: there are potentially negative aspects that come with my position. There is the always-present threat of transphobia, of course, as well as the pervasive sexism and misogyny so ingrained in our culture. And perversely, there are people who claim that trans women are "faking it" to gain some kind of advantage in society. Add to these things, for me, the possibility of being perceived as *actually* faking it (because Derek still exists), and of being seen – however inaccurately – as a hostile or unwelcome male in a female space.

I have been lucky in such social situations so far, although I do occasionally feel a bit like I am trespassing, in spite of my dual identity being accepted largely without question. Until I am familiar enough with the others present to fully relax, there is always a tiny sense of uneasiness in the back of my mind, waiting for the resentment and accusation of "but you're not completely female" to be levelled at me. Fortunately, this hasn't happened. Most of my group interactions are in casual circumstances, such as a girls' night out, but I have been accepted even when attending the women's group at my workplace on a day when I am presenting as Derek.

In nearly twenty years of being Meredith, I have had only two memorably negative experiences regarding my identity and presentation. Most people simply seem to accept that I am who I say I am, and treat me accordingly. While there may be plenty of mainstream institutions and systems still hostile to transgender people, I have found that on an individual level people are generally benign (I am aware that Meredith is considered attractive in a conventionally feminine way, and acknowledge that this helps a lot with my social interactions).

I would even suggest that, apart from an extremely vocal minority of activists, usually referred to as TERFs (Transgender-Exclusionary Radical Feminists)[38], cisgender people tend not to scrutinise trans identities anywhere near as much as transgender people do to ourselves. There is a period when a transgender person first emerges during which they can be hyper-sensitive to any kind of attention that calls their gender into question (this period can vary significantly in duration across individuals; for some it doesn't happen, and for some it never ends). Constantly checking and second-guessing themselves, a person in this state may perceive someone

---

[38] Specifically in feminist circles, TERFs pose a significant threat to the acceptance of transgender people, trans women in particular. In recent years, public discourse has seen TERFs aligning themselves with right-wing authoritarians and fascists – people who are traditionally opposed to the ideas of feminism. This just shows how hypocritical bigotry can be.

else "doing transgender differently" as a challenge, or even as an invalidation of their own identity. This can result in active avoidance, or even hostility, wasting energy that could be better spent working towards understanding and towards a wider acceptance of diversity.

Whether it comes from a transgender or cisgender person, this kind of dynamic reinforces my belief that people who object to how others identify are themselves quite insecure in their own identities. They are always vigilantly guarding against anything that might cast doubt on their own convictions, whether or not they actually stop to examine or recognise those convictions as a work in progress.

Understand that I am not judging anybody here – the reasons for this kind of insecurity can be insidious, pervasive, and traumatic. Recognising and rectifying problematic beliefs and behaviour is difficult and confronting work. I am as susceptible as the next person to the desire for an easy way out, and I have made choices of my own that I'm not proud of.

* * *

The first time I attended Seahorse, the experience was surreal. It was 2006, and there was still very little awareness or representation of transgender people in mainstream society.

The meeting was held in a community function room in a local council building, after normal closing time. The atmosphere reminded me of the classrooms from my 1980s childhood – cold fluorescent lights, laminated tables and beige everywhere. I sat at a table with a few others but nobody spoke much. I felt nervous and lonely, in a room full of strangers from diverse realities far outside anything I'd ever experienced. The only thing uniting us was that we were all wearing women's clothes.

I looked down at my drink in front of me and listened to the room. I heard deep, resonant voices. Sometimes rough and gravelly. There was a disconnect upon looking up and seeing long hair, floral dresses and high heels. But then, looking closer, I could see large hands, five-o-clock shadows under heavy make-up, slouching in chairs with legs spread.

Later, when I went to use the women's room (Seahorse was the only organisation present during the evening; there were no issues with restrooms), I noticed an interesting phenomenon that led me to create the following joke:

Q: How do you know that you're at a crossdressers' convention?
A: You go to the women's room and the toilet seat has been left up.

I do have to concede, after many years of Seahorse meetings, that this hasn't happened to me again. I don't tell this joke anymore; I include it here not just because it's indicative of how I felt and thought at the time, but also because it illustrates the cultural ideas we have about gender. Furthermore, it demonstrates the importance of language: the terms "crossdresser" and "transgender" have distinctly different meanings, but the nuances of each may vary depending upon whom you ask.[39]

I kept going to Seahorse (and still do to this day), but the feeling I didn't quite belong persisted for a long time. This was supposed to be my tribe, but the truth is: *I didn't feel much desire to want to get to know anyone there.* I continued attending because it was the only space where I could be female without imposing on my friends and asking to use their homes. It took me a while to become comfortable enough to move beyond small talk and start engaging the other Seahorse members in actual friendship-building conversations.

When I began heading out to Monroe's with some of the others after the meetings, I wasn't just nervous at being Meredith out in public. I'm ashamed to admit it, but I felt uneasy being seen with transgender women who didn't "pass". I didn't want to attract the wrong kind of attention from

---

[39] At a simplistic level, one is about clothing and one is about identity. It's not always so simple, though: the assumptions, nuances, and various forms of baggage that accompany much of the language around gender are involving enough to warrant an entire doctorate thesis. And they are constantly changing.

the rest of society: curiosity, scorn, pity. *Look at these men in dresses and make-up.* I'm not proud of this. Internalised transphobia – the inability to fully accept and appreciate one's transgender self, often resulting in shame and regrettable actions towards others – is very real and very difficult to overcome.

I don't think I was ever actually ashamed of wanting to be female. My anxiety stemmed from knowing that society treated what I was doing as a joke. Even though I thought I looked pretty good as a woman, I simply wasn't secure enough in myself to overcome the fear of ridicule, and I didn't want the world reminding me that it thought I should be ashamed of myself.

I wanted the affirmation of being seen as female without the complications that came with the discovery that I was an impostor, or pretending, or any one of a dozen words de-legitimising what I was doing. I existed in the uneasy space between being noticed for my attractiveness and being noticed for my deviance.

* * *

Rather than welcoming new perspectives, some people jealously guard their identity, and their own definition of it, because they perceive it to be under threat and not secure enough to persist without constant, active defence. Unfortunately sometimes these people go on the offensive, which means that we end up in a culture war over "identity politics" which has ramifications not just for people's emotional and psychological well-being, but also for very real, practical societal resource allocation. Suddenly, it's not a zero-sum game anymore – it's more like a *negative*-sum game: allowing people freedom of identity and self-expression takes nothing away from anyone, but *denying* them the same will absolutely cause tangible hardship. And it does. Transgender people are one of the most marginalised groups in society.

Yet the arguments, which repeat themselves across all styles of bigotry, are so easily countered:

- "But you don't have a uterus, you can't call yourself a woman." (So your sister, who had a hysterectomy, isn't allowed to call herself a woman anymore either? Also, do you really want to align yourself with people who reduce women to their reproductive parts?)

- "You're just a man wearing a dress to sneak into the ladies' room and molest women!" (This ludicrous argument refuses to go away, in spite of many years of exactly zero evidence to support it. If a man wants to assault a woman, he's not going to put on a dress first and risk getting assaulted himself. He's just going to barge into her space and assault her with impunity; there's plenty of evidence that this actually happens. Trans women use the women's bathroom because we're women who need to use the bathroom. Using the men's room would cause dysphoria, and risk us being physically assaulted by transphobic men.)

- "Trans people are erasing me! This medical form says *birthing parent*. I'm not allowed to call myself a *mother* anymore!" (*Birthing parent* means anyone giving birth – including mothers. People can always call *themselves* what they choose, but assuming things about others can be harmful. There are pregnant trans men and non-binary people who have to navigate the medical system, who must constantly deal with incorrect assumptions on a scale that would be exhausting.)

- "If people are allowed to change their gender, then how can I trust anyone?" (A great deal of our society is built upon trusting people to be who they say they are, and other qualities besides gender are usually much more relevant. Focusing on gender alone demonstrates this to be a disingenuous argument. Gender might be an important concern when dating, but the people most at risk of harm in that context are trans people, not their mistrustful potential partners.)

Sadly, these opinions persist and get recycled by conservative pundits over and over. Other writers have analysed and debunked these arguments more effectively and thoroughly than I can – this is a memoir, not a polemic. I include them here because they represent the kind of attitude that transgender people are always alert to encountering, consciously on the lookout for potential danger. The anxiety this creates can be exhausting, and is something that many cisgender people might not consider in their interactions with trans people.

Because I do not hide my dual-gender nature, I run the additional risk of being seen and used as evidence for the "not really transgender" argument, coming from cis and trans people alike. I could be accused of somehow betraying the cause, regardless of how authentically I live in my dual identity. The simple fact that my existence *can* be misappropriated by those who wish to oppose trans rights is enough to make me nervous about how other trans people receive me.

Luckily, I have encountered this attitude in only one person – if there have been others judging me as "not trans enough", they have not confronted me. The incident still affected me deeply, though – perhaps because it was so unique in its hostility. The memory serves to remind me why I believe we must be generous in our appreciation for the stories and struggles of other people.

The other party in this interaction is Eleanor (not her real name of course) – someone with whom I share connections, and periodically cross paths with as a result, but with whom I don't interact very much. At the time of this exchange she had recently come out publicly as a transgender woman. I don't know what kind of community support she had sought out, if any, but I offered my own, in spite of the fact that we had previously found ourselves at odds regarding what I felt to be important social and humanitarian issues.

Trans Enough

Eleanor was navigating a situation with parallels to my own – she had a partner and children – and had known for many years about my existence as Meredith and Derek. Because she was not overly receptive to my offer of support, I had been observing her journey mostly through comments and gossip I overheard from third parties, and through the occasional encounter when we crossed paths in person.

Prior to this exchange, Eleanor and I both attended an unrelated social event (not transgender-focused). I presented as Derek that day and briefly interacted with Eleanor through a group conversation with others. We did not discuss anything personal; the subject of Harry Potter came up, and I assertively voiced my displeasure about J. K. Rowling and her increasingly public TERF opinions.[40]

I didn't think any more about the conversation after that day. In the circles I frequent, J. K. Rowling is viewed as an annoying, ongoing threat that periodically surfaces to make noise and waste our energy and time in having to explain to onlookers why her transphobia is harmful. Revisiting her bigotry is tiresome, and a single conversation about her is hardly ever going to stand out in my memory.

A few days later, Eleanor started a conversation with me over instant messenger:

> [Eleanor] I get that you are stuck in your world but you seem happy to be where you are. If you ever need to talk I am here. I don't judge others but I feel freedom of speech is important and everyone can have an opinion whether right or wrong. I feel some negativity and toxic views from you that I personally do not like. Because I do not like your actions does not mean I don't like you. Don't take it personally.

---

[40] Rowling's transphobic opinions are apparently not considered problematic enough by many to stop them purchasing Harry Potter stuff and sending her the royalties.* For many people, personal entertainment is more important than the safety and well-being of people they don't know (and sometimes do know), even when you can draw a direct line connecting the two.

* Rowling is on record gloating about how the royalty cheques make it easy for her to ignore the fans she's losing. Obviously she's not losing a significant number.

To me, this came completely out of the blue. I had no idea what she was on about.

> [Meredith] ?????
>
> [Meredith] I've been supportive of you. I have never intended to be negative about anything regarding your journey. What did I do that you don't like?
>
> [Eleanor] It is when you get angry about TERFs etc. I saw the anger in you the other day. I didn't like what I saw.

She was having a go at me over J. K. Rowling? Seriously?

> [Meredith] I happen to have a problem with people who have a problem with other people's identities. JKR has made it clear where she stands.
>
> [Eleanor] I like that people have opinions and I don't feel angry. Why get angry?
>
> [Meredith] Because she, and others like her, do actual harm.
>
> [Eleanor] Well I'm transgender and it didn't harm me.
>
> [Meredith] You are one person.
>
> [Meredith] It didn't harm me either.
>
> [Eleanor] You speak for everyone?
>
> [Eleanor] You too are only one person you made that clear.

Oh nice. She was trying to school me in empathy now, immediately after her previous comment?

> [Meredith] I do not speak for everyone, but I am going to call out hate when I see it.
>
> [Meredith] If you don't like seeing or reading my activism, feel free to ignore it.
>
> [Eleanor] It's militant and harmful.

[Meredith] I'm low key. You don't know militant.

[Eleanor] Makes it harder for everyone in my humble opinion.

[Meredith] There's a thing called the paradox of (in)tolerance.

[Meredith] You can't just "let everyone have their opinion" when one of those opinions seeks to do away with everyone else.

[Eleanor] Well we are very different people and you are gender fluid apparently and I'm transitioning to be transgender.

[Meredith] I never said we were similar. You're the one who keeps reiterating that we are different.

[Eleanor] I'm transgender you are more non binary to me.

[Eleanor] So no we are not going to agree.

I guess nobody had told her that it's rude to decide someone else's labels for them.

[Meredith] I am dual-gender, if you must put a label on it.

[Eleanor] How can you be both with testosterone? It makes you angry.

[Meredith] The fact that you don't agree with me has nothing to do with your gender or mine.

[Eleanor] Like you can't get angry all the time how is that being a good human?

I couldn't even begin to unpack this argument, so I just shook my head.

[Meredith] You think I'm angry all the time?

[Meredith] You don't know me at all.

[Eleanor] You dress up just for attention.

WHOA. Did she just say that?

[Meredith] WTF?

[Eleanor] That is my thoughts and it pisses me off that you even call yourself transgender to be honest.

There it was. Her real problem with me. Nothing to do with arguing about TERFs or being an activist. I saw no point in continuing to try to be nice.

[Meredith] I knew it.
[Meredith] Well.
[Meredith] Suck it up.
[Meredith] Trans is a big umbrella.
[Eleanor] You are toxic.

She blocked me at this point and my next two messages did not get delivered.

[Meredith] No, my existence makes you insecure in your own identity. It doesn't have to. Just let people be who they are. I do.
[Meredith] If I'm "not trans enough for you" that's 100% your problem.

Yeah, I dress up for attention. And I will fucking flaunt it whenever I please. As is the right of any woman. Of any human being. We can still appreciate and accept the reality of other people's presentations without judging their motives or insisting that the stories behind them make sense to us.

Thankfully, even though I'm wary of the Eleanors out in the community, the majority of people I meet seem to accept the deeply personal nature of identity and self-expression. This probably says something about the progressive environments I find myself in, but I do think society as a whole is becoming increasingly comfortable with diversity.

I am indeed trans enough. Eleanor is trans enough, and denying her own anger will just make her more miserable, not more trans. We can never fully appreciate the internal struggle that another person experiences; we might never understand them. But it doesn't matter. Understanding someone's identity is not a prerequisite for acceptance.

Part Twelve

Chapter Fifty-One

Spotlight

March 2020

The crowd's excitement isn't a surprise, since they've been the same for every model who walked before me. Still, it feels surreal to have more than two hundred people cheering and clapping for me. Just me, alone on the runway. Trying not to trip on the elaborate flowing train of my ballgown as I walk slowly forward, attempting to be graceful. I twirl around, letting the fabric spread and billow sensuously, teasing the air with swirls and flutters. Like the background of a romance novel book cover. I stop, strike a pose, one leg held out between the sides of the thigh-high split in the hem of my dress. The cheers grow louder and fill the cavernous hall. Sexy lace and sparkles and joyous encouragement.

Today we are honouring women. All women. Everyday women. Women who might otherwise be overlooked, silenced, marginalised or hidden – by society, or even by themselves. Any women: cisgender, transgender, disabled or not, migrants and Australian-born alike. Thirty women will step into the spotlight today; each will walk the runway to words and music of her own choosing, wearing whatever outfit she feels comfortable expressing herself in: from a ballgown or ceremonial robes and traditional headdress, to gym workout gear or a t-shirt and jeans. Fashion as a window into each story within. Stories of triumph, of trauma, determination and despair, of hope or heartache still unresolved. All linked together by one common thread: acknowledgement. The need to be seen is universally human, even if it's only for five minutes in an experimental fashion show. Being acknowledged in the moment allows us to imagine a future we have a say in.

We are affirming and authentic, embracing without judgement. Hurt and healing. Fortunate and fated. Raw and polished. Women expressing our humanity side by side. The event is named appropriately: *This is Me*.

I claim the runway proudly and unapologetically, a woman existing on my own terms. It's not exactly a coming out; I stopped hiding Meredith two and a half years ago. But it feels different, testifying in front of a live audience of hundreds of people. It feels like celebration.

A celebration I wish Lisa was here to see. But she has not come today. She remains distant from Meredith, supportive but not interactive. As much as it saddens me, I try not to dwell too much on the situation, preferring instead to focus on the joy of moments like this one I'm having now.

Two hours before stepping onto the runway, I am frozen.

I did this dozens of times at Domicile, but never with the expectation that someone from my "normal" life would see me. Domicile provided an escape from normality: exploring the strange and the unusual was key to the nightclub's attraction. And it was one of those places where, if you did run into someone you already knew, you would both keep quiet about it in front of people who didn't also frequent the same establishment.

This is different. This is a fashion show, and it's the middle of the afternoon. The Grand Ballroom of the Collingwood Town Hall is open, airy and filled with light – far from the muted, shadowy strobes of Domicile's dark underground play space. Today's audience hasn't come in search of secretive shenanigans; they've come to loudly and publicly show their support for the women sharing their stories. Women including myself, in the final act of the show. But before that, until intermission, I have taken this opportunity to be a living mannequin.

There are friends of mine attending today who have no idea that I do this. I feel exposed – which is kind of the point, since I'm deliberately pushing past my boundaries to have this experience. Domicile was safe and familiar, but its closure two years ago left me without an outlet to satisfy my peculiar needs. Until this event came along. And while it scares me a bit, I have always dreamed of posing in a more mainstream, public environment.

When I suggested the idea to the event committee, they were wholeheartedly supportive. Anything to increase interest in this experimental event – as long as it was suitably aligned with the event's underlying philosophy and feminist principles.

Given my own struggle to address the contradictions that my dollhood posed against my politics, I wanted to make sure the committee understood the possible ramifications – even if I didn't delve into the finer points of my doll fantasies. "People might interpret it as objectification," I suggested. "Will the audience think we're giving mixed messages?"

Rani, the event founder, was unconcerned. "I think they'll focus more on the skill of your performance. People love living statues. They'll wonder how you can stay so still."

"Maybe," I answered.

She continued. "Besides, you said it's something you've dreamt about forever, so it's important to you. The whole point of this event is to embrace these things about ourselves."

That was true. I would be publicly embracing my womanhood at this event. Wasn't my dollhood also an important, vital part of that?

When the doors open, I'm already frozen in place, nervously anticipating the arrival of the audience – particularly my friends. I haven't told anyone outside the committee about my posing because I want to witness people's genuine reactions. I wait, standing motionless on a small pedestal, wearing a rainbow dress and pink heels. Imagining my body in rigid plastic. People do double takes as they pass by, entertaining me as much as I do them.

The first person to recognise me is Fiona, who clasps her hands and smiles with delight when she realises it's me. "I don't suppose you can talk to me, can you," she winks as she takes a photo.

I get similar reactions as my other friends discover me. Disbelief and amazement and squeals of laughter as they wave their hands in my face and threaten to tickle me, trying to see just how dedicated I am to my art.

Nobody succeeds in breaking my stillness until Fiona comes past again and unexpectedly makes a goofy face at me as she walks by. Completely taken by surprise I burst out laughing. Sideswiped! Fiona walks off with an air of triumph as I re-freeze, feeling amused and slightly embarrassed.

Mischievous provocation notwithstanding, I'm well practised and have no further trouble staying motionless as the hall fills up and the show gets under way. Another hour on display brings me no closer to understanding what's behind my fascination. As I step down to go backstage and change into my runway dress, a couple of my friends ask me why I do it. I simply say, "It's fun."

It's more than that, but I will need a whole memoir to explore why.

The duality of my dollhood and my self-determination will occupy my thoughts for much of the next five years. Today, this dichotomy is far from my mind as I slowly, proudly swan along the runway. I'm too focused on making sure I don't stumble, too fascinated by the novelty of hundreds of people applauding my presence. I know that this moment is meaningful, but it will be several years before I understand why, before I comprehend the deeper significance of the things I've done today. For now, I am just drinking it all in, the feelings and the atmosphere, the cheers, the overwhelming support for me simply being who I am.

The music playing behind me is dramatic, almost haunting, resonating with strength and solidity. Intimately familiar to me, absolutely unknown to everyone else in the venue. It's a song I am certain has never been played in public before. For it is my own music, recorded two and a half decades earlier, long before I had any idea how my life would unfold. Part of a collection of songs that emerged from countless days and nights spent distilling the emotions and lessons of my early twenties into my earnest, grasping, often naïvely idealistic creativity. Songs that I shared with my friends at the time, but which stayed mostly private in the years that followed, not forgotten, but kept quietly treasured as part of my life's story.

> *A single note can shatter walls*
> *Turn the world upside down*
> *And as the tears of freedom flow*
> *Out of the night, our hearts unbound*
> *With the sound of thunder*
> *To shake the land and take back our own*
> *Shine on my friends*
> *For you have the strength to walk this road*

I walk the runway to a song of solidarity. Twenty-five years ago, as a young man, I already knew how strong women were. How strong they had to be to survive. I was thankful for my appreciation and for the brief glimpses of sisterhood I was fortunate to experience. Twenty-five years ago I sang about strength, the strength to weep, to cry, to be vulnerable. To openly show emotion and to welcome the affirmation of being fully human. Strength that women need to cultivate in order to exist in this world on their own terms. Strength that even today is difficult for many men to accept, let alone embrace. In the women around them, and in themselves.

Twenty-five years later, I am a transgender woman, proudly one side of a dual-gender human being, revealing the strength and vulnerability to claim my place in society as my song resounds throughout the gloriously emotion-filled chambers of the Collingwood Town Hall. A song inspired by women. A song that Lauren would have surely treasured, had she still been in my life when I created it. Lauren, who never saw how she changed my world, how she unknowingly predicted and taught me who I really was, even if it took me years to understand it myself.

I think she's just... you.

The years continue to reveal their insights. Another five spent writing this memoir, and I understand that the definition of who I am cannot be fixed. I am: a woman, a man, a contradiction, a complication. The doll and the defiant. Willingly objectified, simultaneously claiming and asserting my power. Endlessly inspired to reflect, to create, to continue.

Forever learning and discovering. Fashioning my existence on my own terms.

What does it cost to be yourself? Infinitely less than the cost of denial.

I know that I am one of the lucky ones, and I want to show the world what is possible.

Chapter Fifty-Two

Dance Like Everyone Is Watching

"To be is to do." - Socrates
"To do is to be." - Sartre
"Do be do be do." - Sinatra
"Don't just do something, stand there!" - Gabel

April 2023

It's Saturday morning. I'm standing frozen on my display stand, happy and content being my mannequin doll self. I'm wearing a cream coloured lace top and a cute red miniskirt, with high heels of course; I'm enjoying showing off my legs, which are highlighted by the shiny, glimmery pantyhose I'm wearing.

I have a semi-regular gig as a living mannequin now. I volunteer at an op shop where I know some of the staff, and on days when I'm not rostered on for actual work I sometimes come in to pose instead. It feels like a day off — many people express amazement that I have the discipline to stand so still for so long, assuming that it must be mentally as well as physically taxing. But apart from sore feet and a few tired leg muscles from standing in my heels for hours, I actually find it relaxing. I usually feel refreshed and recharged the following day.

I am so thankful that I've found this opportunity and that the staff at the shop are so supportive. The first time I posed it was an experiment, and the reactions from customers were so positive (and occasionally hilarious) that I was invited to come back whenever I wanted. Eventually I signed on as a volunteer to make it official, and so that I could contribute in other ways when they needed more helpers (doing "real work" instead of "standing around doing nothing"!).

When I'm doing a "work" shift, I usually show up as Derek – it's easier to lift and move things around in the shop without flowing skirt hemlines and frills getting in the way. The other staff and volunteers were surprised to find out that I had two genders but they have warmly welcomed and embraced both of me.

When I am posing I am always Meredith of course. I love feeling beautiful, wearing all of my pretty outfits, doing my best to combine classy with sexy and flirty. I am the objectified expression of my own femininity: my dollhood on show for the whole world. But I will happily do this even when nobody is there to witness it. The shop can be busy or empty; the presence of others does not affect the joy this brings me: an inner glow that I feel spreading from my frozen form and filling the space I'm in – and beyond – with its energy. Affirmation of my feminine soul; I feel blessed and at peace.

My pose is uncomplicated and easy to maintain. Legs slightly apart, hips inclined just a little bit to one side, arms and hands spread expressively. My smile is real; I was made to be frozen in place. I imagine my body made of plastic, alive but enchanted into rigid stillness. It's all self-imposed, of course – I know that my brain is telling my muscles to stay exactly as they are – but it is effortless and automatic, and it feels completely natural. Any conscious attempts to trigger *motion* that surface in my mind are blocked as soon as they appear; the messages never travel through my body to their destinations; they are never received. Staying perfectly still is the easiest thing in the world to do.

In my life outside this fantasy of timeless immobility, I am restless and active. I move and I speak and I write and I create. I flounce and I flaunt. I *do* many things in the world.

Today, right now, I don't do anything except *be*.

I *exist*. As an object of beauty, to be appreciated by everybody. Or even by nobody but myself.

It is enough.

My femininity is a complex and multilayered subject, and even after spending five years on this memoir I still find myself unable to adequately address all the nuanced considerations it demands: self-realisation, social conditioning, agency and the willing lack thereof, aesthetic appeal, sexuality, vulnerability, the giving of oneself for others. It is certainly enough to appreciate the essence of my being when I am alone, but the introduction of other people brings some insight into the importance of being visible and authentic.

I discovered during my nights at Domicile just how appreciative strangers can be of another person's presence. People would stop to tell me, as I packed up my display stand, how much they loved me. People who never tried to interact with me, whom I didn't recognise, who had never stopped to inspect me while I stood frozen. Yet they would still thank me for bringing my beauty into this space for them to enjoy.

At the op shop, it is the same story. Regular customers are delighted when they see me and disappointed when I'm not there. Whenever I message the shop manager to propose a day for me to come in and be a mannequin, I get the reply "Yes! Please!!!"

Sometimes it's hard to separate what I *do* from what I *am*, particularly when I create things. But as a living doll, my identity is made real not by *doing*, but by *being*.

Me, having an impact on other lives, simply by existing.[41]

* * *

Ding!

I click the notification icon every time the little number pops up. One new notification, maybe two, maybe if I leave it for a while there will be four or five. Occasionally, when I check using my phone first thing in the morning I'll see a dozen. Today there were fifty-one!

My post last night in the "I Love To Op Shop" group showed an ensemble typical of my style: quite feminine, with soft colours and lace; demure fitted top, knee-length flared skirt, classic high heeled pumps. I've been posting in this Facebook group for many years, so the comments are predictable by now, but they remain as affirming as ever:

"Gorgeous, such a stunning outfit!"

"You are always so stylish, and your legs are amazing!"

"Your posts always make me so happy!"

I know that it's very shallow to count the reactions and "Likes" and comments on Facebook posts, but to be honest, it's delightful to see them. I don't think my self-image would change much without them – I was already pretty happy within myself when I joined the group – but it's a nice bonus to have so many positive vibes come my way. This morning, when I woke up to fifty-one notifications, someone in the group had "Liked" a new post of mine, and then looked at fifty of my old posts and "Liked" all of them too. That simple act of clicking sends an acknowledgement to me

---

[41] Acknowledging the fact that I have privilege here is important: if people didn't find me attractive, I might have very different experiences. Even though my doll fascination started in early childhood – predating my gender and sexual development by many years – it's hard to say how much my ability to present the way I do affects how I feel inside about it.

that I've been seen and appreciated, but it also tells me that I touched someone's life, even in this very small way, and they cared enough to let me know.

As I sit here writing these words, I think about identity and how so much of who I am is reflected in how I present myself. It's more than just my clothing and my appearance, even if those are the first things that draw attention. There is my demeanour, my mood, and my intentions. How do others receive who, and what, I am?

It is springtime, and the view from the window out into my suburban backyard is alive with birds making themselves busy nesting and foraging in the trees and bushes. I watch as a rainbow lorikeet alights on the grass. Its little head darts this way and that, hunting and pecking for food, the vibrant colours of its feathers so striking and beautiful. Why does its presence make me happy and thankful? I don't know. The rainbow lorikeet simply *is*, and I appreciate it for no other reason.

* * *

"Do, or do not. There is no try." - Yoda

I have spent a lot of time struggling with the thought that people will see my doll fixation, and by extension my identity as Meredith, as nothing more than a weird sexual fetish – particularly given the things I have included in this book. But my dollhood is not one-dimensional, and the feelings it elicits in me are complex and not easily categorised. Sometimes it is simply the joy of perfect stillness. Or the artifice of decorating and dressing up an image of my femininity, including all of the cultural baggage that goes with it. I have been drawn to these things since I was a very young child, and equating my feelings to a sexual kink trivialises my entire experience of being female. It's much more complicated than that.

I am careful not to overcompensate in my explanations, partly because I do not want the reader to say "the lady doth protest too much, methinks".

But I also want to question why it matters. Should we automatically judge unusual or overtly sexual content in a negative light? I feel nervous about revealing these things, but that's a socialised response. I don't think I should have to feel nervous or try to justify anything.[42]

Sometimes it doesn't matter whether I do, or do not.

I'm on display in the shop, and the only thing on my mind is making sure my pose is stable and comfortable. It's a busy morning and I don't like to reposition myself when there are customers watching.

About an hour into the day, a middle-aged man and woman walk past me. They have the demeanour of a married couple, but I can't know for sure.

The woman does a double take and gasps, and then steps back, grabbing her companion.

"Oh my God. Look at that! It's horrible!"

Well that's a new one. I've been called creepy but never horrible.

"Looks real, doesn't it?" The man seems amused.

"Oh no, it's disgusting. I can't believe they put that here." Her voice drips with moral judgement. In my peripheral vision I can see the revulsion on her face.

I'm puzzled and kind of intrigued, but I impassively maintain my pose and my frozen smile, trying not to blink.

She can't help herself, and reaches out to touch my arm.

The man begins to say something. "Oh, I don't know, I think-"

She cuts him off as she recoils in horror from the feel of my skin. "Oh my God, it's so disgusting! Feel it! Ugh!" She turns away and tries to get the man to follow, but he stays put, still scrutinising me.

---

[42] Transgender women used to frequently get accused of *autogynephilia* – the idea that we are really men who obtain perverted sexual gratification from dressing as women. This theory was debunked years ago: cisgender people, women and men alike, are allowed to find themselves sexy without fear of being labelled mentally ill, so trans people should be afforded the same consideration. However, the ghost of its legacy still lingers.

The woman is still muttering "disgusting!" when I've had enough and I shift my pose. I can't tell if the man is still watching me but I don't care. Hands on hips, I turn and fix myself to look at the back of her head with an expression of "are you serious?" frozen on my face and in my body.

She turns back around to talk to the man and ends up looking right into my eyes. I remain completely still as she nearly jumps out of her skin.

"Ughmnbhgh!!! Oh!!" She shakes herself and grabs his arm, pulling him away. "It moved! Why would they put that thing here??? Oh it's horrible! Disgusting!"

She still doesn't think I'm alive.

The couple spends some time browsing the nearby part of the shop, out of my sight but still within earshot. At one point, as they walk through the display area behind me, I hear the woman say somewhat dismissively to the man, "You like that thing, don't you?"

I feel a little bit sorry for him.

An hour later, I'm still on my stand, but I'm animated, taking a short break and chatting with some of the shop staff about people's reactions. Customers are usually delighted to figure me out. Some people, usually teens and young adults, find me creepy – I blame horror movies and too many Internet memes. However, nobody has surpassed that woman.

I mention her. "Did you hear that woman call me disgusting?" I look around. "Is she still here?"

The manager shakes her head. "I don't think so."

"She didn't think I was real even after I moved! Can you believe that? She even felt my arm!" I mimic her voice and actions: "Oh, that's disgusting!"

Suddenly I notice movement from across the shop. I hadn't got a clear look at the man earlier, but now I recognise him standing next to the change room where a curtain has just been pulled back and the woman is looking at me. I think they heard us.

"Oh. Hi!" I call out, waving.

The curtain closes again.

Ten minutes later, I can see in a reflection that the couple are leaving the shop. They never came back around near my spot.

Two days later, while I'm telling some friends about the experience, laughing and puzzling over the woman's reaction, it suddenly dawns on me. Her behaviour was too extreme to be explained by an aversion to mannequins, lifelike dolls, and other "uncanny valley" representations of human beings. Some people find living mannequins creepy, but this woman's disgust and moral judgement was on another level.

It's affirming, unfortunate, and hilarious all at the same time.

I'm pretty sure that she thought I was a donated item for sale, and not a shop fixture.

A second-hand robotic sex doll.

* * *

"Be yourself. Everyone else is already taken." - Gilbert Perreira (sometimes attributed to Oscar Wilde)

In music, the space between the notes is just as important as the notes themselves. The way a piece breathes is an essential part of how it resonates with the listener. I know very little about dance, but it seems to me the same would apply: balance, counterpoint, context. Stillness and movement go hand in hand. When I stand frozen, it is part of the dance of my life. The doll is an ever-present part of my multi-faceted identity, and there is freedom in being wholly visible. Everyone is watching anyway, so I might as well be true to myself.

The more I embrace the idea that *being* is tragically undervalued in this world that emphasises *doing* – particularly *producing*, for the capitalist machine – the less I care about my material achievements. Even as someone who builds and crafts things with my hands, I would rather be known for the way I strive to *be:* kind, attentive, compassionate, insightful. Even if I remained fixed to my display stand, forever a living doll, unable to move – I would still be all of these things.

Who you are is a story. If you only dance when nobody is watching, then the world misses out on something valuable and unique. Yet, by dancing alone, you may learn to truly appreciate who you really are – and who you want to be. Eventually you risk dancing in front of somebody else, and their affirmation makes you realise that being yourself is enough. It doesn't matter whether anybody is watching, or everybody is watching.

When I first joined the "I Love To Op Shop" group in 2016, I was not yet fully out as Meredith, and I would hide my face in the photos I posted. At the time, there were already thirty thousand members, and you never know who knows who on Facebook, so I was a bit cautious about revealing anything that could link Meredith back to my life as Derek.

Fast forward a few years. It's now sometime in late 2020, and a lot has happened in the time since I joined the group. I am comfortably out to my children and to my workplace, and I no longer worry about anyone tracking me down online.

It's Transgender Awareness Week. I post a message in the group about being dual-gender, with two photos of myself side by side: one of Meredith in a sparkly top, miniskirt and heels, dancing for the camera, and one of Derek in a T-shirt and shorts, doing star jumps on a trampoline and making a goofy face.

Here I am, visible for the world to see, just being myself. Glamorous and beautiful on one hand, silly and ridiculous on the other. Both photos capture "the real me" – and this is not lost on the people who comment on my post.

"*Pure joy from both sides of you. 2 sides to a shiny coin x*"

"*I've always believed it's what's inside that counts and as I've watched your posts over the years I've seen your beautiful nature, the rest is just wrapping and you do that so well too.*"

"*Thanks for sharing your wonderful photos. Your beautiful personality shines brightly in all of them.*"

"*So much happiness exuded by Merri and Derek.*"

I am not surprised by the supportive nature of the comments. The attentiveness of the moderators and many active members ensures that the group remains a safe space. Negative comments are uncommon and they quickly get removed.

I am happy because being allowed to express who I am makes me happy. Being celebrated for it makes me happy. I still have my off days; everyone does. There are things that persist in this world that make me angry and sad. But I have no doubt that whatever part of myself I share to this group, I will find appreciation and support. If you are visible here, you will be seen and you will be acknowledged. Anyone who shares a part of themselves here is received in the same manner as I have been. No matter who they are, they are enough.

It gives me hope.

I am enough. We all are. Dance if you feel like it.

Chapter Fifty-Three

Present

Meredith is a gift. I feel like the universe has granted me an extraordinary ability to experience this life in full, allowing me to cross the great gender divide and immerse myself in the mysterious world of the "other" that roughly half the population never gets to see from the inside.

This is, of course, my own take on things. The "gender divide" is a social construct: the way we conceive of and discuss gender is inextricably bound to human cultural norms. Norms that I have spent my lifetime learning to navigate, consciously or otherwise, in order to make sense of my own experiences.

Gender – no matter how you define or relate to it – is still a very real thing, and I happen to have two of them in a world where we are usually expected to have exactly one. But expectations can change, or disappear, and I hope that my story, along with the stories of others like me, and of non-binary, genderfluid, agender, and transgender people of all experiences, demonstrates that the possibilities for human existence are rich and endlessly varied – and not static. Holding ourselves to outside expectations about our identities, or to old ideas that may no longer apply, is a waste of time, energy, and happiness.

* * *

June 2025

As I write this, much of the world is still a dangerous place for me to exist the way I do. I have been incredibly lucky in my life and I do not treat this fact lightly. In many places, any deviance from prescribed gender expectations is severely punished – and in some countries, the USA and UK in particular, a lot of hard-won progress for transgender rights has recently been significantly jeopardised or reversed outright.

Even for cisgender people, particularly men, the envelope of "allowable" expression is still woefully narrow, regardless of whether transgression is actively punished or simply frowned upon. The systemic forces that dictate social norms are powerful and slow to change, and those who stand to materially benefit from the status quo are always the ones with the most influence. I am fortunate that my own social nonconformity, no matter whether viewed through a cisgender or transgender lens, seems to be palatable enough in its presentation that I haven't faced significant pushback – though even after spending five years thinking and writing about it, I still don't know how much of my expression comes naturally and how much was learned.

On a personal level, my relationship with Lisa has been stable and positive for many years. She still prefers to avoid interacting directly with Meredith, and I won't deny that this still makes me sad, but I know that this isn't an actual rejection of my female reality. My wife accepts that Meredith is an intrinsic part of the person she loves, even as she keeps her distance. I believe her, and I trust her, and she doesn't have to justify her reasons to me or to anyone else. I know that Lisa has a strong sense of justice and loyalty, and I know that she would defend the truth of my identity and its expression to anyone who questioned it.

Writing this book has been one of the most difficult creative projects in my life so far. There have been times when I questioned why anyone would want to actually read it, and times when I questioned if I would actually want anyone to read it. However, even if nobody were to ever read it, the rewards I have already experienced while writing it have made it worthwhile. I have gained a deeper understanding of myself – not just my gender, but also my passions, my values, my neurodivergent quirks – and the complexity and nuances of my ongoing journey. This memoir is a gift to myself. A reassuring embrace to younger me, a knowing acknowledgement to who I am now, and a talisman to carry into the future. A reminder and a testament to possibility.

I hope that you, the reader, also consider it a gift. I hope that you have taken the time to sit and contemplate the ideas and perspectives in this book, possibly challenging yourself, perhaps giving yourself a greater appreciation and understanding of your own identity, and reinforcing your respect for the identities of others.

And if you happen to have found something of yourself in these pages, I offer you my hope and solidarity in discovering the joy of being authentic, and my staunch support in fighting whatever battles are necessary to realise it. You yourself are a gift. You are present, and you matter.

You are not alone.

Much love,
Derek/Merri

Supplemental

Stones Unturned

1995

The butterfly on the screen twirled slowly around, the light from the virtual room glinting off her wings. Other avatars floated past, birds, fish, humans, aliens, each with a name tag jutting out above its head, if there was a head to speak of. Howdy, Ted, BoomBoom, C-U-2, Sexxxy, they were called. They came from all over the United States and the world, logged into this Internet chat program to shoot the breeze, joke around, make lewd conversation. Sometimes the less sexually obsessed ones were fun to talk to, but right now they were a distraction. Leah, the butterfly, was unusual – something of an enigma, Australian, twenty-five, philosophical, quietly interesting. A student of some sort. She hadn't given him the usual "What, you're responsible for all those computerese manuals?" when she found out he was a technical documentation writer. He certainly didn't want to sit around in a crowd making the usual small talk with her.

Let's go find a private room somewhere. Leah suggested it first, opening a private channel between them. She had already turned and was heading for the room's portal. *I found a secret maze yesterday.*

Richard, alias Mr. Bear — his avatar was an orange teddy bear with a blue T-shirt and sunglasses — hurried to follow, careful not to lose her beyond the visibility limit that existed to avoid cluttering the screen. *Wait up, I'm still not too good at navigating in here...*

Walking along the shore at Torrey Pines beach. Children playing at the water's edge, their parents watching from a blanket littered with miniature shovels, buckets, magazines, ice cooler. Surfers silhouetted on the breaking waves by the setting sun. This was Richard's beach — even when he was courting Tina he didn't bring her here much. She didn't have the same affinity for the ocean that he did. Now he watched the children playing and sighed. Tina was great with the kids, but she would never think to take Tommy and Stephen to the beach. A young couple jogged past while he stood alone, watching the children scatter and regroup in front of the water's edge. Only a week ago, his last attempt at getting his family to do something "together." A picnic and afternoon at La Jolla Shores, where he hadn't been since his college days. But Tina wasn't interested, she had made other plans for the afternoon, the kids were going to a friend's anyway — like always, she just planned things and went off without telling him about any of it. They fought, the same words, the same arguments, he said he'd had enough. Finally. She said to consider moving out. A good idea, she said. She needed time to think. Why can't we ever talk, he asked. Never speak to each other anymore except to argue.

Do you ever wonder why we try so hard to explain everything? Like we're always afraid we're going to miss out on the most important answer. The flamingos behind her seemed to dance on the walls as she moved.

What do you mean? Such a predictable answer. Oh well, maybe he was a predictable guy. Boring. Tina didn't find him worth the effort anymore, he'd grown too familiar.

If I answered that, I'd ruin this whole line of thought, wouldn't I? Can a butterfly shrug? Maybe it was interference from the flamingos on the wall.

The secret maze seemed to go on forever. They had wandered down six different corridors and encountered only one other person, a toad on a toadstool who knew what a private conversation was and hopped away.

Don't you think life is more interesting when you leave a few stones, the pretty ones, unturned? Her words appeared before he could enter anything.

But what about the joy of discovery? he asked. *People are driven to explore, they always will be.* At least the ones you read about in National Geographic.

What do you find worth exploring? Leah asked some interesting questions.

A childhood memory popped into his head from nowhere. *When I was little, my best friend and I used to dig huge pits in the sand at the beach and pretend we were exploring unknown caves.*

What did you find?

The usual stuff — buried treasure, maps, old skeletons.

What about now? Are you a frustrated archaeologist?

No, not really. *Umm... I don't think I could handle unearthing a real human skeleton. What about you? What do you like to explore?*

I really don't know. It's not a tangible thing for me. People, relationships, things like that. I studied science and engineering once, but as nifty as some of it was (and a lot more of it was just plain awful...) I didn't find it satisfying.

What do you study now? You said you were a student.

She took longer than usual to reply. *I... I don't really know, to be honest. It sounds strange... but I'll have to explain it some other time.*

Richard made a note to remind her of that.

She continued before he could enter anything. *Don't you ever wonder how people can devote their whole lives to studying things like physics or biology? I realise that a lot of good comes out of it, but sometimes I wonder if they push it too far sometimes.*

You mean like runaway technology? Artificial intelligence, genetic engineering, stuff like that? Science is just a tool, he thought. The old saying. Human beings make the policy.

Not so much that. She might have read his mind. *Some mad scientist going off and mis-using secret technology, X-files kind of stuff — that's not what I'm afraid of.*

A long pause. Leah didn't strike him as the kind of person who was afraid of much. Just something about her manner, even over a computer chat line. *What then?*

Her wings seemed to glow, shimmer iridescently. *We *attach* meaning to things everyday, that's not anything new. What I'm afraid of is, I think sometimes we seem to be *looking for* meaning in science, in black holes, in subatomic particles. We don't question whether the answers should be there in the first place. Why do we need proof of God's existence? Do we really need to know why two people love each other? Isn't it enough that they just do?*

They had agreed to a trial separation. A change. Room to breathe, to think without having one's guard up constantly. Better for the kids to not see their parents fighting all the time. He'd take Tommy and Stephen to the beach next weekend.

Only a week, and he missed her already. But it wasn't the Tina he left that came into his thoughts — it was, he realized, the Tina he had been missing ever since their marriage became difficult. It was the Tina who could make him laugh, the Tina who always seemed to know what he was thinking. It was the woman who loved him. The woman who would bear his children. It was nine years ago, when he was just out of grad school and she was just starting, a pretty, flirtatious young thing who was always one step ahead of him. Only she delighted in watching him, delightfully puzzled, in his attempts to keep up. When was it that he lost the knack? She didn't wait for him anymore.

Richard took his computer with him to the new apartment. Just him, some clothes, an old set of pots and pans, his portable stereo, his CD collection. Nothing to do after work but log on and wait for Leah. The kitchen he hardly used, subsisting mostly on sandwiches and Chinese take-out.

He felt drawn to Leah somehow. Dangerous, he knew, stories of false identities and net relationships gone sordidly awry. But he found comfort in her earnestness, her questions made more meaningful by the fact that she seemed well-grounded, in a universe of flaky netizens.

<---+++--->

Of course he wanted to know more. *I really enjoy chatting with you, but I don't really know that much about you. Beyond your questions – you get pretty intense sometimes.*

We don't have to get so deep all the time. I can joke around if you want. I don't know, I always end up philosophising too much.

I don't mind – it's a refreshing change from most of the "conversation" around here. But you haven't told me much about yourself. He remembered what she said about her indeterminate studies.

Actually, it's something I've been thinking about. There's something I need to tell you if we're going to be chatting a lot – I don't want to mislead you.

Oh, great. *Mislead me? How?*

It's kind of strange... I'm not really sure how to explain it.

Try. Richard honestly didn't know what to expect.

I'm a literary creation. A fictional character in a book.

A false identity! But a strange way to explain it. **Which book?**

The one my author is working on now.

Who is your author?

I can't tell you that. This is kind of an experiment. My author wants to know if I can be a believable character.

He had been chatting with a person who didn't exist? No, "Leah" was voicing her "author's" thoughts, surely. **So Leah's not real then?**

Excuse me, I am very real. You are talking to me, aren't you?

Is your name really Leah then?

My name is Leah. I can't tell you what my author's name is.

I am confused. Who am I really talking to?

Leah.

Then who is your author? Am I not talking to Leah's author?

My author is actually hitting the keys on the keyboard. But you are talking to me.

Huh??

Weird, for sure. **Now you're confusing me more. Whoever you are, please stop playing games.**

Please understand that it's not a game. You don't mean to, but you are trivialising my life. It was just given to me, and I'd like you to accept it as I have.

He was totally lost, or she was a mental case. **Just tell me who you are.**

Arrrgh!!! The whole reason I told you was because I don't want to deceive you. I am trying to explain exactly who, and what, I am...

There was a pause.

I am not physically real, in the sense that I can walk around, eat, break my arm, whatever. But I am real nonetheless. I have emotions, feelings, hopes, dreams.

Pause. **Go on,** he typed.

You know when you watch a really good movie? Or read a really good book, for that matter.... you sometimes forget that the characters are fictional? You kind of grow with them, feel for them, even learn from them. They are real in every sense except physically. I am the same – only this is real-time. I am a character that has stepped out of a book. I can live in your world through this computer chat program.

Pause.

Does any of this make sense now?

It was an intriguing idea. I think so. But I assumed you were real before. Why bother telling me?

I want to be honest with people that I get to know well. I'm afraid of leading people on only to have them feel betrayed or cheated in some way. Besides, don't you think it's a nifty idea?

He was, in fact, interested in her. He could accept her claim, think of her as "Leah," only without the quotation marks. But he had a sneaking suspicion that the Leah he was talking to, in fact, bore a striking resemblance to her author.

Their conversations got more personal. Significantly, Leah never asked him, but Richard told her his real name, even gave her his e-mail address. She remained cryptic about her "author's" identity, and Richard stopped pressing her. Her fictionality became a non-issue, as he grew to think of her and her author as one in the same. If she was indeed a fictional creation, her author had done a remarkable job.

He didn't tell her about his troubled marriage. His day at the beach with Tommy and Stephen was "a beach barbeque with some friends." In fact it went quite well, and the kids spent most of the afternoon trying to dig a hole so deep they could stand in it without seeing over the edge. They succeeded with a little help from Dad. Something to tell Leah about, but he was afraid she would lose interest in him if she found out he was married.

He was torn. He dreamed about going back to Tina, back to the kids, and somehow making things right. As they were gathering their things to leave the beach, Tommy asked when he was coming home. What could he say? If he tried to answer, he wouldn't be able to explain the tears.

But during the long days at work, he dreamed of dropping everything and catching the next flight to Melbourne, on the other side of the world, chasing the mysterious Leah who made him feel alive, valued, trusted. Only the kids anchored him in the present, swinging between a dream of the past and a longing for the mysterious, the unattainable, which, by stretching the corners of his imagination, was just absurdly possible.

Tell me about the book. What is it about?

It's mainly about my life, over the past three years or so. Mostly about an experience I had in Japan.

What happened?

I guess you could call it my first love. But it was more — that was the beginning, or maybe the centre, of everything that happened. It was one of those experiences that changes your whole life. I know it might sound naïve, but quite a bit happened to me. At least it feels that way.

Well, love could do that. **What was he like? Was he Japanese?**

No, he was another exchange student. It's kind of hard to describe him. The whole thing, actually. I remember everything I felt, all the changes I went through, but it's going to be hard to translate that into a good story. You'll have to understand if I'm vague at times — I haven't sorted everything out myself yet.

Richard had gotten used to it. Leah could be really fuzzy sometimes — whenever the conversation approached something that could link her to the "real" world. He was drawn to the restless nature of her mind and her heart, which came through very clearly online, but he hardly knew any concrete facts about her life.

Like, for instance, if she had a boyfriend. **Are you still together with him?**

Alas, no. I guess you could say I've been single ever since.

Why would she volunteer that? **You haven't sworn off men, have you?**

No, I haven't. Why do you ask?

Oops – was she reading his mind? **No reason. :-)** But a little flirting never hurt, said the smiley.

You're not flirting with me are you? :-)

Flirting. It was just flirting, he says. **Whatever gave you that idea?**

Oh, nothing. Just a hunch.

Well, she was a literary creation, or so she said. What did flirting mean then? But she seemed to welcome it. Real or not, it was something. But now he felt uneasy – real or not, she didn't know he was married.

<--- + + + --->

"How are you?"

"Okay, I guess. I'm getting by."

"I miss you."

"Rick, don't. I'm not ready for that yet. We're taking this slow, remember? I still have a lot to think about."

"So do I." More than you'd realize, he thought. He wasn't going to insist this time. "I... I'm sorry, I just wanted to see if you were okay, see if maybe..."

Pause. Well, she didn't want to talk yet. "Nevermind. I'll see you when I pick the kids up on Friday."

"Fine."

"Okay, I'll see you then."

"Rick -"

"Yeah?"

"I do realize that you're trying. You should know that."

"Thanks." But does it make a difference?

Stones Unturned

Imagine life without Tina. Not just living apart, but gone for good. Would theirs be an emotional parting? He couldn't know if she still felt anything. Maybe for her, they already said goodbye. But the kids, how could he leave the kids? Stare at the breaking waves. Wind in his hair, calling him to freedom. What was freedom? The waves were endless, no answers. Running to Leah wasn't a smart thing to do, it was an act of a desperate man trapped by fate. Or was it?

Tell me, what did you love about Adrian?

He wondered what Leah's face really looked like as she recalled memories of her love in Tokyo. He pictured her: sandy brown hair framing an easy smile, bright eyes, clear and honest. When asked, she had said that she was average looking. But Richard saw a simple, down-to-earth beauty. The kind where you don't notice unless you stop and look closer. Come on, Richard, he thought. How much of this is real?

He had a quietness about him, like he kept most of himself hidden in some inner world of his. Sometimes bits would escape, the best parts, and the "real" Adrian would make himself known in the outside world. At least that's what I like to think. Unless you really knew him, you'd have a hard time explaining it. But it was beautiful, like a ray of sunshine. I fell in love with him when one of those rays shone on me.

I think I understand. The difference between real and imaginary was perhaps only a reflection of the hidden aspects of ourselves. Who was Leah, for instance? And who was he to her? Certainly not the same person that Tina knew. He never talked about things like this to Tina. Seven years ago he could have, but that was before life had taught him seven years' worth of lessons.

Well, he still entertained his idea of escape. **Do you think you could fall in love again, the way you did with Adrian?**

Everybody is different. It wouldn't be in the same way. But I do believe I will fall in love again. What about you? Have you ever been in love, really in love?

Ouch. Well, if he was going to talk about it with anyone, Leah was the right person. He just felt that way. She really cared, he could tell. Or he just believed, which was good enough – if the things Leah philosophized about were true.

Here goes. *I have been in love. It seems like a very long time ago. Her name was Tina, and she was the most wonderful thing that ever happened to me. It was the happiest time of my life.*

This sounds like a real story.

It is, believe me. How much time do you have? :-)

I would love to hear everything you feel like telling me. But please don't feel pressured – I understand if you don't want to get too personal.

When was the last time he really opened up to someone? **Don't worry. I want to share this with you.**

Well then, please go on...

So Richard began the story of his life with Tina. From how they met in Croce's Bar on Fifth Street downtown (funny, he actually met her in a bar – he never thought himself the type to pick up a girl in a bar), to the way he chased her as she led him around all of her haunts in the city, to the moment he finally realized he had fallen for her (it was when his brother's family came to visit from Seattle and she hit it off instantly with the twins, who were six years old and normally shy around strange adults). He knew then that he wanted to marry her and raise a family together.

It made him sad to recall such early, happy days. Leah was amazingly compassionate, considering that they were separated by two computers so many thousands of miles apart. They chatted for hours that night, until he realized he had to work the next day, and then for hours again the next night. He lingered on his days of courting Tina, painting a picture of her that he hadn't seen in years. He married a wonderful, warm, playful, intelligent woman. It wasn't until the third day that he touched on the reason it was such a sad story.

It all sounds a bit storybook, doesn't it? Maybe I'm looking through rose colored lenses at the past.

Were you really that happy together?

I have tears in my eyes remembering all of this. I'm sorry, maybe I overdid it a bit.

Not at all! One thing I can tell, is that you haven't made anything up. Funny that I of all people should say that, but I can sense the sincerity of your emotions.

Don't you want to know how it ended?

I've been killing myself trying to keep from asking. :-)

It hasn't. We're still married, and we have two beautiful young sons.

Was he imagining silence? How was Leah supposed to react to that?

Tell me why you're sad.

No reaction at all? You don't think any differently of me, knowing that? I never told you about my marriage or my kids before.

I never asked. Should it make a difference to me?

I don't know. I thought it might.

I suppose if you finished your story, I might be able to let you know. But somehow I doubt it will.

What did she feel for him? A married man, running and confiding in someone he met in a chat program? He really wished he could see her face. *Well, I won't hold my breath... don't be afraid of hurting my feelings. Okay?*

Tell me why you're sad. I think it might help me, and help you, if I understood more.

Before I go any further, I want you to know that you are one of the most wonderful people I have ever met.

Thank you. Really, you have no idea how much that means to me. I could never have asked for this experience to be so rewarding. Oh, there I go getting all mushy... :-)

Well, I started it. And I meant it.

Don't feel bad about keeping things secret. I'm sure this is a new experience for both of us. And you haven't finished your story...

So on he went, past the good times and into the lean years. Where did things go wrong? He couldn't tell. It just faded. Tommy was a difficult first child, he had to switch jobs, they had to move out of state for a couple of years and Tina had to suspend her graduate studies. Then when they moved back, it was with a new baby. His new job was too demanding and she had to deal with the kids alone most of the time. She said she wasn't forced to give up her Master's degree, but he knew she regretted the decision in spite of how much she loved Tommy and Stephen. It just went on and on. And never seemed to change for the better. His job, never that interesting, had become a chore. Tina talked about going back to school but never acted on it, no matter how supportive he tried to be. The only bright spots were his sons. Yet five years later here he was, living alone while his kids slept without a father near. And no way of knowing if there was anything left between him and his wife.

It was well into the wee hours of the morning when he decided that there was no more to tell.

So is that what you expected? Pretty grim, huh?

I didn't know what to expect, I guess. It's a terribly sad story. I wish there was something I could do.

You're helping me a lot just by listening. It's good to let it out – I feel trapped sometimes, and talking about it really helps.

Are you really trapped?

It certainly felt like it. To be honest, I have thought about getting away from all this, just a break, somewhere far away. Australia, maybe. If it wasn't for the kids, I'd leave tomorrow.

Why Australia?

To meet you. I've been thinking a lot about it.

Uh-oh. Hold on. You do remember what I am, don't you?

Yes, but I know so much more about you now. I really want to meet you.

But you can't. You must know that.

Why not? You don't really live in Melbourne?

I do. But not physically, I told you I'm a character from a book.

I guess I assumed that I was really talking to your author. I mean, since we started having really close conversations. Aren't I? It doesn't seem fair otherwise.

Wait a minute, I never made any bargains. I told you honestly what I was, and you accepted it. Or at least that's what I thought.

She couldn't have made everything up! So you've been pretending this whole time? That really seems unfair.

Pretending? As far as I'm concerned, I am real. My interest and my emotions and my *intentions* have all been honest. Please don't accuse me otherwise. I really do care, and I really do value your friendship.

All this time I have been more and more interested in knowing your author, who I think is really you.

Oh dear, oh dear... let me think...

Pause.

Let who think? You or your author?

You know, we're treading on dangerous ground here. I never expected it to go this far, honestly. I really don't know what to do.

You could tell me who you really are.

I can't. I mean, you know who I am. But my author... I can't. I want to, but you have to accept that I just can't. I'm sorry.

Even if I came all the way to Australia to meet you?

Please don't do something foolish like that! I mean, if you need to get away, do it for yourself, don't come here to meet me.

What would you do if I told you I already bought a ticket?

You didn't. Tell me you didn't.

What would you do?

Another pause.

Please don't make me feel guilty for not telling you who my author is. Remember that anything you do is your choice. I want to be here as your friend, but I can't make you do anything, and I don't want to be responsible, I can't be responsible.

Okay, I haven't bought a ticket yet.

You know, I'm beginning to think I went too far with this. Maybe it would be better if we stopped.

If you do that, then what harm does it do to tell me who your author is? You said you wanted to.

Did I? Oh yes, I did, didn't I... No, it's just not a good idea. I can't. I'm sorry.

Just do it, Leah! Then you can stop. Let your author take over.

No. Some things are better left alone. If my author goes online you'll never know who it is. Anyway, remember about looking too hard for answers? They might not belong where you want to find them. I think this has to stop. I won't be logging in again.

Are you serious?

Yes.

Just like that?

How else? I think it's time anyway. I've learned what I wanted to find out. All I can see now is ending up like this again, if not with you then with someone else. I really don't want people falling for me.

How could she just leave, after all he told her? Surely she wasn't just using him for her "experiment?" I won't say I really understand, because I don't. It hurts. I consider you a close friend.

I know. I'm sorry, God I'm so sorry. I never wanted to hurt anyone. I hope you can believe that.

I'll try. I think I need some time to think about it.

If it helps, I'd like you to know that I'm losing a friend too.

It doesn't really help, but thank you anyway.

I just hope you're not angry with me.

Angry? No, I don't think I could be angry. You really have helped me. I just don't understand why you have to go, and why you can't tell me who you really are.

I can't explain it any more so I won't try.

Silence. Richard honestly didn't know what to say, to make her change her mind. She was really leaving.

I really don't want you to go.

I have to.

Please?

Really.

Well, he wasn't going to beg. All that time spent getting to know each other, gone. Back to square one.

I guess I'd better accept this and say goodbye, huh? Or we'll be here all night.

If you do accept that I have to go then it would make me feel better about leaving.

I don't have a choice, do I? You could just log off.

I won't. I want to say goodbye properly. It's been an experience I won't forget. My only regret is that ending it will hurt you.

She meant it, he knew. *Well, I must say that I don't regret it at all. I've learned a lot from talking to you. Even if you won't tell me who your author is, I'm really sorry you have to go.*

I'm sorry too. I want you to know that you are and always will be important to me. You have taught me that my life is as real as I could hope or imagine it to be. *I have learned more than I ever hoped to through our friendship, and if I have hurt you I am truly sorry.*

I know.

Pause.

I guess this is goodbye then.

She was going, forever. Not even a chance meeting somewhere on the net? **Are you really going to swear off chatting for good?**

I think so. I need to think much harder about the consequences of what I do. Maybe this was a one-in-a-million adventure. But I don't want to hurt anyone else.

What about going online as yourself? I mean, as your author?

That's an entirely different question. But like I said, if my author was online you'd never know it was my author.

Silence. Richard wondered what she was really feeling. Of course, now he would never truly know. **Well, I guess this is goodbye then.**

There is one last thing I would like to say, if you want to hear it.

Please.

I don't think I ever could have provided you with the answers you want. Perhaps there are others you should think about talking to, and telling everything that you feel. As you have told me. You are a good, honest, caring person, and your children know that. You shouldn't worry about it. Just be who you feel you are, who you want to be. It's worth the effort. Take care of yourself.

<<Leah has left the conversation>> said the computer screen.

For a long time afterwards, Richard sat in front of the blank screen. Scared, hurt, bewildered. Who had he really fallen for? Was he so easily fooled? Well, he wanted to be fooled – Leah had been honest the whole time. But was it her own naïveté that did it? She said she never expected to go so far with her experiment, and he believed that. It was true, she should have known better. She knew that already. But he couldn't fault her for her curious mind – and her curious heart. One could say that she could afford to be detached, hiding behind the computer and her fictional character, but "Leah" could get hurt – if only by realizing that she had hurt someone else in her innocence. Richard knew there was a woman somewhere in Australia, sitting in front of her computer with a lot to think about.

Three days later, Leah's last words to him were still fresh in his mind. It was amazing how much you could learn from really reaching out to another person. And she was right – he wanted answers she didn't have. He was just on the verge of realizing the questions himself anyway. There was more than he had tried to see in the past – he wasn't trapped, really. It wasn't exactly life and death. It was, well, life, and he still had a lot to find out about it. And he couldn't expect anyone else to teach him, or show him, or respond in the ways that he thought they should. It wasn't fair to himself, to his children, or to Tina.

Tina. He needed to talk to Tina. He knew what to say to her this time.

"Hello?"

"Hi, it's me."

"Hi. What's up?"

"Can we meet for an afternoon? There's something I want to tell you, and ask you. I won't pester you, or pull any emotional tricks. I just want to share one afternoon with you, and share something very important with you. After I'm done, you can do whatever you want, and I won't try and stop you. Really."

There was a short pause.

"I must admit, you have me intrigued. I'll meet you, but you have to pay for the babysitter."

It didn't matter what Tina thought, really. It could be her, but if it wasn't, then it wasn't. The reason wasn't that important anymore. His children would always be his children. For the first time since he could remember, Richard's hopes didn't rest on Tina's answers.

Copyright © 1996 by Derek Moo

Acknowledgements

I live and write on the unceded lands of the Bunurong people of the Kulin Nation. I pay respect to elders past, present, and future, who continue to survive the ongoing injustice of colonisation.

This book would not have been possible without the assistance and support of many important people, for whom I am deeply grateful.

To my beloved writing colleagues – Amanda, Cynthia, and Suzy: Thank you so much for all of your encouragement, patience, and insightful feedback. My writing would be nowhere near as rich and thought-provoking without you.

To the owners and staff at the best cafés in Frankston: Eeny Meeny, Rosie's, Mr. Frankie, and Baxter's Two Cow Dairy: Thank you for giving me the space to sit and write for hours on end, over months and years, and for providing me with so much warmth, welcome, and amazing coffee.

To Chloe Higgins, for teaching me the basics. Your guidance as I learned this new craft was essential and much appreciated.

To Bellie Chocmonster, for supporting me every step of the way on this journey (my very own crayzee walk): can we has Together Coffee soon?

To Marianna Sunshine, my favourite weirdo-in-arms: meow.

To the members and committee of Seahorse Victoria, for providing a safe and welcoming space for newly hatched eggs and old chooks alike to express themselves. Thanks especially to Greer McGearey for her years of dedication and steadfast guidance making it possible.

To Marillion, Fish and Steve Hogarth, without whose music I may not have made it this far: You have been a constant part of the soundtrack of my life since 1986. Your music has carried me through the despair of my darkest hours, and has filled my sails with light when I needed to soar. I have long admired your humanity and your uncompromising approach to creating art that reaches people and connects us all.

To friends and family who eagerly read all of the excerpts and drafts I drip-fed you for the last five years: Your encouragement and belief in me have been a source of joy when I have felt the heaviness of exploring and reliving some of the most difficult times of my life. You make me feel well-loved and immensely lucky.

To everyone who has encountered Meredith and treated me with dignity and respect: Thank you for your kindness. You give me hope that the world isn't as bad as I am constantly told to fear it may be.

And finally, to my wife Lisa: Thank you for everything. You have weathered a daunting and emotionally dangerous journey that you didn't sign up for, and I am forever thankful that you elected to stay with me. Your grace in allowing me to reveal some of our most intimate conversations, and your own vulnerability, reflects the depth of our love and trust which I have at times sorely tested. I take nothing for granted and love you with all my heart. Even if you still deny being a punkin bottom.

About the Author

Derek Moo and Meredith Lee are two sides of the same person, living a life openly in two genders, male and female, which occasionally complicates things. Like when updating employee records at work, or writing Author bios like this one.

Smart, sassy, loud, authentic, caring, creative, resourceful, open-minded – these words have all been used to describe the author. The word 'stylish' has also been frequently applied to Meredith but almost never to Derek, which is both an insight into their respective interests, and also a commentary on how society expects, and provides for, male versus female expression.

Meredith can occasionally be found browsing the clothing racks, or simply standing around doing nothing, in one of Melbourne's many op shops. Derek is more often preoccupied with tinkering on some upcycling or repair project, looking after his wife and children, or doing Meredith's laundry and figuring out how to squeeze yet more of her clothing into an already overstuffed wardrobe.

When not occupied with a day job, either one can be found a few mornings a week at their favourite cafés, now with much more time to read other people's writings, seeing as this memoir is finally finished.

Transgender Resources

If you want to learn more about the transgender community and the issues we face, here are some excellent starting points.

> Seahorse Victoria
> seahorsevic.com.au
>
> Transfamily
> www.transfamily.org.au
>
> Transcend Australia
> transcend.org.au
>
> Transgender Victoria
> www.tgv.org.au

www.ingramcontent.com/pod-product-compliance
Lightning Source LLC
Chambersburg PA
CBHW020512080526
44583CB00013B/574